# WHERE TWO
# OR MORE
# ARE GATHERED

To Megan ~

In celebration of life!

Ellie Hawel

# WHERE TWO
# OR MORE
# ARE GATHERED

## A New Church
## for the 21st Century

Ellie Harold

NCM Press
Atlanta, Georgia

Published by
NCM Press
P.O. Box 803
Atlanta, GA 30091-0803

orders@thenewchurch.com

The situations described in this book represent actual events; however, some names have been changed to protect the privacy of the individuals involved.

**Publisher's Cataloging-in-Publication Data**
*(Provided by Quality Books, Inc.)*

Harold, Ellie
    Where two or more are gathered : a new church for the
21st century / Ellie Harold. – 1st ed.
    p. cm.
    Includes bibliographical references.
    ISBN: 1-931268-08-8

    1. Christianity—Forecasting.  2. Church history.
  3. Psychology, Religious.  I. Title.

BV600.2.H37 2001           270.09'05
                           QBI00-1056
**Library of Congress Card Number: 00-192981**
**ISBN: 1-931268-08-8**

**Printed in the United States of America on acid free paper.**

*To my mother,*
*Charlotte Webber Harold,*
*and my father,*
*Charles Louis Harold,*
*for bringing me to Life.*

# TABLE OF CONTENTS

# FOREWORD
## RICHARD MOSS, M.D.

YOU ARE ABOUT TO READ a very courageous and important book. It is courageous because Ellie Harold does not flinch in speaking from her own religious experience and the conviction born in her through that experience. It is courageous because she is a woman minister in a field largely dominated by men. And women, in our culture, have to overcome a tremendous taboo against speaking out from the depths of their own truth, thereby facing the possibility of scathing criticism or even worse—being completely discounted. This becomes all the more true when what Ellie seeks to challenge is the failure of our churches to be true vessels for the transmission and support of genuine spiritual awakening.

I am privileged to know Ellie over many years. Long ago she has worked through her anger and disillusionment with her own Catholic roots. This book is not born of rejection of Catholicism or of any Christian faith. Nor is she grandiose in making her fundamental assertion that Jesus becomes more (not less) than the mythic "one and only" Son of God, when we appreciate him as a man who came to have a profound realization of God and sought to transmit the freedom and "good news" of his understanding to others.

A reader, if he professes to be a Christian, might argue that this assertion categorically denies the most foundational claim of Christianity. Speaking as a teacher who seeks to help individuals awaken to their own essential nature, I strongly support Ellie's interpretation of Jesus. Whether this is the correct or best understanding of

Jesus is not the issue for me nor, I hope, will it be for you. What is truly important is realizing that even if one were to unequivocally accept that Jesus was God incarnate, his greatest value in your life is not in having someone else tell you who he is and how to believe, but rather attempting to find his meaning for yourself by drinking from the same fountain from which Jesus himself drank.

Indeed, this is Ellie's assertion: in attempting to come to grips with God for himself, Jesus realized God in/as himself; we too, with grace, can do the same if we have the courage to really listen to our hearts. Jesus, she states, never intended to found a religion—he already was a Jew—but simply lived his life trying to free his contemporaries from religious dogma so that they too could have a direct experience of God. And as anyone knows who has had some taste of Self-realization, we are impelled, indeed obliged, to attempt to share our understanding with others. In this way we each bear witness to and help catalyze spiritual awakening in each other. In this very manner, consciousness evolves.

If we will accept this premise, that each of us has the capacity for immediate religious experience, then it is out of our own experience we have the basic criteria upon which to evaluate whether our churches are really serving this potential in us. This is where Ellie takes the important position that the purpose of a church is not to foster religion, but religious experience. She has taken on a big issue here. If a church, whatever church, exists as a place where individuals are supported to have authentic religious experience, then, she asks, is it the purpose of religion to yoke a person to a system of belief or to free each individual to discover their own spiritual essence—the very thing she asserts Jesus was attempting to do?

*Where Two Or More Are Gathered: A New Church for the 21*[st] *Century* is a gutsy, insightful critique into a part of our lives that most people do not trust themselves to examine critically. Once someone "joins" a church, the collective energy of such a group is a powerful force that is difficult to differentiate from. This is especially so when members are told that the beliefs uniting this group have absolute truth and to question them in the process of coming to terms with one's own sense of truth can lead to rejection, even judgments about the righteousness of your own soul.

Equally important, the congregation often doesn't understand the financial and other pressures that preoccupy the minister and can rob the minister of the very time and energy he/she requires to maintain his/her own spiritual connection. Ellie takes the reader behind the scenes, graphically describing these forces that can compromise the mission and integrity of any church. She pulls no punches when it comes to pointing out how often the business of church, which she aptly calls "Churchianity," uses people in service to its ends, rather than in service to genuine spiritual rebirth.

Perhaps the most important thesis of the book involves clearly discerning the different levels of need that church experience in general can serve, and that not every church can or should try to provide for all needs. Ellie's description of three basic incarnations of church experience—Old, Transitional and New—reflects different levels of spiritual readiness and provides each reader with a model in which to sense toward one's own level of readiness. She clearly points out that not everyone, indeed only a minority, is ready for a church that acts as a transformational vessel in which the very structure of one's own ego must be challenged in order to become transparent to spirit.

The new church for the twenty-first century that Ellie herself has devoted ten years to creating and which she describes in detail, is not an institution that can be copied. While readers will laugh and ache at the trials of her creative process; building such a living spiritual environment requires being a disciple of spirit in ones own heart moment by moment. The vulnerability and uncertainty of such a path is not for everyone, but for those who understand the need of a context in which faith, not belief, can be engendered, it is not a path that can be refused.

Richard Moss
November 2000

# INTRODUCTION

FOR TEN YEARS I MINISTERED to the Unity-Midtown Church in Atlanta, which I founded in October 1990. Since its inception I experimented with the creation of a new kind of church. This "new church" is inspired by and modeled after Jesus' statement, "Wherever two or more are gathered in my name, there am I in the midst of them." Rather than being a new religion or denomination that promotes a new twist on the traditional Christian belief system, this church is designed to provide access for its participants to the direct experience of God. As such it is more a spiritual than a religious venture and represents an evolutionary leap in Christian faith: for the sole intent of this church is to facilitate the spiritual growth and development of individuals toward the realization of their essential spirituality—the full recognition and expression of their human/divine nature. It does so within a context of committed relationship, self-inquiry and spiritual practice described within these pages.

This book recounts how and why I came to commit my life to the transformation of traditional notions of what church should be and to the unfoldment of a New Church for the twenty-first century. There are three parts. For the greatest understanding of this proposed New Church, I suggest you read them in the order presented.

Part One of the book is autobiographical. It chronicles part of my life story beginning with the religious influence surrounding the circumstances of my conception and concluding with my decision to pioneer a new church. I've included this narrative of the highlights of my life to show how in many ways I was an unlikely candidate for ministry. Despite my refusal to follow a traditional religious path, I still found the need for a community in which to deepen my spirituality and returned to church, albeit this new kind of church.

Part Two gives an analysis of the traditional Christian, or Old Church. In it I attend to the task of naming and discussing what I think are the major problems that have developed in Christianity over the past two thousand years. I will show how these problems, stemming from the early Christian founders' interpretation of Jesus' words, reflect their somewhat limited psychological stage of development rather than the enlightened one attained by Jesus. The result is a major distortion of Jesus' intention regarding church.

I analyze six aspects of the Old Church in the chapters of Part Two. I approach each of these as "partial truths"—ideas and practices that may have been appropriate for the time in which they were formed, but which lose much of their validity when seen from an evolutionary perspective that takes in a wider view. The viewpoint informed by two millennia of psychological and technological development is able to form a more complete context, more of the whole truth.

I offer my critique of traditional Christianity with the understanding that those responsible for promoting the distortions described in this section were ignorant of their motivation for doing so. The benefit of seeing and articulating the negative consequences of that ignorance is not to place blame so much as to open the door to a more complete understanding. Then, it is hoped, the suffering caused by past misdeeds might in some way be redeemed by the resolve to learn more effective ways of doing and being.

Part Three suggests what that resolution might be, provided there is a wider or relatively more whole perspective in place. It describes a new kind of church, or New Church, and how to create one. In Part Three, I give a point-by-point response of the New Church to the six major problems of the Old Church. I present an evolutionary framework that includes those religious and spiritual forms inspired by Jesus. This lays the theoretical foundation for a Curriculum for Transformation which describes the New Church, as well as an important bridge to the New Church that I call Transitional Church. Finally, for those with an interest in implementing New Church ideas, either by expanding the services offered by an already existing church or by starting a new one, there is a set of basic guidelines based on my experience of doing this.

&

When I speak with people about the ideas in this book, they object something like this: "Well, Ellie, what you're describing sounds really great—but it isn't church!" Or another complaint: "I'm turned on by what you're describing, but I hate church and don't want to go to one. Can't you call it something else?!"

After ten years of experimenting with New Church ideas and practices, I've also wondered why I've insisted on calling my discovery "church." Why not let church be as it has been for the last two thousand years? Why not call this kind of transformational work by some other name?

Rather than discouraging me, this line of conversation simply renews my passion for sharing the ideas in this book. Ideas about church are deeply embedded in our culturally conditioned minds; everybody already thinks they know what a church is supposed to be. They accept this definition as gospel and are stuck, either in trying to fit themselves into this too-small box, or resisting it altogether.

The New Church I describe challenges the conditioned belief of what a church is and should be. The New Church invites us to reflect anew on what Jesus really intended when he spoke of founding a church. Did he mean an institution dedicated to the worship of the person of Jesus, that condemned those who didn't believe in him to eternal hell? Or did he intend some vehicle by which people could learn the truth of the divine principle he embodied when he said, "These things that I do, greater things than these will you also do?" Did he want to confine our experience to religious observances that would guarantee a future salvation? Or could it be that he really desired we should taste the bliss of spiritual awareness in our own realization of "I AM" and "The Father and I are One?"

My devotion to the mission of expanding the idea of what is considered church is fueled by a persistent urge—one I sometimes wish would go away—to discover and honor Jesus' original intent regarding church. Perhaps I've projected my own feelings that I haven't been properly understood by those around me, or maybe I am operating from some other neurotic motivation. Or is it possible that there actually is a shred of truth in what I've observed, and this simple form I call the New Church—for all its dissimilarity with traditional forms—is really like the transformational and spiritual church that Jesus intended to create? I invite you, then, to open your mind to the possibilities contained within these chapters, and decide for yourself.

# PART ONE
# A Wanderer's Path: Finding a Way

*Wanderer, the road is your
footsteps, nothing else;
Wanderer, there is no path.
You lay down a path in walking
In walking you lay down a path*

*and when turning around
you see the road you'll
never step on again.
Wanderer, path there is none,
only tracks on the ocean foam.*

**ANTONIO MACHADO**

Like many baby-boomers, I grew up with the sense of entitlement that comes from being one of a large, privileged generation. Everything—from the Barbie dolls of our youth, to present-day TV commercials that play "Louie, Louie" instead of ad copy, from Volkswagen bug's (original and revived versions) to rock 'n' roll church music—has been targeted to those of us born after World War II.

When my generation began to come of age in the late '60s, we suddenly became aware of the power in our numbers. Our student strikes could shut down most of the universities in the country. Our flowers in "their" guns could stop a war. We turned a cynical cold shoulder towards any institution that hinted of repression. The Establishment—schools, governments, religions— would not ruin our lives for us. We would not be held back by any authority! We would create a way of life in which we could be the free spirits we knew ourselves to be! We would do things differently.

Many of us have tried our best to do just that. In some areas we've succeeded, or so it seems. We keep an eye out for injustice, and, in our own minds (if not in practice), try to keep ourselves slightly left of center. But we've also been seduced by the sort of success we never thought we'd want as idealistic flower children. When we were growing up, we were so widely indulged with the benefits of middle-class life, it wasn't too hard for Madison Avenue to convince us as grown-ups that our greatest freedom and ability to make a difference lies in having whatever we want and feeling good about it. After all, as one cosmetics ad reassures us, we deserve it. And so we've figured out how to have it all—a conscience and a fat stock portfolio!

In other domains it seems we've succumbed to a more confined lifestyle than we dreamed possible. We can identify more with our parents' middle-aged frustrations, with the compromises inherent in trying to be good parents and providers. Our black-and-white principles have faded somewhat, and we've resigned ourselves to living more or less in the gray areas of life. We are constantly tied up in traffic, slaves to our cell phones. We thought we could change the world, and it turns out just answering a days' accumulated e-mail feels like an accomplishment.

In our spiritual lives, however, the longings of our youth refuse to be assuaged. No matter how effectively we may have distanced ourselves from the spiritual reality glimpsed in earlier days, the urge to find spiritual fulfillment persists. The quest for spiritual realization has been like a thread running through our lives; even when we've not been aware of it, it forms the very fabric of our existence. We can think of that thread as our unique spiritual path. Our rediscovery of its meaning puts us directly in contact with the deepest reasons we have to live our lives and truly impact the world of the present and the future.

My purpose in telling you about my own path is twofold. First, to help you know who it is that lived the life which yielded the conclusions leading to the creation of what I've called the New Church. I have no doubt that many others have walked their version of the meandering spiritual path that drew me out from a devout Catholicism to an angry rejection of *the* Church, finally leading me to moments of profound mystical experience. Like so many others of my generation, I sought to understand what was happening to me, occurring within me. To a large extent, my perception of the need for a new church grows out of my personal search for meaning, and so I share my process of realization to give a background for the assertions I make regarding the problems with the Old Church, and for the claims I make about the possibilities of the New Church I describe.

But, perhaps more important than this, I hope to help you reconnect with your own spiritual experiences; for the New Church is based, not so much in what you were taught to believe, as in what you've experienced. I believe your inner life and your unique experience of the Divine form the most important and vital link to spiritual fulfillment you will ever find. In sharing my story, I want to help you validate your own inner life so you may trust where it will lead you to go in order to be who you really are.

As you read about my path, you'll see that I never became a scholar in the academic sense. The highest degree I've earned in an institutional setting is an Associate Degree of Science in Nursing. However, you'll discover I have a full roster of degrees in experience; as is true for most of us, Life has been my greatest Teacher. For twenty-five years or more, I have learned that to be a disciple of one's own life it becomes necessary to trust in the process of that life's unfoldment, in the meaning that can be attributed to the events within that life. The most beautiful thing about developing such trust is that an inner authority arises that, when claimed, becomes the access to an abundance of originality and creativity.

I hope you won't find this sharing to be too narcissistic or arrogant. Since I have certainly not yet transcended my personality I know that I have the capacity to be both. In my reality, I have come to view the extraordinary events in my life as neither personal tragedy nor personal triumph—but instead as a demonstration of possibility, whether negative or positive. With that in mind, I hope accounts of my personal foibles will help the reader to discern "how-not-to" lessons, even as the tales of miracles contained within the story might give you an idea of "how-to."

# 1
# Child's Play

*When I was a child,*
*I spake as a child,*
*I understood as a child,*
*I thought as a child.*

**1 CORINTHIANS 13:11**

My mother tells me I was a diaphragm baby. "The diaphragm," she laughs, was in the dresser drawer." It seems I was conceived as a direct result of my mother's religion. Ordinarily not the strictest of Catholics, every five or six years she'd have a "religious fit" and follow the church no-birth control rule by the book. After the resulting pregnancy produced yet another unplanned child, she thought better of her decision and resumed using the diaphragm. None of my four siblings or I was planned. My father, whose only religious expression was a rendition of "I've Got That Ole Time Religion" bellowed forth in some inebriated state, quipped on the subject of reproduction in our family, "I'd rather have two good basset hounds than five children." Alas, my mother was Catholic, albeit a wavering one, and he never did get those dogs.

I grew up under the influence of my mother's ambivalence. Even though it was sometimes boring and made no sense, I was enchanted by religion and the Catholic Church. In the fifties, the Roman church was still mysterious, filled with strange smells, flickering candles and ringing bells. The priests wore rich, satiny robes like kings. The nuns were strange creatures, little faces encased in stiff white cardboard, the rest (did they have bodies?) hidden in endless swaths of black cloth. Church was

Mass, an odd repetition of rituals I didn't understand, characterized by foreign words sung in monotone. For no apparent
reason, I stood, sat or kneeled along with everyone else, mum-
bling Latin responses that, in lieu of knowing what else to do, I
translated for myself. When the priest thundered, "Dominus
vobiscum," and the congregation responded "Et cum spirit tu
tuo," I thought we were reciting God's phone number—the
name of His exchange plus 2-2-0.

Because Mass was so often beyond my ken, I whiled away
the time flipping through the Missal which listed the feast days
of the various saints canonized by the Church. When I discovered there was no saint celebrated on my birthday, I decided
that I would try to be so holy that when I died they would
make the ninth of December *my* feast day. I didn't know much
about holiness except I gathered it involved suffering—doing
things you really didn't like to do and pretending you didn't
mind. Going to church was one of the many things a holy person would do even though it always gave me a headache. As my
Aunt Nornie would frequently remind my cousins and me, we
should offer up all of life's unpleasantries to the Souls in Purgatory.
After all, our prayers were the only way these unfortunates could
get to heaven, and who knows, if we weren't careful we'd be in
the same boat with them with no one to pray for us. I did my
best to help out.

As a child of ten, one of my favorite games was "Saint and
Martyr." I secluded myself in a niche I'd made in the hedge that
bordered the back yard and spent hours there, pretending to pray
or making grass soup for what I imagined was an ascetic meal.
Sometimes, instead of playing with other kids on a summer day, I
would indenture myself to the nuns who taught at the parochial
school I attended just around the corner from my house. Weed-
ing in the convent garden, I cultivated suffering, offering it up for
a lofty spiritual ambition. Other times I took my game into the
church, kneeling in the sanctuary until I was in pain, thinking
about how if I hurt enough my martyrdom would be noticed and
I would eventually be canonized.

I often helped out in the church office after school by sorting
the offering envelopes. I longed for the recognition of my holiness so deeply that I also offered up my discomfort when the
parish priest began backing me into a corner and tongue-kissing

me. This lasted for about a year. When, in the eighth grade, my classmates and I were invited to examine our conscience to see if we had a religious vocation, I was disappointed to discover that I didn't. By this time the priest, who'd evidently been molesting other girls in my class, had moved on. In my confusion, I took his departure as a personal affront to my religious strivings. Since God didn't want me, I'd drop Him too!

It wasn't hard to find other things to be religious about. Puberty brought with it a zealous preoccupation with the opposite sex, while high school opened my mind to ideas. I was turned on. Like others of my '60s generation, I was ripe for conversion to alternative ways of thinking and being, especially when the Establishment presented us with such unattractive options as the Vietnam War and the draft. In my bedroom, decorated with psychedelic posters and a red light bulb, I'd lie in bed listening to The Doors. One of my favorite songs was "Break On Through to the Other Side." I'd let the music seduce me for hours on end, teasing me with its promise of something else besides a humdrum middle-class existence, something more than a life in Marietta, Georgia. By the end of high school I'd smoked marijuana for the first time, slept with my boyfriend, read most of Camus, all of Oscar Wilde and J.D. Salinger, and I was ready to leave home.

When I arrived in Boston in 1969 for the start of my first year of college at Boston University, I had more than academia on my mind. Smoking dope, hitchhiking around town, ecstatic dancing and chanting at the Hare Krishna temple, and going for bagels after midnight were a lot more interesting than attending classes. One fine spring day of that freshman year found me on the Boston Common, incited to riot by Abbie Hoffman. That night in Harvard Square, fires burned in the subway station and police tear-gassed the hordes of us who raced through the streets. I tasted some of the terror of what seemed to be the new order, the revolution we were attempting to bring about. When four students were killed by National Guardsmen at Kent State, I cried, realizing it could have been me. I was outraged that the government of my country might want to do me in. At the same time it was exhilarating to participate in scenes like ones to which Time magazine devoted cover stories.

Within in a few weeks I'd added to my non-academic syllabus an LSD trip, a protest march on Washington, and a massive student strike. I was lucky the university administration decided to pass all students that term; otherwise, I surely would have flunked out. After spring semester, I returned to my hometown in Georgia to my summer job as a copy girl for the local newspaper. A few days into it, however, I was impatient for the freedom I'd sampled in Boston. The younger brother of someone I'd dated in high school turned up and we fell in love. Without our parents' knowledge, we embarked on a hitchhiking trip that took us north to Ontario, west to Vancouver Island, and south to San Francisco. I had eighty dollars to my name. We ate a lot of peanut butter and honey sandwiches by the side of many long and desolate roads and soon fell out of love.

After a couple of months away we returned to Marietta. My mother informed me that my father had declared I was no longer welcome in the family home. The youngest of three daughters in a family of five children, I was by far the most rebellious. Undaunted by my father's declaration and by the fact that I was penniless, I moved to another town where I took up residence in a friend's closet. We subsisted on French toast made from bread, eggs and milk from the day-old store, as well as brown rice and vegetables. We raised food money by selling pink lemonade on the street corner late at night. A sign decorated with Day-Glo paint announcing "Lemonade 5 cents," glowed under the black light. While there was no LSD in our lemonade, passersby thought it was "electric" and we did nothing to discourage them from this assumption. We gave a free glass to the first person to pass by after 1 a.m., calling him Steppenwolf, although he was more likely the cook at the Waffle House. We had fun being as playful and carefree as we could be, making magic happen with lights, smoke and a willingness to suspend anything resembling adult responsibility. We improvised life and learned to trust our power to have a good time regardless of circumstances. If we were unable to afford marijuana, my friends and I smoked rabbit tobacco, a local weed, and got just as high.

For me, as for others of my generation, the now-proverbial sex, drugs, and rock 'n' roll, as well as radical politics, all held a great deal more interest than any other religion I was aware of at the time. After a while, however, the lifestyle that provided access to these experiences began to wear on me. At one point I lived with a group of people in a rambling house in the country outside of Atlanta. I worked at home making sandals for a living, and often I was alone with one of our roommates, an actively paranoid schizophrenic. Albert spent entire days sawing out screeching non-melodies on his cello. Or he'd stand for hours in front of the stove burning potatoes in a dry frying pan. I was afraid to be alone with him, but when I'd appeal to the others in the household for support, they'd respond by getting him drunk or stoned and encouraging him to hold forth in nonsensical German, assuring me that what we were doing was caring for this man better than his family or an institution could. I wasn't so sure and I was greatly relieved when his dad sent the police to take him to the hospital. A short time later I decided I'd had enough of living this hippie lifestyle and moved out.

While I was relieved finally to be on my own, moving into my own apartment felt somewhat like a failure. I hadn't been able to live an ideology that valued the collective over the individual. Without this to identify with I was forced to admit that I was just another single twenty-something living without any particular sense of meaning or direction for my life. A gnawing emptiness increasingly marked my days. By now, I was far behind my more conservative high school acquaintances, who had finished college and launched careers and families, and I was hungry to find some purpose for living. I longed for something, anything, to which I could commit myself. I enrolled in classes at the city university and bussed tables in a huge Chinese restaurant six nights a week for all of 1971.

For the next seven years I lived as if I were a somnambulist. I went through the motions of how I imagined normal people managed to live their lives, but was barely conscious that I was doing so. In somewhat mechanical fashion, I invented a life. I studied nursing and worked as a Registered Nurse. I lived with a man for four years. I planted a vegetable garden every spring and cooked meals with the produce. I had cordial relations with my family and my boyfriend's family. I took up weaving as a hobby and made nice scarves and rugs.

Toward the end of this period, in what I presumed would be an act of solidifying my existence as an adult on this planet, I got married. On my wedding day in 1977, it poured rain and I had a sore throat with a bad case of laryngitis. It was six weeks after an abortion I didn't really want to have. My communication with my fiancé, which had seemed to take place through a thick sheet of Plexiglas ever since the first month we were together, was limited to cryptic sarcasm which revealed his resistance to the whole notion of marriage. But I was so accustomed to ignoring my feelings about everything, it never occurred to me it might not be a good idea to go through with the wedding. I recall forcing myself to consummate the marriage on our wedding night, having lost most of my sexual desire several years before. After the wedding, I worked at trying to figure out what being a wife was all about and concluded it meant ceasing to exist as a person, and so I did.

# 2
# Awakening

*"Come to the edge ," he said.*
*"We are afraid," they said.*
*"Come to the edge," he said.*
*They came. He pushed them.*
*They flew.*

**GUILLUAME APOLLINAIRE**

Marriage took me to Missoula, Montana. My husband wanted to go to graduate school in Environmental Studies, and the program he was drawn to was 3200 miles from our home in Atlanta. In dutiful fashion I offered to work to put him through the two-year program. After he finished his Master's degree, he would support me while I went on to become a Nurse Midwife. That was the plan, at least until the day he announced he was having an affair with his office mate. Their long hours poring over air pollution statistics had led to romance. I already knew I couldn't compete with his fascination with the deterioration of air quality so I kicked him out of the house just before Thanksgiving, 1979.

A few months later, early on a chilly March morning, I woke up to the phone ringing. It was my older brother calling. "Daddy died yesterday morning," Brent said. And then, pausing, "It looks like it was suicide." Shocked, I called my husband with whom the day before I'd been sitting in a lawyer's office signing marriage dissolution papers. That night I flew back to Atlanta to be with the remaining family and to puzzle over the circumstances of my father's death. His suicide note, written in water-soluble ink, was largely illegible; it was mostly washed away when the bottle of vodka he'd used to swallow the Darvon had spilled on it. The words "my right testicle" remained as the only clue to his motivation. A subsequent autopsy showed nothing pathological in process, and the whole event seemed a tragic mystery.

Several days later I visited with a therapist I'd seen years before. He asked me what the timing of my father's death meant to me. A simple question, yet I was dumbfounded. Now long accustomed to a life pretty much void of such considerations, meaning was as foreign to me as a snowball in San Juan. Until Dan asked that question I'd been living in a world in which it appeared that things just happened randomly, and for the most part, absurdly and unpleasantly. With a divorce pending, my emotions scraped bottom while my cynicism scaled the heights. I was caught off-guard by this talk of meaning.

When I reflected on the timing of my father's death, I discovered that he died in exactly the same hour as I'd been signing the divorce papers in the law office. A coincidence? I began reading some books by Carl Jung and discovered otherwise. Synchronicity—an acausal, meaningful relationship between events—seemed a more apt, even plausible explanation for what had happened.

In one fell swoop I lost the two men I was most connected with. The result was that I was on my own without a man. I was a woman alone, and I needed to find some ground I could stand on with my own two feet. As painful as it was real, I found deep comfort in the possibility that my suffering could be redeemed through the insight that this sort of non-rational perspective offered.

Back in Montana, I pursued the question of meaning like a cat chasing a mouse. I purchased a copy of the oracular *I Ching*. I devoured Jung's introduction to the text and plunged into the practice of throwing the coins to divine the meaning of various situations. It seemed remarkable how accurately the hexagram images described whatever I was considering and how often the "judgements" reflected my own intuitive response to the question I'd asked. While I by no means relinquished all of my skepticism, I became curious about processes others used to find meaning in life, and, when I heard of an opportunity to have a psychic reading performed for just seven dollars, I signed myself up. At the very least I thought it could provide a few laughs, which I was in sore need of at the time.

The reading took place as part of a psychic meditation class held on the second floor of a decrepit office building in downtown Missoula. The man who seemed to be the leader of the group told me my energy field would be described by three of the students, "readers," who sat directly in front of me about five feet away. Another student sitting in a corner had instructions to ground the energy in the room, while yet another student was to act as scribe, recording the words of the readers.

The readers then closed their eyes and took turns speaking, using the metaphor of a rose to describe their findings. They told me about the thickness of the stem and the color and fullness of the flower. The roots of my rose were somewhat shallow, they said, and the plant in general seemed thirsty for water. There were leaves on the rose; however, one leaf appeared to have died. One of the readers, a woman, then matter-of-factly described the death of an unborn child, possibly due to an abortion.

I got an anxious feeling in my chest. I had never seen any of these people before. No one in Montana but my almost ex-husband knew anything about the abortion I'd had a year and a half before. There had been an ultimatum: no abortion, no wedding. Unwilling to confront him with the unfairness of such a choice, I terminated a pregnancy I'd longed for; I was certain that marriage would soften his position regarding children in the future. Of course, now I was fully aware that from such a beginning the marriage never had much chance of succeeding, and I was left with the ungrieved loss of the child whose life we aborted. This, apparently, could be seen by total strangers sitting in the same room with me with their eyes closed. I was stunned and ashamed. How could this woman know?

About the time I was recouping from this revelation, another of the readers spoke up. She was perceiving, she said, the presence of a departed soul in the room, hovering on my left side. As the reader spoke, I felt an urgent desire to leave the room; things were getting too bizarre for me. But despite my discomfort, I stayed, protecting myself with a promise that I could leave whenever I wanted to if it got too strange. When I was finally able to listen to her, she was describing how my father had attached himself to me with some invisible cords; that he was afraid, although she didn't know why. She was silent for a moment, then she continued. She was getting the impression that this soul had recently died, and… something else. Yes, could it be…? With this she opened her eyes and looked directly at me asking the question, could he possibly have killed himself?

I shivered and stuttered some affirmative response. A short time later, the reading concluded. I was handed the scribe's notes and I stumbled down the dark staircase out onto the bright, bustling street below. In a daze, I struggled to make sense of what had taken place. The content of the reading had come as no surprise to me, but the fact that these things, which could only have been known by me, could also be known by strangers was amazing. Having seen the invisible, they knew; and I knew that they knew. About that fact, I had no doubt.

After this reading, I lived more and more in an awareness that no matter what seemed to be going on in my life there was probably more to it than met the eye. My work as a nurse in a critical care unit presented a great deal of life-and-death drama that begged for this kind of understanding. I was rarely privy to a full revelation of that "something more", but occasionally I found peace in the midst of this chaotic environment. I discovered a way of being with people that allowed us all to face the terror of the pain and death that surrounded us simply by being present to it, yielding to the mystery of it, and leaning heavily on a faith-filled longing that more would be revealed. With this surrender, more courage, more love, more life, more meaning—whatever was lacking—inevitably seemed to come forth.

The miracles I began to witness sometimes manifested as physical recoveries for my patients, but often they did not. To my mind they were nonetheless healings. Accompanying them there would sometimes be a sense of *kairos*—a feeling that the ordinary realm had been penetrated by something extraordinary—creating a sense of divine timing or order. Yet this penetration did not seem to originate with an external source, but rather from within the people involved, who frequently revealed a power or grace that seemed to transcend accepted human limitations.

I recall one gentleman who was admitted with crushing chest pain in the midst of a major myocardial infarction. The doctor ordered an intravenous injection of morphine sulfate to be given until the man was comfortable. This was a fairly typical order under the circumstances. Given the extent of his pain, to make him comfortable would mean to sedate him until his respirations were so depressed he would stop breathing. I went to my patient's bedside with a dose of morphine that could permanently ease his pain. Checking his vital signs before administering the medication, I found his systolic blood pressure was barely audible at fifty millimeters of mercury; his pulse was rapid, irregular, and thready; his skin was cool and clammy. But he was conscious and coherent as he looked me directly in the eye and asked me if he was going to die.

In the chaos surrounding his admission to the hospital, no one had told him about his condition and prognosis. Following orders, I was about to give him a drug that would likely end his life, and he wouldn't have had the first clue. Typically, the hospital staff would think we'd done the man a favor by making him unconscious, but, by his question, he let me know otherwise. I told him I couldn't say for sure, but all the signs pointed to that likelihood. I told him I could give him a shot to put him to sleep and out of his misery.

He then asked how long I thought he might live without the injection. I checked his blood pressure once again and it was so low I could not even palpate his pulse this time. Not wanting to frighten him, I replied that I couldn't say exactly. I asked him if there was something he wanted or needed to complete before he died and he said he'd like to say goodbye to his brother. Not knowing anything about his brother's location, I told him I believed he could stay alive long enough for that to happen if I gave him just enough pain medication to dull the pain, but not kill it and him. He assented to this. I gave him enough to take a slight edge off the pain and then rushed off to call his brother who, as it turned out, lived in a small town several hours away by car. The patient's doctor and I looked on with amazement as our patient lived without any discernible blood pressure until his brother arrived five hours later. They spent five minutes together saying goodbye and then he died, unassisted by medication.

Incidents such as this one reminded me of Viktor Frankl's experiences of life in a Nazi concentration camp. In *Man's Search for Meaning*, Frankl describes the difference between those who survived the horrific conditions of the camp and those who succumbed to them. The former seemed to grasp the truth in Nietzsche's words: "He who has a why to live for can bear almost any how." If only for a few hours, this man's purpose, expressed as intention, kept him alive in spite of intense pain and vital organ collapse.

A great deal of the time during the period I worked in critical care, however, I was depressed. For every moment I witnessed a profound transformation in a patient or family member, there were hours spent struggling with a medical system that dehumanized people I came to love.

In the Coronary Care Unit, I once admitted a man in his early sixties who had suffered a relatively mild heart attack. He was frightened, though, and as we went through the admission procedure he began to cry. "You know," he said to me shyly, "this is the first time I've cried since I was six years old. I didn't think I knew how to cry anymore." I assured him it was a good thing for him to just feel his fear and sadness. He continued, "I've worked so hard, trying to be a good husband and father. I am just so tired. I guess it took me almost dying to realize how much I want to live. I don't want to work so hard. I really want to know what I can do to slow down and take care of myself."

I recall his complete sincerity in that moment. I was heartened that now, motivated from the depths of his desire to live, there was a possibility he would learn an important lesson from this frightening experience. But all of that vanished as soon as his physician approached his bedside. "Don't worry about a thing," his doctor declared. "We'll have your plumbing fixed in no time. A little bypass and you'll be back on your feet better than ever." I could not help but think that a deep healing had been foiled once again by a superficial quick fix of the symptoms.

One evening shift in Intensive Care the nurses on duty anxiously watched for hours as another man who'd undergone bypass surgery earlier in the day bled excessively through the tube in his chest cavity. Hours after the man should have been returned to the operating room, his surgeon dramatically called for the O.R. team to prepare to reopen the man's chest immediately, without benefit of anesthesia. When the surgeon proceeded to remove the incision staples and apply the rib spreaders, it became obvious that the man was awake and aware of pain for he started kicking his feet. My own heart literally ached as I watched this travesty, which would undoubtedly go down on record as an unavoidable emergency procedure.

From that time on, night after night I found myself blankly gazing at the life support machines that pumped away in the bodies of my patients. Increasingly, it was becoming clear that my job was to nurse the medical machine, not people. To the rhythm of various beeps and blips and whooshes, for two more years I addressed the universe with this mantra: There's got to be more to life than this.

The winters in Missoula were long and cold. I had moved to Montana in 1978 to meet the coldest winter there in fifty years. My husband left me in November about the time of the first snow. During a three-week period around Christmas, the temperature dropped to thirty degrees below zero at night and never went above minus ten Farenheit during the day. The heat in my Volkswagen didn't work below freezing, so I'd drive around town with the windows down to keep the windshield from icing up too badly on the inside.

Subsequent winters were warmer but imperceptibly so. My second winter in Missoula, an alcoholic Blackfoot man I'd met as a patient in the hospital, died from exposure after he spent the night in an alley. I thought I'd freeze to death myself sitting in the unheated church awaiting his funeral. The third winter had some cozy moments spent with a man with whom I was deeply in love, and I cross-country skied to and from the hospital on the railroad tracks when they were covered with snow for the winter. But the next year, the relationship was on the skids and the snowfall was disappointing.

It was in February of this, the fourth winter, my best friend left town for the West Coast. We met for breakfast at the Queen of Tarts, a local café, the day she was to leave. As a parting gift, she presented me with a copy of Scott Peck's recently published book, *The Road Less Traveled.* For hours after we said good-bye, I wandered aimlessly around downtown Missoula, clutching the book and feeling like a lost dog.

Eventually, hungry and sad, I went into the Mammyth Bakery, usually a place where I might see a friendly face or two. But this day there were only a few others in the café, none of them familiar. I started to eat my meal and was actually finding some small comfort in the good food when I noticed a fellow at the next table looking a bit peculiar. By the time I recognized why his strangeness seemed familiar, he lurched from his seat toward my table and vomited all over it. As a metaphor for my life at the time, it was a revolting but an apt gesture. I drove home, went to bed, and read Peck's book.

The next morning I awakened early and continued reading. Still glum, the book at least offered validation for my feelings of depression. But Chapter Five gave me something even more. "The Case of Theodore" described a young man, full of promise, who encounters tragedy at an early age, makes an embittered decision against life, and hides out until his suffering is so great he must seek help. Through therapy, he rediscovers his childhood loves and aspirations and is able to integrate his spirituality into his adult life. As this is accomplished, he is able to fully experience his love for God, which he'd felt compelled to keep secret for most of his life. As his cynicism falls away, he initially rejects, but then embraces, the idea of expressing his love of God by becoming a minister.

As I read this chapter I was absorbed in a surreal sensation. I could not shake the feeling it had been deliberately written about me and for me. The details of Theodore's life were different, but our reactions and decisions had been identical. So deep was my recognition of myself in this character that, by the end of the chapter, I was sobbing uncontrollably. Love and counsel seemed to pour through Peck's writing, and I bathed myself in permission to drop into my most ancient, tender longings.

I remembered an afternoon in early autumn when I was about six. Lying on my bed, I had been put down for a nap but was not yet asleep. I could hear leaves rustling in the breeze and gentle family voices out in the back yard. Alone, drenched in the pool of sunlight that poured through the window, I had a feeling of being exquisitely myself, fully innocent, loved completely and unconditionally. I basked in this sunlit presence until I fell asleep. When I woke up some time later, the room was dark and cool; however, an inner glow continued to warm me. I moved cautiously out of my room and down the stairs to join my family, now raucous with activity in the kitchen.

Before primitive people knew how to make fire themselves, they preserved their lightning-made fire as they moved from one camp to another by wrapping hot coals in layers of leaves. As a child in an alcoholic family, I was already aware that my mystical sunlight experience was precious like fire and needed protection from the teasing condescension that would likely follow any open disclosure I might make of what had happened during my nap time. So, I buried the burning embers deep in my heart under layers of humor that became sarcasm, intelligence that developed into cynicism, self-sufficiency that turned to contempt for need of any kind. I buried the intense love I'd received and my longing to have more of it so well I couldn't find it when it was most needed.

The story is told of how the gods, desiring to guard the se-crets of the universe from humans, sought a safe hiding place. After considering the tallest mountain peak and the deepest abyss of the oceans, the gods finally decided to place the cherished se-crets in the one place where human beings would be least likely to look. And, as the story tells us, throughout the ages humans have looked high and low for those secrets, which from the crea-tion of life itself, have been hidden within their own hearts. On this cold Montana morning in February 1983, I am sure the gods laughed with delight. After dissolving the layers of pain with which I had protected myself for so long, I discovered the sunlit fire of love within my heart for the second time. Like the most prodigal of children, I was overcome with joy.

Past, present, and future seemed to melt into a Now full of love, meaning, purpose and direction. Years of living in the ques-tion of What am I here for? resolved in an instant. It was clear that I was, like Theodore, a lover of God. At the time, I couldn't have given any theological description of this God I loved; I had no conceptual belief in God. But I simply knew I loved It, It loved me and we longed to be together in love always. I also knew that my life work from that point on would be about pro-claiming this presence I had experienced first-hand. I saw that the crafts and trades I'd explored until that moment dealt with material of secondary value. No wonder sandal-making, weaving, and even nursing, couldn't hold my attention. I was called to live and work in meaning and in love. This was my right livelihood: I was to be a minister.

In that moment, doubt cast no shadow. The next moment, however, I found myself in familiar darkness. Ten years earlier, when I told my mother I'd decided to go to nursing school, she retorted, "You can't be a nurse! You never wanted to be a nurse when you were little! You don't really want to be a nurse!" Now my own objections surfaced: "I can't be a minister," I reasoned. "I'm not the type." In my mind, ministers were good and holy and nice; I was just a cynical old hippie. Besides, I argued to myself, "I hate church. I'm not even sure I believe in God. There must be some mistake!" Underneath these considerations, I still knew the truth, and I also knew it wouldn't be easy this time to hide my knowing.

# 3

# Broken Down, Broken Open

*The fates guide them that will;*
*them that won't they drag.*

**SENECA**

I was a lot like Jonah in the early days following what I came
to regard as my calling to ministry. In the Old Testament
tale, God, or Yahweh, tells Jonah to go to Nineveh where he
had a job for Jonah to do. But Jonah, an independent kind of guy,
doesn't really feel like it.

To get away from Yahweh and his demands, Jonah jumps on
a ship headed to Tarshish—in the exact opposite direction from
Nineveh. As the story continues, we learn that Yahweh is not
pleased; he creates a big storm that wreaks havoc for the ship on
which Jonah has set sail. The ship's crew looks around for who
might be responsible for bringing down the wrath of God and
before long all eyes turn to Jonah. Whether he deserves it or not,
Jonah takes the heat and lets the crew throw him overboard.
Then, Yahweh sends a great fish that swallows Jonah into its
huge belly, where he stays for three days, after which the big fish
vomits him up. When Yahweh yet again commands his servant
to go to Nineveh, Jonah obeys.

Even though I felt I'd been called to be a minister, it was easy
for me to think of other, less bothersome things to do with my
life. In meditation one day, I began visualizing an ocean scene. I
saw a sunny beach with blue-green water; the surf with its frothy
white foam curled gently upon the shore. I imagined myself div-
ing in the water, then surfacing, floating, completely relaxed and

at peace, soothed by the sound of waves…and then the telephone rang. Still halfway in this reverie, I answered and heard the voice of a friend who lived on the beach in Florida. What a meaningful coincidence! We talked and our conversation eventually led to an invitation for me to come to Florida to share a waterfront condo with Dawna and her husband. Within a very short time I was convinced I was being called, not to ministry, but to Florida and to a life at the beach that seemed a lot more appealing than life as a stuffy minister.

Within six weeks, I'd sold everything I owned except my house and what I could pack into my VW Bug. My plans to leave went smoothly except for the acute eye condition that afflicted me shortly after I'd decided to go. The iris of my left eye became suddenly and painfully inflamed. When I viewed the symptoms of this condition metaphorically, I was troubled because my vision was blurred and it hurt to be in any light. As I'd now become accustomed to making decisions according to signs and symbols, I strained to discover if there was a message in this regarding my move from Montana. But every time I considered the possibility of staying or going, leaving was by far the strongest impulse. I treated my eye with medication and bought the darkest sunglasses I could find for my travel east. Not wanting to miss any opportunity for religious significance, I left Montana on Easter Sunday to begin my trip to St. Petersburg, that is, Tarshish.

By mid-afternoon my travel was halted by a blizzard that closed the mountain pass east of Bozeman, Montana. The next day, the weather seemed to have cleared, the pass opened and, despite the bitter cold, I resumed my trip. Only a few minutes from the town, I was already approaching the summit of the pass. I noticed I'd only seen one other vehicle on the road, a tractor-trailer, yet the road was snow-packed and my studded tires seemed to be holding well. Then suddenly I drove into a thick cloud full of wind and swirling snow. Without warning, I hit ice and the car started sliding. The thick snow blew directly into the windshield; even with time to look, I wouldn't have been able to see a thing. The car spun around 360 degrees three times on the interstate highway crossing Bozeman Pass. Although I resisted the impulse to brake and I steered into the skid as I'd been taught years before, I had no sense of being in control of the outcome of this drama. I did have a sense of being tested. Would I trust?

Would I surrender? Would I let God have my life? Silently, privately, I assented. The car came to a stop with headlights pointed east. Without further equivocation, I put my foot to the accelerator and drove on.

For three days I drove through the most desolate parts of Montana, Wyoming and Colorado in a virtual whiteout. Unable to see the side of the road for the wind-driven snow, I simply prayed to stay on the pavement—and I did. The heat in my car still didn't work so I wrapped my down sleeping bag around my legs and feet and prayed for warm places to stop so I wouldn't get frostbite. Roadside restaurants appeared miraculously from time to time and I was renewed with cups of hot soup. When I was too exhausted to drive in the afternoon, neon motel lights beckoned like a ghostly specter on the horizon. Each night of this storm, I considered turning back, but the next morning weather reports assured me the clear skies were ahead, not behind me, and I pushed on.

A week later, I was in St. Petersburg, an oasis of warm sun and palm trees. I lived in what came to be known to me as the Surrealistic Palace. The building was painted white and designed with stark lines. The condo had high ceilings and plain white walls with large sliding glass windows on both sides of the living space, the view looking out over wide expanses of ocean and the bay. There was no solid ground to be seen from our apartment, and I spent my first weeks there with my mind bobbing along with the gentle waves, feeling empty and slightly bored with the endless seascape. Although the weather was a lot better than in Montana, the same feelings of dissatisfaction with life persisted in my new location.

I still needed money and I needed something to do. I was tired of nursing but as I was uncertain how else to earn as much money, I applied for a Florida license to practice. Soon thereafter I got a job as a relief nurse for the local hospice. My first weekend on call I was paged repeatedly, and three people died.

I also had two car accidents. The first happened on Saturday night as I was driving to Clearwater to attend the third death. Someone rear-ended me, smashing the lid to the engine compartment into the engine. I had to get the car towed back to the Palace. The next day I banged the lid out, and, despite the big oil spot I found under the car the next morning, it started.

I went off-call Monday morning at nine, and to celebrate surviving the weekend, I drove myself to a little café. While I ate, a tropical storm swept into the area. I lingered over my coffee thinking the downpour would eventually let up, but it didn't. Tired of waiting, I waded through the ankle-deep water in the parking lot to the car. I thought it was a good omen that the car started so well. Visibility was poor as the rain continued to fall in torrents and deep water collected in the streets. Nonetheless, I drove on without too much difficulty. About a mile from the condo, I stopped for a traffic light. As the light turned yellow on the road I was going to turn onto, I noticed a car coming from my left speed up to make the light, while a car coming from my right turned left into the intersection. I then watched as in apparent slow motion the two cars collided and careened toward me.

"Here goes my front end," I remember thinking as we played bumper cars for real. "Here goes my car. Here goes my job. Thank you, God, I get to leave this place." Sure enough, with the two accidents in thirty-six hours, neither of which I had apparently done anything to bring about except sit in traffic, I had a car that was a total, undriveable wreck. It wouldn't take a Mack truck rolling over me to convince me my Florida vacation had come to a crashing halt. I was ready to leave.

Later that night, my mother called to see how things were going. I told her I didn't have a car anymore, and without a car, no way to work. I was miserable. With a surprising lack of chiding or criticism, she invited me to pack my things and come to her new summer home on Martha's Vineyard. Within a week I arrived. I secured a job in the ICU at the local hospital, worked into the fall, and spent time with my family. When it turned too cold to stay any longer, I drove my cousin's RV to her home in Colorado, and eventually landed back in Missoula where I'd started out seven months earlier.

Several weeks later I attended a service at the little Unity church I'd attended off and on for several years. It occupied a humble white-shingled building a block down the street from my house, and I had initially been drawn to go there when I felt quite lonely. The people congregating on the front steps seemed interesting, not like regular churchgoers, and I spent many Sundays taking solace in the message of self-acceptance and forgiveness that the minister typically presented.

On this first Sunday back in Missoula, during the social hour, David, the minister, took me aside and asked if I was still thinking about becoming a minister. I said yes; I was a true believer now—I truly believed my life would not work ever again unless I agreed to follow my calling. David was typically an easygoing guy with a non-directive approach to everything, so I was taken by surprise when he asked me to make an appointment to meet with him later in the week.

David and I met early on a blustery November morning in the shabby add-on to the church that served as David's office. I wasn't sure what David wanted to talk about, although I definitely felt I was on the spot. As we sat across from each other in that ramshackle little room, the import of this meeting began to dawn on me. I sat up straight and listened to what the man had to say.

David said that if I was serious about becoming a minister there were three things he wanted me to do to prepare myself. Later I discovered these were standard steps every local minister would ask a prospective applicant to take as part of the process for admission to the Unity ministerial training program. But in this context, I heard his requests as if they were from a fairy tale—the tasks which must be fulfilled before the fairy godmother would grant a cherished wish; or, from an esoteric tradition, as the required steps for initiation into a mystical priesthood. Looking back, perhaps I wasn't so far off base.

First, David asked me to begin facilitating a small discussion group. I had been a part of that group at different times and knew it would be easy for me to do. No problem, I told him, I'll start on Friday.

Next, he needed someone to serve as his platform assistant on Sunday mornings during the service. The platform assistant opened the service with a welcome statement, read the announcements, and led the congregation in The Lord's Prayer. Because there was a script to follow, this reading to the group didn't seem too difficult. I readily agreed to take this second step, beginning the following Sunday.

"There's one other thing," David said, his voice deepening. I sat up straighter with even more attention to hear his third request. "I'd like you to give the lesson one Sunday morning in February when I'll be out of town. That's all."

That's all! I heard those words and something told me that my response to this third request would determine the entire rest of my life. I plunged into fear as if I had fallen through a crack in the earth and was tumbling through an abyss toward infinity.

I revisited the moments in my life when I'd been asked to speak freely before an audience. In grammar school, I'd always panicked when it came time for Show & Tell. For years, teachers wrote comments on my report card: "Ellie is so shy, it is difficult for her to talk in front of other children." "Ellie needs to improve her oral expression."

Things didn't improve. Later on, as the editor of my high school newspaper, I was supposed to introduce the staff at an assembly after the staff's annual promotional skit. When I took the microphone, however, all I could see were the faces of twelve hundred students all looking at me. Then I stared at the staff members, all of them turned expectantly toward me. I went totally blank. I recognized them, yet when I tried to say their names aloud, nothing came out. I stood there suffering mightily until, after what seemed like eons, someone removed the microphone from me and did what I'd been unable to do.

Now David was asking me to speak, not about anything trivial, but about what for me was Ultimate Meaning...Universal Truth...God. This seemed impossible. If I couldn't simply announce the names of people I knew well, how could I say anything about a subject of which I was basically ignorant? At the same time, it became clear I was being asked to try. I had been called to be a minister months before but I hadn't yet accepted the invitation. I was being given another opportunity.

I took a deep breath and said Yes!

As the word left my mouth goose bumps jumped up from their epidermal hiding places. I felt breathless and dizzy. When I opened my eyes, everything in the room seemed to be swirling around.

David sat across from me smiling. "The room is moving," he stated matter-of-factly. Amazed, I could only stare back at him. We went to the window to look outside. Trees swayed and power lines bounced up and down. I thought the nuclear reactor in Hanford, Washington, had blown up and we were feeling the first effects, just as two years earlier we'd heard the explosion hours before the fallout from Mount St. Helen's eruption covered the town. I imagined death was imminent and was glad one of my final acts was to have said yes to my calling. In the tradition of the Native American people, I felt it was a good day to die.

The rocking and rolling settled down after a few minutes. David and I sat down once again and he chuckled. "Well," he said, "Earthquakes have always been a great symbol for the breaking open of consciousness."

Evidently, I had just received an unmistakable sign. Life as I had known it was over and a new one lay ahead.

# 4

# Life Is the Present

*People who have not been in Narnia
sometimes think that a thing
cannot be good and terrible
at the same time.*

**C. S. LEWIS**

It took me a couple of years to tie up the loose ends of my nursing career and rent the house I owned in Missoula. When I was finally ready, my admission to Unity's ministerial training program proceeded smoothly. Still, I had some concern I wasn't the type to be a minister. I chose not to misrepresent myself to the admissions committee by dressing myself up to conform to what I thought they would find acceptable. Instead of a business suit I wore a nice flowered dress. One interviewer, noting my non-conformity, asked if I'd be willing to assume a ministerial image if I were accepted to the program. I told him I'd be willing to do whatever it took to fulfill my calling, so I spent the next two years playing dress-up. One of my classmates showed me how to put on makeup; another introduced me to the wonderful world of the local mall.

Another interviewer marveled at the story of my calling (complete with the confirmation by earthquake) and at the deep, resonant quality of my voice. "You'll go far with that voice," he assured me. I concluded from these early conversations that ministry might just be as simple as looking good and sounding good. If so, it seemed I was off to a promising start.

The first few months of school were great fun. I landed in a class full of other refugees of the 1960s and '70s, a number of whom were in recovery from alcoholism and drug addiction.

While I had feared I wouldn't be holy enough to be a minister, I found myself in the midst of a group for whom excessive piety was not a problem. In fact, most of my classmates had a great sense of humor about their spirituality, even as they were sincerely devoted to it.

As much fun as I was having with my classmates, dancing at Kansas City blues clubs, riding around with the T-tops off and listening to the Pointer Sisters' "Jump" blasting at full volume, the real enjoyment came with the rediscovery of my mind. My metaphysics professor, Marvin Anderson, a man whose mind I greatly admired, early recognized my ability to develop original ideas and communicate them with some clarity in writing. I fell in love with ideas again and loved nothing more than entertaining them in my meditations, on long walks around the lake near where I lived, and in conversations with Marvin. I no longer felt I had to wait for signs and wonders to indicate God's presence. God was as close as the next idea that revealed itself to me. All I needed to do, it seemed, was be still enough to receive those ideas.

One morning, our Prayer and Meditation class was dismissed with the instruction to spend an hour in free-form spiritual practice. While I could have used the time to go over my notes for a talk I was to give immediately afterwards, I decided to spend the hour in silence in a meditation hut I'd discovered a few days earlier. Making my way through the shrubs hiding the old stone building, I was disappointed to find a woman retreatant already sitting on one of the benches inside. I noticed from the tag she wore that her name was Marietta, the same as the Georgia town I'd grown up in. She welcomed me with a warm smile, but, when I indicated to her that I was keeping silence, she respectfully withdrew into her own space. I took a seat on another bench facing an obelisk that stood about four feet tall in the center of the hut. As I did so, a sense of presence came over me similar to what I'd experienced previously only with hallucinogens, but this was more powerful—and at the same time far more gentle.

For a moment, I was overcome with bliss, saturated with a feeling of deep intimacy with everything in the scene—the woman, the obelisk, the rock benches, the bushes rustling in the breeze outside the hut—everything at once familiar and profound. Marietta finished her meditation and stood up to leave. I had tears in my eyes as I watched her go. Then, sitting alone in the silence, words formed from some place deep within that no longer felt like me, "Blessed is the silence; blessed are the words that issue forth from the silence."

Still in a very altered state of consciousness, I knew I was destined to deliver these words to my class, which was to start a few minutes later. The instructor habitually chose someone to open the class with prayer, and I sensed that today it would be me. The words I'd been given were the prayer that wanted to be prayed that day. Gradually, I returned to a more normal state, although I remained aware that something quite profound had just taken place. I kept silent as I walked back to the classroom building and took my seat inside. Just as if the scene had been rehearsed a hundred times, when everyone was in place, the instructor turned to me and asked me to open the class with prayer. On cue, I went to the front of the room and opened our communications class with the words that I'd been directed, it seemed, to deliver. Then, fully back to normal, I went on to give the talk I'd been scheduled to give, which happened to be a telling in my own words of the Old Testament story of Jonah. As clear and direct as the prayer had been, my own words were as muddy and hesitant as ever.

Later I told Marvin what had happened and my uncertainty about what to do with it. "You don't need to *do* anything," he said. "Just enjoy it. Mystical experiences don't come along all that often, so just enjoy that you had one." This was an entirely new order of fun. I had gotten to play on the multi-dimensional playground, drug-free. I appreciated that a new world seemed to be opening its portals to me and that I had someone to guide me through them.

And so it was, a couple of months later I called Marvin at home to tell him I had just been diagnosed with cancer. He laughed, "Well, Ellie, don't worry about it. You just signed up for the accelerated training course, that's all! Most Unity ministers don't get cancer until they've been out in the field for six or seven years." He went on to say that cancer was easy to heal; it was the common cold that was difficult to treat. I was shocked by what seemed like his flippant response to my dire situation.

That morning I'd found my mailbox stuffed with pink message slips from the office of the oral surgeon who'd biopsied a smooth, round, painless bump on the roof of my mouth a few weeks earlier. The office staff wouldn't tell me anything over the telephone, so I knew the report wasn't good. In meditation class, I visualized a pathology report. It read, "malignant neuroma." At lunch, I saw myself floating in the room above the rest of my class. After lunch, I went with a friend to get the pathology results. The initial report did indeed read, "malignant neuroma," although this was later discovered to be incorrect. The condition as described on the final pathology report was actually a "muco-epidermoid carcinoma of the palate." I was immediately set up to see a Head and Neck surgeon the next day, although the way I felt, a trip to the guillotine seemed more in order.

Marvin assured me the reason cancer was easier to heal than a cold was that cancer gets our attention so effectively. We believe a cold will eventually go away and it does, but only after a lot of snuffling and snorting. On the other hand, we don't believe that cancer eventually will go away; instead, we believe cancer will kill us. But if we are not paralyzed with fear, a cancer diagnosis can actually mobilize us to take action that can heal it.

The surgeon, Dr. Rogers, was direct. "We're going to do everything we can to save your life, young lady." Including, as he described it, a surgical procedure that involved pulling all the upper teeth on the left side of my mouth, and the removal of the roof of my mouth on that side, leaving a permanent opening from my sinus to my mouth. If lymph nodes in my neck were involved, there was also the possibility of a radical neck dissection, which, from my nursing experience, I knew to be a very disfiguring procedure. Dr. Rogers explained that the mouth surgery might also distort my speech and prevent me from smiling properly ever again.

As a nurse, I'd seen how often the treatment of a disease was far worse than the cure. I'd made up my mind years before that if I ever got cancer I would not treat it at all. Given my diagnosis, however, this was a difficult position to maintain. I was frightened, and the forces of the tradition that were automatically scheduling my blood tests, X-rays, CAT scans, and the surgery itself, offered what seemed to be the only way out. Dr. Rogers seemed to believe my life was worth saving, and since I'd spent so much time wondering if that was so, his conviction impressed me. Without sufficient awareness of an alternative, I agreed to his treatment plan. The CAT scan was set for my birthday, two days hence. Surgery was scheduled to take place in nine days.

When Marvin described the action we could take to heal the cancer, however, he had a different approach in mind. As a metaphysician, he understood that real healing occurs in the realm of the cause, not the effect. While Dr. Rogers could work on the effects, Marvin and I set out to discover and heal the erroneous beliefs that were manifesting as this malignant condition in my body. Marvin, my spiritual surgeon, proposed an inner treatment plan.

We set aside specific times during the day for deep meditation. In the meditation, I was to seek illumination about the cause of the cancer and listen for guidance on healing it. I was to devote myself to this endeavor full-time: this was to be my work until the healing was accomplished. We began immediately.

Laser-beam mental attention, alternating with frantic fear, deep sadness, and sweeping emotion marked the days following my diagnosis. To help me keep my focus, I moved in with a friend, Bill, who had also committed himself to my healing. I slept on a mattress in his spare room, my dreams filled with roses and light. Waking up each day in early morning sunlight, not remembering where I was, I basked in the sweetness of my dream, but zooming back to the reality in which I'd been delivered a death sentence, I awaited my guillotine execution scheduled for eight, seven, now six days hence. My tears seemed to flow without end.

Reclaiming my focus with meditation, a mantra took up residence in my mind. "God loves me," some distant voice whispered from within. Of course, I didn't believe this. After all, I had cancer! I was going to die, or at the very least be permanently disfigured. "God loves me," the whisper echoed, louder now. I was angry, hurt, confused. How could God love me and still I was in all this pain? More tears. The voice persisted. "God loves me." I did not want to hear those words anymore; they were a slap in the face of my disease. Nevertheless, "God loves me" repeated again and again.

Bill and I meditated together the day before my CAT scan. He sensed a message from my father and asked permission to deliver it to me. Sure. Your father says you don't have to die to prove you love him. More tears, more "God loves me." We prayed The Lord's Prayer aloud. At the end, where the words are about the Power and the Glory, the room seemed to flood with light. Bill and I were both in tears, feeling the Power and the Glory in the light, in us, all around us. Laughing, crying, yes, God does love me, this cancer—it *is* a gift. All of this pain, such deep openings to God, what I've longed for all this time, here it is, now. I love God. I love this cancer. I am healed!

The next day, my birthday, we were off to the hospital. The mantra repetition was ringing now like bells in a town square celebrating the day. Yes, through it all, God loves me. I had never known this before. God was always an abstract, faraway principle, not something personal. Now God was moving in closer than my thoughts, closer than my breath. No explaining it, but it was alright. The technician had to start an IV for the CAT scan. It hurt but I was supported by the thought that God loves me; God's love dissolved the pain. I was strapped to the table that moved in and out of the scanning cylinder, but when I heard the buzz of the radiation I simply felt more of the Power and the Glory penetrating to the core of the ancient hurts of my wounded past. I am free!

The CAT scan was negative, but the surgery was still scheduled to go ahead. Each day now offered me the possibility of loving myself as much as God did. I explored the myriad ways in which I was unkind to myself. Money, for instance. I had no health insurance and, one day I panicked. I thought, I'll never be able to pay for all this. The expenses are mounting exponentially. Perhaps I should just go ahead and die.

With that thought, I found myself in a spontaneous meditation on my own death. What would it be like to die? Instantly I had a vision of two doors. On the left, through the door called Death, different forms, but still more life; on the right, through the door called Life, the familiar characters of this lifetime. No judgement, simply a choice of Life or Life, where do you want to live it?

I recalled a decision I'd made somewhere along the way to die young, a tragic death, having accomplished the writing of the Great American Novel. Since I'd just turned 34, except for the novel, this cancer was right on schedule. The train had pulled up to the station and all I had to do was climb aboard. I heard the engine running, felt the energy of this large machine ready to take off to parts unknown called Death. Yet, a last glimpse through the door of this Life intrigued me. My life here was clearly a work in progress. I wanted to know how this story would unfold. What would the young heroine actually do with herself, with her calling to minister, where would her longing for love lead her next? Curious to live this story out to its conclusion, I let the train pull out of the station without me this time. As the vision faded, money seemed less of a problem. Certainly, it was nothing to die over, and why treat myself poorly for the lack of it? I could love myself with or without money.

Other problems, my perennial difficulty with relationship, career dissatisfaction, and antagonism with my family were like bowling pins now. My love of life just knocked them over. From this new perspective, I marveled that the fear and misery I associated with these worries could have dominated my existence as they had for so long.

Surgery was just around the corner now. One of my sisters and my mother arrived the night before. I was grateful they came, although their familiar presence made it more difficult to maintain my blissful contact. Early in the morning as I got ready to go to the hospital, I looked in the mirror at my mouth to see it intact for the last time. I knew when I saw it next my mouth, my face, everything would be different, not whole ever again. I was surrendered, but sad. I drove to the hospital with my sister. The roads were very icy. I checked in, and while I waited for the lab work, a chaplain came to comfort me. Her conversation was irritating, filled with platitudes, and I tried to be nice to her. I could tell she was more afraid for me than I was. I found my mantra and once again my mind and heart were filled with peace.

In the holding area, a resident started my IV. He missed the first time and apologized. I knew just how he felt, so I showed him the vein I used on patients when I was a nurse starting IVs. He was grateful and slipped the needle in easily. In the operating room, I was blinded by the bright lights. I asked the anesthesiologist to let me know when he was about to inject the anesthesia. The liquid sleep was cold as ice sliding up the vein in my left arm. My last memory before slipping away was the feeling of "God loves me."

Eight hours later, I woke up in the Recovery Room. Disoriented, the endotracheal tube was still in place. I was gagging and there didn't seem to be anyone around. Dangling over my head, a garish Santa and reindeer. Christmas music blared from the P.A. system. Over in the corner, I heard voices discussing holiday food recipes. Nauseous, frightened, I thought I'd died and gone to hell. Finally, I was extubated. My face was throbbing and I touched it lightly to find it swollen, huge. The fact of my new deformity hit me hard now, and I struggled to conjure up my soothing mantra. It was there, but I could not quite regain the peace I had before.

When I was rolled out of the recovery area, however, my friend Bill was in the hallway. He was very excited, practically jumping up and down. He exclaimed again and again, "They didn't find any more cancer! No more cancer!" The frozen section of the bone in which the tumor had been embedded was sparkling clean, he said, there were no cancer cells there. I was amazed. This was the best news I'd ever heard. I really wasn't going to die. The precious life I had discovered in the last ten days—there was going to be a lot more of it. I felt deeply grateful.

Then Bill spread the icing on the cake. The surgeon didn't remove the whole roof of my mouth. Pleased with the results of the frozen section, he'd only pulled a couple of teeth and taken off a corner of the palate in the back. The prosthedontist later assured me he'd seen worse deformity from a wisdom tooth extraction.

The next day, I went back to my own room at school. I watched TV and ate oatmeal. The swelling in my mouth gradually receded, and a week later I gently returned to normal. My sister and mother went back east to spend the holidays with the rest of the family. They asked me to come along but I wanted to be alone with my rediscovered self. On Christmas Eve, I ventured out to a candle lighting service. The first song I sang through the new hole in my mouth was "Joy to the World!"

It was the first Christmas in my whole life when I wasn't disappointed that Santa Claus isn't real. For the first time Santa didn't need to be real because Christ was. Not the baby Jesus of the manger scene from my Catholic childhood. Not even the Jesus that was crucified, although I could certainly relate to that experience more than ever before. It wasn't Jesus Christ who became real to me that Christmas Eve, but *the* Christ, my own divinity, the Christ of Ellie. I recognized my deepest and most essential self as Ellie Christ. I didn't need to look under the festive tree to find my Christmas present, because it seemed my own divine essence had healed me, spiritually and, very possibly, physically as well. Perhaps I had simply discovered a wholeness that had been there all along. I didn't really need to figure it all out. I had life and I had it abundantly. I now recognized, as the Christ within me whispered, "The gift has already been given." The rest of my life I was to unwrap that gift, to enjoy the present moment.

# 5

# The Power of No

*To know your mind, you should mind your no.*
*Without the ability to say no, one's assent is*
*merely a form of submission and*
*not the free expression of one's will.*

**ALEXANDER LOWEN**

Following the initial elation of my healing, I plunged into a depression. Money concerns resumed and I reluctantly took a nursing job to pay the bills. It was difficult, because I was too identified now with the patients. It had become impossible to objectify their pain; when I needed to give someone a shot, I'd secretly cry in sympathy.

Ministerial training classes seemed boring and irrelevant. Just being with my friends and classmates was trying. Meaning well, they did not seem to know how to relate to my surgery. To me it felt as if they pasted a cardboard faith over the terror they felt whenever I came around. I didn't know how to communicate to them the experience of my spiritual healing—how the bad stuff revealed such a tremendous good and how real optimism comes of a process far deeper than mere positive thinking. I could not yet find the words to explain that the abyss we fill with our fears is actually lined with floating feathers; that it is okay to jump in, far less painful than hanging onto the edge by our fingernails. I felt isolated in this awareness, which I tried to tone down. I had to learn how to act normal again.

My periodic visits to the doctor aroused apprehension and caused me to summon the mantra into service once more. At first check-ups were fine, but then a small lump appeared in my neck which needed watching. In another month I was told, if it's still there, the surgeon would need to biopsy it. Marvin and I got to work again. He claimed there was no substance to this physical growth, and I wanted to agree, but I found myself sad and confused. Despite my best efforts to think otherwise, I felt victimized. At this point I found a therapist and we began doing the work that has come to be called "healing the inner child."

Marvin was right; the next surgery revealed only a benign swelling of a salivary gland. Another reprieve, and although I was grateful once more, I was no less depressed. But more was being revealed, through the therapy, through my dreams.

One dream seemed to summarize my life's dilemma:

I am in a house with many doors and windows, all of them open. I feel terribly exposed, and I begin to close and lock each window and door. I am almost finished, with only the back door remaining. As I go to shut the screen door, a man approaches out of the darkness of the back porch and barges through the door. I push him out, but he shoves his foot between the door and the frame so I cannot close it completely. He demands to be let in. I refuse. He becomes seductive. "I only want to come in to use the phone for a minute." I don't budge. "Please," he implores, "I want to use the phone to call you for a date." I feel an ancient pull to comply, then find a strength to say no, to push him finally, completely out the door. Breathless, I close and lock the inside door as well.

Awake from the dream, I realized that in many of the unfortunate relationships I'd had with men in my life, I often said yes when I needed and wanted to say no. I didn't know how to say no. I didn't seem to have a self who could form that small word. Cancer was the first thing to invade my life to which I had a memory of clearly saying no. I said no, and, like a miracle, it backed off. I began to realize there was more power in me than I had ever dreamed.

A few months later, in the spring of 1986, my depression lifted and a newly discovered ability started to be unleashed in me. A fearless torrent of words seemed to pour through the hole in my mouth whenever I was called upon to speak. Whereas before my surgery I had been terrified each time I was to present a talk, now I began to put my notes aside and simply let my thoughts and feelings flow. I had prayed, a few weeks before my diagnosis, that everything standing as an obstacle between me and my ability to be an instrument of God's will be removed, and evidently it had.

It seemed, too, that I finally had something to talk about. God was not some abstract principle to intellectualize about, but a presence and an energy to be experienced now, in the telling of a story, in the expounding of an idea. My words came not from my head but from my core. They were filled with energy and animation; they evoked thought and stirred emotions, my own as well as my listeners.

I marveled at my own transformation. In my mind, I was still shut down and shy when it came to speaking in public. I did not recognize this new figure who seemed to have taken the platform. I liked her a lot, but it took some while before I could agree she was really me. Eventually I realized this lovely creature was the embodied expression of my healed inner child. I came to think of myself as "we"—my inner child, who'd been long neglected, and me, the adult trying my best to re-parent her. When I stood before eight hundred friends, families, and ministers to deliver the address at the ministerial licensing ceremony, I had no notes, no thoughts of what to say, yet "our" every word rang clear, true and full of purpose. I knew we were there to tell the truth as best we understood it, and to be as much ourselves as we could be in the telling of it. There was simply nothing else to do and nothing else we'd have so much fun doing.

Three weeks after licensing, I was on my way for a job interview at a Unity church in the Bahamas. Nassau was colorful, sensual, and intense—for me it was love at first sight. A cacophony of horns honking, people shouting, and the deep bass vibration of reggae blasting at full volume filled the narrow streets that twisted around the city. On the bay side, there were lovely, crumbling pastel stucco estates, verandas wrapped with wrought iron, elegant windows shuttered with louvered blinds, invisible residents protected by high walls and locked gates. Over the hill, people lived packed together in brightly painted one-room shacks jammed up against each other on garbage-filled lots. No plumbing, a communal spigot on each block supplied water, with outhouses an obvious necessity.

The harsh contrast within the city was softened, however, by the dazzling turquoise sea that bathed her shores, and by the breeze-filled palms and casuarina pines that lined the pink sand beaches. The hypnotic surf of the sea erased Third World nightmares for the natives as easily as it dissolved First World stress for tourists. A travel poster dream come true, I thanked God for a ministry in paradise.

I was hired, although it took several months for a work permit to be issued. I arrived in Nassau in the heat of September. Crossing the tarmac at the airport I noticed my sandals sticking to the surface. When I reached my tiny apartment, I found all my belongings in a pile on the floor—the boxes I'd sent ahead had all been ripped open for customs' inspection—their contents pawed through and never put back. My first trip to the food store revealed that milk cost $5 a gallon, a pound of bananas $1.25, a stalk of wilted broccoli $2. Gas went for two dollars per gallon. Wild dogs roamed the neighborhood where I lived. The first time I rode my bicycle around the block, a pack of eleven dogs chased me home, biting my ankles while I pedaled as fast as I could, scared to death. I couldn't get a telephone hooked up for months, and the power failed daily.

The smell of ever-present rotting garbage swiftly overpowered the sweet sea breezes as I began my expatriate life in the Bahamas. The jitneys I rode to work were commandeered by what seemed to be drug-using juveniles who were themselves driven by the beat of the deafening music I'd earlier found so energetic. When I'd get to the church, housed in the old Christian bookstore on busy Shirley Street, I'd often find someone urinating on the side of the building, rats scurrying through the car park, the back door smashed in, the contents of my office and the refrigerator strewn about, the sound equipment stolen.

The church I ministered to had been founded four years earlier by a colleague who was much loved by the congregation. He'd had severe medical problems secondary to a kidney transplant; and, when the kidney failed, he was air-lifted from the island to the States. He left behind a congregation that had never gotten to say good-bye. Many of these people were still grieving his loss. They were ready to crucify anyone who tried to take his place, although neither I nor they knew this at the time.

It turned out I was the only white, female, foreign minister of a non-traditional religion ever to take a church in the Bahamas. While my predecessor had some advantage in that he was African-American, I literally stuck out wherever I went. As I made my introductions around town, wary Nassau folk would say, "Oh, you're that *lady* minister." After all, there were no women clergy in the entire country, and strong religious beliefs prevailed that would keep it that way.

Unity also was regarded with suspicion. Ninety-nine percent of the population of the Bahamas attended church, many abiding in the faith of the more fundamental sects. The current government, well-known for its corruption, took pride in beginning every parliamentary session with prayer. A religion that empowered individuals to find God within themselves was undoubtedly threatening to a political system that used religion to maintain control.

Once, a shop owner friendly to the political party in power, refused to sell me a basket from her shop. I had looked at it one day, noting the price to be more than I wanted to spend. But I went home and thought about it, and decided it was worth it. I returned to the shop the next day. "It's not for sale anymore," she announced. I didn't understand. She went on to tell me that another woman who'd been in the shop at the same time as me said she would buy the basket when she had the money. Disappointed, I told her that if the other woman didn't come through with the cash, I was willing to buy the basket. I'd leave my name and phone number for her to call if the other deal fell through. She emphatically replied, "I don't need your name. I *know* who you are! You're at that Unity church down the street. This basket is *not* for sale!"

I was devastated with loneliness. I'd never before been so aware of being the object of discrimination. The rejection stung and I felt helpless to change the attitude prompting it. Since I was in the Bahamas, however, to do my work in the church, I decided I would focus all my energies there. Filled with the fresh indoctrination of my ministerial training, I was licensed to minister to a congregation and build a church. Why not just go ahead and do it?

I am certain my full-steam-ahead energy in an environment already overcome with heat and humidity must have seemed ridiculous to most of my congregants. Others, curiously, found it infuriating. I jumped in to bring order to the chaos I perceived all around me. Whereas my predecessor had been known to get high on marijuana with certain of his flock, I was a teetotaler, instituting Twelve Step groups to save the Bahamas from drugs, alcohol, and co-dependency.

I didn't realize the scale of the problem I was attacking until the day a congregant approached me with a strange request. A smart, educated woman from Canada, she'd been working illegally in the Bahamas for years. She habitually fell in love with dysfunctional Bahamian men who seemed to replicate the abuse of her childhood. Her current boyfriend, Reggie, wrote political editorials for the opposition party newspaper. A well-respected writer, he'd been drunk when Anne introduced us at a New Year's Eve service at the church.

"Reggie wanted me to tell you he'd like to sample the minister," Anne said. I told her I didn't know what she was talking about. "You know," she replied with all sincerity. "He said he'd like to *sample* you, and he wanted me to see if you'd agree."

Like a brick hitting the pit of my stomach, I realized the sexual implications of what she was suggesting. Pity for her washed over me, and also the realization that not everyone who came to the service on Sunday was there to learn and grow.

Blinded by my missionary zeal, I naïvely assumed that people wanted me to help them. One by one many of the ideas I had for growing the church collapsed as they met a culture and individuals resistant to change. I became discouraged by the focus placed instead on how I did or did not measure up to the standard of ministerial perfection. I was critiqued, not by the content and delivery of my message on Sunday morning, but by what I wore to the grocery store on Friday afternoon. I found myself trying harder and harder to please those who seemed to have a vested interest in being impossible to please. It seemed ironic that while thousands of tourists fled to the Bahamas for a restful vacation I could not find a place to relax within the entire country.

Beginning on Friday and continuing through Saturday night I worked on notes for my Sunday lesson, even though I knew I could speak perfectly well, if not better, without them. I arrived early at the church on Sunday morning to set up chairs and clean the bathrooms. Sunday afternoons I spent on a mental rack, torturing myself with an unforgiving analysis of what I'd forgotten to say, what I said that I shouldn't have, and what I could have said differently. Without fail, the church treasurer who also doubled as the music director, called wanting to know what songs to prepare for the next Sunday's service. Each week the cycle repeated without relief.

I was desperate for support, but found no place to turn to find it. It cost a dollar a minute to phone the U.S. and I wasn't making enough to justify the long calls I occasionally allowed myself to friends and family. Letters from the States took two or three weeks to reach me and they came rarely enough. Desperate, I began to look forward to the monthly meetings of the American Women's Club, when wealthy, bored Junior League-types gathered for lunch to discuss worthwhile charity projects and complain about the Bahamas. Otherwise, my social life outside the church was a blank.

Fourteen months into my tour of duty, I'd settled into an uncomfortable ennui. I had adjusted to certain aspects of life in the Bahamas. I'd moved to a lovely cottage situated in the lush garden of a waterfront estate called Seeker's End. I swam every day from the private beach. I avoided the traffic and intensity of the town life as much as possible, preferring the vacant boredom of Eastern Road.

I reduced my involvement at the church to a routine I tolerated three days during the week, plus Sunday, and spent time working on a writing project for John Templeton, the mutual funds magnate who was also a member of my church. Mr. Templeton (or Sir John as he was known locally) had engaged me to organize the writing of a collection of essays based on the wisdom contained in ancient and contemporary proverbs (eventually published as *Discovering the Laws of Life*). I was paid by him to research topics and write essays, and to enroll other ministers to do the same.

But even as I found ways to cope with my situation I still had a nagging longing for personal intimacy which I'd been unable to find except in rare encounters with unavailable, unsuitable men. While other aspects of my life improved, I could not imagine staying in the Bahamas with no prospect of relief from this lone-liness.

On the night of December 5, 1988, I wrote in my journal:

> My body is in weird shape—I have a urinary tract infection that is quite uncomfortable—I am weak and tired. I feel very confused about life and myself.
>
> In some aspects of life, there is beauty (the new church building, for example). In other aspects there are things I am not proud of, nor do I feel like I've treated myself well (by falling asleep, both literally and figura-tively with J. the other night).
>
> There is a thick emotional overlay. I have little at-traction to this work—or any real relationship to what it represents. There *is* a quality of richness to life at pre-sent that I experience sitting in my new office, enjoying the light. God—Spirit—not sure where that's at—is it so internalized it now feels like a normal part of me—or am I missing it all together?
>
> *I need a sign!*

At midnight, I put the journal on my nightstand and turned out the light. Around two I woke up and heard a small rustling sound coming from the kitchen. I assumed the mice I'd been dealing with for several weeks were at it again, turned over, and went back to sleep.

At 4 a.m. I was awake again; this time I had the feeling some-one was in the room with me. I felt disoriented, confused. I called out. In the dim light from the street lamp outside I saw there was a man standing near my bed. The next thing I knew, I felt cold metal on my throat. Was it a knife, a gun? It didn't matter, the threat was clear. The metal pressed harder. The man was con-fused, unsure whether the voice he'd heard was male or female. Ever-sensitive about my deep voice frequently being mistaken over the telephone, especially first thing in the morning, I let him know I was a woman. A mistake, perhaps, since in an instant he threw his whole body on top of mine.

I talked to him, genuinely trying to figure out what was hap-pening. He spoke with a thick Bahamian dialect, yet I was able to make out that some drug deal he was involved with went bad.

"Five thousand kilos down at the marina got ripped off," he mumbled. I asked him, "Do you think I've got your drugs? I don't have any drugs here!" I was confused. I tried to console him about his loss, to assure him that I had no part in it. But this didn't matter to him. It was clear he intended to rape me.

I continued to talk. Invoking the widespread Christian fundamentalism of the Bahamas, I told him I was a minister. "God will punish you if you hurt me—you'll go to hell if you do this." I realized, of course, that he was already in hell, and this was no threat to him. He continued to fondle me.

My mind was racing through sleepy torpor to find a way out of this horrible nightmare and at the same time a part of me calmly observed. I was a victim once again. I felt angry about this. I wondered what part of me still needed to work something out by constructing these scenarios. I had worked so hard to take responsibility in my life, but it was difficult to see my responsibility here. I welled up with compassion for myself in this untenable situation. I tried to dredge up everything I knew about dealing with a rapist.

I strained to recall what I'd read in rape prevention pamphlets. I couldn't remember whether it was supposed to be more effective to fight back or to yield. The weapon at my neck deterred me from the former, but it was viscerally impossible for me to simply let this strange man take over my body without a fight of some kind.

I persisted with conversation. I told him I'd been to the doctor that day. (It was true, I had gone to see about my urinary tract infection). "The doctor told me I had AIDS," I lied. "If you have sex with me you are going to die."

"That's my problem, then, isn't it?" he replied. It occurred to me *he* might have AIDS, in which case, if I survived the rape, my life would be further endangered.

I told him I'd scream, and Marcel, the gardener who lived in another part of the cottage, would come to help me. I was not at all sure about this. Since it was December, all the windows were shut, and Marcel was a very sound sleeper. But that didn't matter because the man told me he'd tied Marcel up before coming into my apartment—he'd be no help at all.

At one point, the man kissed me and, reflexively, I suppose, I kissed him back. The whole event was strangely intimate. It occurred

to me that this man and I were playing out parts in a drama neither one of us really wanted, but couldn't quite figure a way out
of. He touched my genitals and I froze. He told me to relax; I
yelled at him. "Do you think *you* could relax if this were happening to you?!"

But by now I was feeling totally a victim; completely helpless, I resigned myself to having sex with this man against my
will. I told myself to pretend that I was being examined by a gy-
necologist—it would be uncomfortable and then it would be over.
I would survive and then I would recover from this terrible, inevitable thing.

The man pulled back from me for a moment, still holding the
knife to my throat, but reaching down with the other to unzip his
jeans. The euphemism, "Now I'm really fucked!" was rapidly becoming a literal reality.

Finally, a part of me that had been simply observing what
was taking place offered a suggestion. The thought arose in my
mind, "Ellie, you're a minister—pray!" There was an instant of
embarrassment that I hadn't had a more instinctive impulse to do
so, and, yet, even then, I formed no words to pray. But instantly,
in my mind's eye it was as if a movie marquee had been erected.
Bold letters marched across the marquee announcing, "This
doesn't have to happen."

Some impulse in me caused me to sit straight up in the bed.
Gently I put my hand on the man's chest and pushed him away.
A clear, calm, sure voice within me spoke. "This is not going to
happen," I said firmly. "You can take whatever you want from the
apartment, but *this* is not going to happen. I am going to get up
and go to the front door. I am going to open the door and you are
going to leave."

I then did exactly as I said and he did not object. I walked
through the bedroom and down the hall to the kitchen to the
only door to the cottage. The man followed, knife still in hand.
He stood behind me, waiting, as I unlocked the several bolts that
had failed to prevent his break-in. I swung the door open and out,
and stood aside. Obedient to my clear direction the man walked
past me out on to the patio, and disappeared into the darkness
without a sound.

I stood trembling in the doorway for a few minutes, then
called my neighbors and the police. The police never came but

my neighbors did. It was about half past four in the morning. They took me to their house where I curled up in bed and shook uncontrollably for hours. I eventually calmed down, although I seemed to remain in an altered state of consciousness. What had just taken place seemed like a bad dream, yet the broken window frame in the kitchen, my missing watch and money all attested to the reality of what had taken place.

But it also seemed that some kind of miracle had occurred. Just when I felt most powerless to deal with the menacing presence of this man, another force seemingly intervened, and I was saved from the excruciating pain of rape. Curiously, I felt blessed by the whole event.

I found my way that morning to a counselor who helped me sort through the experience. I told her how I had gone to bed the night before in a state of confusion, that I'd asked God for a sign, how this seemed to be an unmistakable response to my request. What did it mean?

At first, it seemed I now had every piece of evidence a sane person would need to leave Nassau. No one would blame me if I packed up that day and took the first plane back to the States. Oddly, this didn't seem to me like the right thing for me to do. It would be a fear-based reaction, justified, yet not satisfying as far as yielding the spiritual growth to which I'd committed my life. I didn't want to run away. Like Jacob wrestling with his angel, I would not leave the Bahamas until I had gotten a blessing from it. I wanted to understand my part in the creation of the loneliness and misery that I experienced there. There was something about this event the understanding of which held a key to my further healing, and I wanted to know what it was.

My investigation of the incident began with the timing of the event. It had taken place exactly three years to the day since my cancer diagnosis, just a few days before my birthday. This seemed more than coincidence. I then looked at the similarities between the two events, remembered the dream I had after my surgery, the awareness of how I'd said yes when so much of the time I needed to say no. Cancer, an internal manifestation of chaos and confusion which invaded my body, threatened my physical well-being, got my attention, invited me to consider another possibility that included a happy life. I had accepted the invitation, and the microscopic invader apparently disappeared. But somewhere along the way I had begun to say yes again when I needed to say no. I reflected on all the unhappiness I had caused myself through my belief that I was responsible for everyone and everything in my church. I hated cleaning the bathrooms and setting up the chairs for the service, but I did it anyway, filled with resentment, because I did not realize I could say no.

Now, another would-be body snatcher had invaded my life, this one large and obvious, certainly an attention-getter, yet with no less of an invitation to make another choice about how to live my life. The message seemed clear I wasn't going to be able to live at all if I didn't say no when it was appropriate. This pre-dawn intrusion was a violation to which I could not agree. From the deepest level of my being, I had been willing to say no to this intruder. And my refusal apparently communicated with the part of him who no more wanted to rape me than I wanted to be raped.

As had happened following my healing of cancer, I experienced a rebirth. Just at the moment of greatest victimization, I was awakened to a tremendous power that was an essential yet untapped resource. I realized myself fully as an individual with the capacity and the right to say no. I reflected on those situations, including my sexual abuse at the hands of the parish priest when I was a child, in which I had felt powerless to say no. How much of that unexpressed negation had simply been applied to myself, denying my own life instead of the unwanted advances of outside violators. This incident had offered me another opportunity to say no; I'd seized the moment and succeeded.

I did not leave Nassau for almost another year. Instead, I went back to my church and began off-loading all the things I'd agreed to do that I didn't want to do. I started delegating responsibilities, and those things that could not be delegated I learned to be content to drop without feeling guilty.

I looked around me, though, at a culture that faltered and failed at almost every turn. While people were quick to commit to undertake a project, they rarely followed through on it. It seemed what a friend called "the disease of nice," with which I had been long familiar in churches, afflicted many others besides myself. Desiring to appear agreeable, they made commitments but didn't follow through. A vestigial reaction, perhaps, to a slave culture or religious systems that fostered dependency to maintain control.

No matter how much I understood its origins, I now found this passive-aggressive behavior increasingly intolerable to live with.

I made my decision to leave Nassau one August day while sitting on the beach with Peter and Jennifer, married friends who were also church members. I liked them. They had spent enough time outside the Bahamas to know another way of life, so we could relate somewhat more easily than others who had always lived in the islands. Peter was in charge of getting a central air-conditioning unit installed in the church, a project I had initiated when we first moved into a new building. At the board meeting in which I had insisted we address the purchase of a larger unit, I'd been chided for bringing up the subject in December, a relatively cool month. Although nine months later progress had been made toward the installation, we were still sweltering without it in our sun-baked storefront.

That morning, Peter had arranged to pick up a worker who was to actually install the unit. The man had agreed to be on a certain street corner at 9 a.m. When Peter went to get him, he wasn't there. Peter wasn't surprised, however, because they'd had the same agreement for the day before, and as it turned out for several other days as well. As much as I was dismayed that the work was not getting done, I was amazed that Peter continued to go back to the corner every day looking for the guy who never showed up.

When I asked Peter if he didn't find this kind of behavior maddening, as I did, Jennifer piped in. "Look, Ellie," she said, "this is the Bahamas. It doesn't do any good to get mad. You've just got to lay back and take it."

I found Jennifer's statement telling. She herself had been dealing with a malignant brain tumor for several years, and felt herself to be a victim, although she was trying very hard to recover. I empathized, but deeply disagreed. "Gosh, Jennifer, as I recall, that's exactly what my rapist said, 'Lay back and take it.' I won't do that anymore. I am no longer willing to accept the unacceptable." I saw that while she had reasons more compelling than mine that would justify her acquiescence, I was no longer bound to serve out my self-imposed sentence in this paradise version of prison. Six weeks later I was on a plane to Boston. The next time I visited the Bahamas, the following January, the air-conditioning had just been installed.

My last month and a half in Nassau I finally gave myself permission to be fully myself in the church. I removed the heavy mantle of ministerial perfectionism and enjoyed sharing myself honestly, authentically. It no longer mattered that some congregants focused on my real or imagined shortcomings. I basked in the warmth of those who were genuinely sad to see me go, and enjoyed the beauty of the island that had for so long been hidden from my view.

I realized I could generate enough income from the Templeton writing project to live on while I traveled, so for as long as that lasted, money was not a problem. Without agenda, destination, or a plan to acquire either, I was poised on the edge of another abyss with every intention of jumping in. I knew I was letting go of everything I'd been planning around for years; nevertheless, I breathed into my anxiety and found excitement. One more step and I'd be falling into life.

# 6

# The Next Step

*Let him who seeks,*
*not cease seeking until he finds,*
*and when he finds, he will be troubled,*
*and when he has been troubled,*
*he will marvel and reign over the All.*

**THE GOSPEL ACCORDING TO THOMAS**

My next step after leaving the Bahamas was literally "The Next Step," a ten-day residential conference with Dr. Richard Moss. As a young physician, Moss had a spiritual awakening which left him profoundly aware of dimensions of non-ordinary reality. Leaving traditional medical practice behind, his work explored the healing possibilities of expanded consciousness, using forms that tap the power of a group's energy.

While in the Bahamas I had read Moss's books *The I That Is We* and *The Black Butterfly,* and I'd gone to a workshop he'd offered at a Unity ministers' conference. What struck me about this man was the apparently absolute congruence of his spoken and written word, and the fullness of his presence shining clearly through both. In addition, I found the content of his work to be highly relevant to me, addressing among other issues, the healing of cancer. Looking forward to having an extensive exposure to Richard and participating in his work, I packed most of my belongings for shipment back to the States, and trundled off with the remainder to the retreat center north of Boston where the conference was to be held.

Forty people from all over the world were registered for the conference. Packed like sardines into the dormitory-style rooms, getting to the shower was a process all its own. Our days began

early with meditation and movement, a kind of spiritual calis-
thenics session. Then we would meet as a group with Richard
and his assistant who conducted a variety of talk sessions and
intense energetic exercises.

One day, we whirled for thirty minutes to a hypnotically
repetitious electronic symphony someone fondly termed "early
morning throw-up music." Another day, we formed into small
groups with the instruction to "sing until the song sings you."
My group finished up at half past three in the morning after
twelve hours in a six by eight foot room. The next morning, we
were up at seven o'clock and spent five hours responding over
and over again to our partners' query, "Who are you?" Then we
were invited into two days of silence and fasting, drinking only
hot water, lemon juice, maple syrup and a dash of cayenne pepper.

As exhausting as these processes were, both physically and
psychically, they were, at the same time, extremely energizing.
Each morning I engaged the work unable to imagine how I
would make it through the rigors of the day. I simply kept
showing up for what was next. Oddly, by bedtime, I slept fitfully
and dreamfully, or not at all.

In the midst of the conference I recalled seeing "Meetings
with Remarkable Men" a few years earlier. The film depicts the
Russian philosopher Gurdjieff's search for and discovery of a
mystery school in the stark, deserted mountains of the Middle
East. Taken blindfolded to this obscure location, he was initiated
into the exercises and esoteric teachings of an ancient spiritual
order. The movie reminded me of what I was now experiencing.

As my sense of time and space at the conference became increasingly distorted, it seemed no other world existed than this
strange boot camp for the soul. I wasn't quite sure how I'd found
this strange place but, like Gurdjieff, I knew it was exactly where
I had longed to be for a very long time. Each day, each hour, was
condensed into a parade of single moments, any one of which
fully experienced would expand into eternity, and, depending on
my degree of resistance to what the moment offered, it was
heaven or hell. But whatever the experience I'd never felt more
alive.

About the sixth or seventh day, we broke our silence. It was
early, about six a.m., and chilly, as it was now late October. A
bonfire five feet tall had been lit in a clearing, and we huddled

close to warm ourselves, listening to Richard as he told us a Native American tale of transformation. I barely heard the story, and surely didn't make sense of it. It was too early, too cold, and I was spaced out from the fast; I was also quite eager to get to the food I was certain awaited us in the warm dining room. His story completed, Richard invited us to toss leaves into the fire to symbolize an aspect of ourselves we wanted transformed. This done, I thought, that's a nice ritual—now let's eat!

Instead, we were ushered inside to our meeting room and given instructions for yet another process Richard called "The Cross of Gold." This involved everyone holding their arms up, crucifixion style. A simple exercise, it was not difficult to do; that is, not for the first minute or two. After that, it was excruciating. As people became uncomfortable with the position, they began to drop their arms. Richard pointed out how the energy in the whole room dropped when one or more of the participants let their arms down, how it became more difficult for everyone if some did not hold the position. As the minutes passed, people moaned with the pain, some even screamed.

Richard invoked the power of the unconditional love we had within us, that was, he exhorted, right now the purifying fire we needed for the transformation we committed to when we tossed our leaves into the bonfire. He invited us to stay present with the pain, to allow it to burn the dross of whatever stood in the way of our transformation. He called on us to hear the cries of those who each day starved to death, to feel the pain of those who died in the tortures of war, to let our own actual pain disintegrate the walls that separate us from those who suffer in the world and from ourselves. Quiet, deep sobbing became audible as an intense feeling of compassion welled up within the participants in the room.

Then, standing directly in front of me, Richard lifted my arms a little higher with his own outstretched limbs. I was deeply touched because I knew from my own discomfort how much pain he must be in, but I was grateful for the relief he gave me for several minutes. It was a gift I wanted to share as well, so I supported his arms for awhile, feeling a lightness in my own arms as I did so. Richard moved on, and I offered my support to someone else. I was surprised. Holding up another's arms was far less painful than holding up my own! Totally surrendered to the process, everyone seemed to float around the room offering and receiving support and love. I felt if we needed to, each of us had tapped into the power that would allow us to continue this process forever.

In fact, eternity only lasted a little more than an hour. At that point, Richard's assistant gave us instructions to let our arms down and to do what we needed to take care of ourselves. Most everyone folded gratefully onto the floor. I curled myself into a fetal position. Classical music played now, washing the intensity of what had been experienced from my mind and body. Embraced by an unfamiliar sense of wholeness, I fell into a calm, gentle sleep. Later that day when we broke our two-and-a-half day fast with a delicious lunch, the food actually seemed inconsequential. I'd been fed already, it seemed, from a source far more nourishing.

The following day, we met as before in the large group meeting room on the lower level of the main retreat building. The weather system that had brought constant cold, dreary rain for almost the entire first week of the conference had finally moved on. Dazzling sunshine now flooded the room in which we gathered.

I cannot remember the subject of our discourse on this particular morning. Perhaps our discussion centered around a dream someone shared from the night before. Or, as was often the case in our meetings, different ones of us might have been speaking of our immediate experience with the group. I do recall, however, feeling that this was the most present to the rest of the group I'd been during the whole conference. Until then, I'd spent much of the time either infatuated with various people in the group or totally alienated and isolated from them. Without an agenda, I was at last able to just be with everyone in what seemed quite ordinary ways—listening, speaking quietly, enjoying.

Then something extraordinary happened.

Spontaneously and simultaneously, without the use of any substance or the prompting of any meditation process, the entire group entered an altered state of consciousness.

Perhaps the Buddhist term *samadhi* comes close to describing what took place. Complete concentration, absorbed contemplation. While awareness of individual personalities continued, any sense of separation between us dissolved. Our souls seemed open to one another and an intimacy of deep spiritual communion took place.

It struck me that this state was what Jesus had in mind when he said, "Wherever two or more are gathered in my name, there am I in the midst of them." For there was a sense of palpable, liquid presence in the room that, like the sunlight, warmed and illuminated each one of us, but from within. I was saturated with an awe-inspired sense of a loving reality. I thought to myself, I am in the presence of the Holy Spirit of God, and I know it.

I laughed to myself imagining what a television audience would think if they were watching us on a "60 Minutes" segment. Mike Wallace describing forty people under the spell of a tyrant guru, finally reduced to sitting around a room, spaced out, waving their arms in slow motion, claiming enlightenment. But this wasn't television; Richard was no guru, certainly no tyrant. And contrary to appearances, we weren't spaced out. I'd never been more conscious in the company of other people in my life. I'd never more fully experienced the pleasure of being alive, nor felt that pleasure as occurring in the most ordinary of circumstances. After all, sitting around on the floor of a room with a bunch of people doing nothing in particular would not get the attention of most thrill seekers.

Richard gently encouraged us to speak from our hearts while in this state. Different ones in the gathering spoke poetry. There was deep emotion—a few tears, occasionally laughter—but mostly there was a deep silence as we drank in the purity of the moment. After a couple of hours the shimmering sense of presence faded, and we returned to a more normal state and ate lunch.

The rest of the conference was relatively unremarkable. One afternoon, several of us went for a walk off the retreat center grounds. I walked about ten miles in the area skirting the local town. At one point, a dog followed me for several miles and I panicked. Thinking it wouldn't be able to find its way home again, I started flagging cars down along the road. I'm sure the ones that stopped found me a bit odd. But I was feeling so deeply about everything by this time, my concern for the dog's welfare overrode my concern with looking foolish. It was just what needed to be done.

When the conference was over, I went to stay with a cousin a few hours' drive from the retreat center. When her husband came to pick me up, I cried. I felt I was leaving my real life behind; I couldn't imagine going back to the artifice of normal existence. The conference experience had been a combination of mystery school, church and womb, and I knew when I turned to look for it after I left, it would likely have disappeared. With a heavy heart, I returned to the "real" world, slept for sixteen hours, woke up for a few minutes, then slept another eight.

For the next several months, I had difficulty functioning in the world in accustomed ways. If a television set was on, it felt to me as if all the energy in the room was being sucked out by it. If someone asked me how I was getting along, I'd reply that my entire life had disintegrated. I had no idea what to do except the next thing that presented itself, which was frequently nothing. I managed to work on my writing project a few hours a day, and to travel, first around the northeast, then to Georgia to see a friend and my younger brother.

It was November 1989. I had not lived in Atlanta for thirteen years, had not visited in six. What a shock it was to arrive in the city and to still recognize the names of streets and other land-marks. Though it had tripled in population and sprouted a high profile skyline, the return to Atlanta was a homecoming.

I looked up old friends and visited the site of the hippie homestead where for five years I'd lived with an organic garden, wood stoves and no plumbing. The old house had burned several years before, and a new high-priced subdivision perched along the creek where I used to bathe. A mile away, a bustling shopping area, complete with four-lane roads and every fast food franchise known to man had usurped the rolling acres cows had grazed just a few years before.

Driving from one familiar location to another, I met the same devastating development. The neighborhood in which I'd grown up had become a major medical center, sprawling out over blocks where my friends' houses had been when we were kids, and over the field where we made houses out of straw, and where I hid from the incessant sad reports that long November weekend when President Kennedy was killed.

The antebellum mansion that had served as a convent and where I'd put in my "Saint and Martyr" time as a young girl still guarded the corner of the church property. A new church build-ing was under construction. I recalled sorting the envelopes for the building fund while I unsuccessfully tried to dodge the priest's advances. All those dollars finally added up, I surmised with no small amount of cynicism.

Finally, I drove to Kennesaw Mountain, another familiar hometown haunt, and I broke down in tears. I grieved the irretrievable loss of the land I loved as well as all the personal losses of the past several years. I climbed the mountain remembering all the other times I'd walked the trail, first with my father, then Girl Scouts, then friends in high school. Now everyone jogged the trail wearing high-tech running shoes and speaking loud New Yorkese. I was more a native here than anyone I saw, even though I'd been long gone, and had only been back in the United States for six weeks.

New Year's Day morning, 1990, I woke up from a very lucid dream. In the dream, I had been writing a book. Its title was "The 21st Century Church: The Unraveling of Religion in America and the Emergence of an Essential Spirituality." The book, commissioned by the Holy Spirit, was to be the inspiration for a movement that would create new forms through which the Holy Spirit could find expression. Old forms no longer sufficed, and the Spirit imprisoned within them was dying. A different kind of church was needed, one in which God could be *experienced*, as I had done at the Richard Moss conference.

I woke up from the dream and recorded as much as I could recall of it. I had the distinct impression I was to write the book.

As I had few ideas of my own on the subject, I spent the first months of 1990 making sporadic visits to a local university, attempting to research material that might be appropriate for a book with such a title. But the buzz of fluorescent lights in the sterile library drove me away. Heeding my resistance to an academic approach, I realized the best research for the book would be to actually create this new church for the twenty-first century.

# 7
# A New Church

*Be patient toward all that is unsolved in your heart and*
*try to love the questions themselves....*
*The point is, to live everything.*
*Live the questions now.*

**R.M. RILKE**

To say I had resistance to starting a church is a wild under-
statement. Given my first experience of ministry in
Nassau, I made Richard Bach's reluctant messiah look
like a eager beaver. My only hope was that a "twenty-first century church," whatever that might turn out to be, would in fact
be different from churches I'd known before, and if the Holy
Spirit could find life there, it might be that I would, too.

Still feeling undone from the Next Step conference, I barely
managed to get out of bed some mornings. I was living with
Robert, my artist-brother, north of Atlanta. Each morning he and
I would call out from our respective sleeping places (mine a bed,
his the living room floor), "Have you figured out the meaning of
life yet?" It was our best joke, since we were both alternately up
in the air and down in the dumps on the subject. I would take a
few minutes each day to review the "Who Are You?" exercise in
the mirror, noticing the variety of my responses and how my
identity changed faster than a chameleon with each query.

I continued to write for the Templeton book I'd begun earlier
in Nassau. Each day I wrote several essays based on a list of eight
hundred proverbs I culled from world wisdom literature. I wondered if life really was as simple as following the prescriptions in
these clichés. I also did some counseling at a nearby Unity
church, and created some workshops that I presented around

Georgia and back in Nassau. From time to time, I'd officiate at a wedding.

Frequently, a guest would approach me after the ceremony to tell me they enjoyed it and to inquire about the location of my church. I would tell them that I didn't have a church, but if I did it would probably be in midtown Atlanta. By now, I had the sense that if I were to create a new church, the people attracted to it would be people like myself: refugees from traditional religion, old anti-war politicos, former hippies, and people with histories of psychedelic drug experiences that had opened them to a spiritual reality. I had lived in the Midtown area twenty years before and remembered it as an area where intellectuals and artists gathered. After several of these wedding guests gave me their business cards, it seemed more feasible that I might actually do the thing I was feeling guided to do.

My reluctance in starting a church echoed the fears I initially had when I considered becoming a minister, and these had been mightily amplified in my ministry in Nassau. I'd resisted the notion of becoming something that I clearly was not. When I went for the interview for ministerial school without make-up and without the requisite business suit and was asked if I would be willing to assume a ministerial image, I said yes, thinking it would be fun, like playing dress-up as a child. Buying new clothes, experimenting with mascara (after all, look where it got Tammy Faye!), getting a sophisticated hairdo was a lot of fun. But I soon discovered the implication in the interviewer's request was the practiced belief that the image was identical with the ministry. Other denominations were clear about this, requiring their clergy to wear collars; Unity's requirement was less explicit, but no less demanding. It was not the person who was expected to minister, I realized, but the idealized image of a minister.

Training seemed in many ways to be about how to assume that image, so much so that I was surprised how many of my classmates who played the part so well told me they'd never had a spiritual experience. Some were miserable about this, though you'd never have known it. They learned to speak uplifting prayers in such reassuring, dulcet tones I was convinced they were far more holy than I. Later, I began to see how many candidates aspired to be ministers to win God's favor the way children try to be good enough to please daddy and mommy.

In Nassau, I learned that my attempts to live up to my own idealized image of a minister had created nothing but an opportunity for my psychological shadow to thrive. I did my best to be what I thought a model minister should be—kind, forbearing, patient, and self-sacrificing. Yet, despite all the warnings we had received in school about intimate involvements with members of our church, I'd fallen in love with a congregant who had been separated for a year from his wife (she had not ever attended the church). Hearing from the man the degree of their estrangement and that they were on their way to a divorce, it seemed within the range of acceptability to pursue a relationship with him. His wife felt differently. She learned of our affair and began stalking me, showing up at the church, eventually attending services.

"Too bad your minister is a whore," she announced to a group during the social hour after the service one day. I cringed whenever I saw her, her presence a constant reminder of my confusion about the distinction between my personal life and my vocational life. As good as I tried to be, some other part of me surfaced that felt more like the real me, which would not be denied no matter how ministerial I might have wanted to appear. I learned I was unwilling to sacrifice my desires in the service of a kind of goodness that dulled my aliveness. Instead I chose to give expression to the more shadowy aspect. Instead of doing what I believed was the right thing a minister should do, I supported myself in exploring the relationship until its nature was fully revealed. A couple of months later, plagued by fear that this woman might do me physical harm (she arranged to have her husband beaten unconscious by a couple of thugs), and the recognition that I did not want to be involved with someone whose life was so complicated, I ended the relationship.

When evangelist Jimmy Swaggart was caught with a Los Angeles hooker several years later, I sympathized. Given the strong claims of fundamental Christianity toward moral righteousness, it seemed likely many religious people had gotten caught in the trap of their idealized ministerial image. In the name of spirituality, sexuality is refused by the conscious mind, leaving the shadow—acting in service to the psyche's call to wholeness—to emerge unconsciously. Even the zealous apostle Paul recognized his shadow and named its expression "sin." He noticed, "I do not do the good I want, but the evil I do not want is what I do....I do not do what I want to do, but I do the very thing I hate." In an attempt to suppress the shadow, Paul heaps condemnation upon what he terms the carnal, and Swaggart must beg forgiveness for his failure to keep his flesh in line.

In starting a new kind of church, ostensibly one that would embody an expression of the whole Spirit of God, I needed to find a way of being a minister that would honor my own wholeness. I made an agreement with God that I would resume ministry on the condition that this church be a place in which I could be myself as I was, with room enough for me to become what I could be. I would minister as a human being with flaws I was aware of, as well as those about whose existence I was completely ignorant. I would work diligently to heal and grow but I would not judge myself to be a bad minister simply because of my imperfections. As time passed and this new ministry progressed, many people cited my willingness to expose the process of my own healing as a primary reason they came to the church.

To the people in Atlanta who showed up in support of the twenty-first century church idea, I was totally honest about the unfinished nature of my personality. "I have been called to minister beyond the shadow of any doubt in my mind," I told them. "And I also swear like a sailor and have sex with people I am not married to." To my surprise, no one in this particular group seemed to care. There were several people in the group whose sex lives made me look like a goody-two-shoes; they were grateful to have a minister who for the first time in their lives did not condemn them for their sexuality. An older Jewish woman, a chiropractor who had just ended a relationship with a man twenty years younger, was deeply entrenched in her own spiritual process. She found it refreshing to meet a minister who was able to move beyond religious formulas into what she considered the real heart of spirituality. Everyone involved encouraged me to be true to myself and to be honest with them. With an inner conviction of the necessity to do so, and with such permission from my early supporters, I moved forward released from the resistance that had until then held my enthusiasm for ministry in check.

Another concern had to do with the financial basis of the church and its ability to support me. A couple of years before, when I was leaving nursing for ministry (with its relatively high pay scale and numerous opportunities to work, my nursing career provided much security), I couldn't quite fathom depending upon an income generated by little more than the words I spoke in twenty or thirty minutes on a Sunday morning. Then I went to Nassau, where I was actually paid for my speaking, albeit with what seemed like crumbs. Although the revenues of the church were quite adequate, there was a good deal of pain and conflict around the money issue. I struggled with several board members against the predominant belief that a minister should be paid, but as little as possible.

Unfortunately, that belief dovetailed too nicely with my own low self-esteem and old notions about the spiritual nobility of poverty. From a church whose philosophy was built around the abundance of God's unlimited bounty, I was earning barely $18,000 a year. I pinched pennies for two years just to buy gas and groceries, and to pay rent. My arguments to the Board of Directors for an increase to a living wage and for decent compensation for guest speakers were met with snide accusations, such as, "You ministers won't even go to the bathroom without getting paid!" I left more than one such board meeting humiliated and in tears. Like other ministers who were not supported fully by their congregations, I quietly turned to moonlighting to meet my basic financial needs.

As I was unwilling to suffer more financial trauma in this new church, I appealed to the Holy Spirit once again to reveal another way to structure the money end of things in this new organization. My guidance was to first trust the Universe, not myself, in providing for all the financial needs of the church. I was not to hold myself responsible for the success or failure of the church. If the Universe supported this effort, it would succeed; if not, it wouldn't and no attempts on my part could prevent the will of the Universe from being done. I was to simply make myself available to do the work that needed to be done and relinquish any attachment to the outcome, including any worry or concern about finances.

I realized, then, I could ask God for anything and everything that I needed to support me physically, emotionally, even financially, and I would either get what I asked for, or not. Operating along these lines, within six months I was able to draw an income from the new church that adequately supported me. As I completed my writing project, income from the church increased to cover my now full-time work with the church.

Regarding the church's finances, it was my practice throughout my tenure as the minister of Unity-Midtown to return to the spiritual bottom line. While the treasurer kept excellent records of such things, I did not regularly check the amount of the Sunday offering each week. I specifically made it a point not to know the amounts of the donations of individual donors. It was my experience that when we were clear in our requests, and open to receive, what we needed as a community was always provided; and when it wasn't, we tended to discover there was no real need. The church always broke even, and, while I did not make a huge salary by contemporary church salary standards, my needs were comfortably fulfilled.

But my largest resistance to starting a new church was my low opinion of organized religion in general. Endless chapel services during ministerial school, sustained my claim that the least likely place I could experience God was in a church. Stained glass windows were beautiful in a way, but mostly they obscured my view of the creation for which I had such a deep longing to be a part of. I felt far more spiritual outside walking in the woods or sitting by a creek than I had ever felt listening to anyone talk about God. And for the doctrines and creeds of traditional religions, I had little but contempt.

As far as I had experienced it, organized religion had been successful in only one regard—killing the very spirit that had inspired it. The nuns in my Catholic school taught us the Baptists would go to hell because they hadn't been baptized in the right faith; and I had been in a Southern Baptist church once where the preacher condemned the godlessness of Catholics. I learned almost instinctively to shy away from anyone who, claiming to be a Christian, wanted to save me; I was certain a contentious "My way is the right way" conversation was likely to ensue.

Someone once remarked that if Jesus did return for a Second Coming he'd never be welcome in so-called Christian churches. He probably wouldn't be dressed correctly, and might have undesirable friends in tow. But truly, would he *want* to go to most of these churches?

He wouldn't be likely to recognize their liturgy as having anything to do with his experience. He would probably wonder where the joy of transformation was and why people were acting so nice when they were really so miserable. If he did attend a church today, would he want to admit to being the fountainhead of the rigidity of thought, word, and deed which has caused more wars to be fought throughout the ages than for any other reason?

Jesus' teaching triumphs because it shows human beings a way out of the suffering caused by their apparent separation from one another by learning to love their enemies and forgive those who persecute them. Most attempts to organize a religion around this teaching fail to honor its intent: for the very act of systematizing religious beliefs and practices creates a wall between people that doesn't exist until clerical authorities form categories of believers and non-believers. Charged with the responsibility for defending their beliefs, religious folk tend not to make love but war amongst those who might not believe as they do.

To be fair, defending the faith is certainly not a preoccupation limited to the Christian religion. When they have enough points of dogma to rally around, groups of all sorts tend to promote their religiously correct differences with a zeal that has the potential for violence. Thus, throughout history, we see at each other's throats Christians and Muslim; Hindus and Muslims, Muslims and Jews, Jews and Christians, Christians and Pagans, and on and on, all in the name of religion, which supposedly binds us together in God.

I certainly didn't want to join in this melee. Unity, for all its claim to being free of dogmatic encumbrances, still asked its students to abide by its "normative" teaching, which Charles and Myrtle Fillmore, the co-founders of Unity, referred to as Practical Christianity. In fact, Practical Christianity is a form of absolute idealism with the practical aspect centering around the power of positive thinking, a notion popularized by Norman Vincent Peale, a one-time student of Unity teachings.

Though Unity came close, I hadn't yet found a theology that covered all the bases for me. My personal belief was that only my experience could lead me beyond doubt and belief into the reality of the Divine. As with the other requests my ministerial training made of me, however, I'd gone along in the spirit of fun and earned kudos for my ability to clearly articulate the philosophy. Then, in my first church, I did my best to sprinkle references to Unity's philosophy throughout my talks to stem complaints that

I wasn't delivering a "real" Unity message. In a pinch, I would invoke Charles Fillmore's statement that he believed the Holy Spirit was constantly revealing itself, that Truth was open-ended, in process. In a setting in which most people wanted their religion to deliver results, however, this teaching was decidedly impractical, and, at times, downright uncomfortable for folks to hear. I feared that such an unpopular message would inevitably reflect in the offering basket, but I persisted because it was what was true for me at my current level of understanding.

But now, on the brink of pioneering my own church, I had to face the reality that I too was organizing a potentially religious body and anything coming out of my mouth could, and probably would, be considered dogma. People would likely rally around the points I'd be making, and it might not be long before some version of religious war could be waged in the name of Unity-Midtown Church.

I constantly asked myself questions my mother could have asked but gratefully never did: Who did I think I was to be starting a church? Wasn't it arrogant of me to set myself up as the spiritual leader of an organization? Where did I get off calling it a "twenty-first century church?" How could I possibly attempt to create a context for transcendent experience within the confines of a Sunday church service? These were all without answers, of course. But following Rilke's advice, I decided to live the questions and see what unfolded as I did so.

# PART TWO
# The Old Church:
# Christianity's Partial Truths

*...a lie which is all a lie may be
met and fought with outright,
but a lie which is part a truth
is a harder matter to fight..*

**ALFRED LORD TENNYSON**

For the past decade I have had a firsthand experience in creating a new kind of church, attempting to be as true as I can to the simple spirit of the "where two or more are gathered" form described by Jesus. Through a process of trial and error I believe I have discovered how and why traditional Christianity has not served that spirit fully. In service to my passion for the possibilities for what a church can be, I offer the following analysis of the traditional Christian Church, not so much as a complete, academic critique on this huge subject, nor as any kind of final word, but more as a personal, intuitive observation of the devolution of Christianity and the emergence of the need for a new kind of church for the twenty-first century.

In Part Two, I present my perspective on how traditional Christianity came to be what it is. I describe what I think was a misinterpretation of Jesus' impulse to found a spiritual church, and how the resulting religion operates from a very different intent than what initially inspired it. I identify the major elements I believe compose the structure or "box" that Christianity has constructed for itself and suggest the ways in which these elements tend to advance religious rather than spiritual agendas, and what the difference is. I will show that the history of Christianity is so enmeshed with the development of the Western world, it has been and continues to be more a servant of culture than Spirit, and, for those who get stuck in it, a place to regress rather than self-realize.

In the rest of this book, I use the term Old Church as a shorthand for Christian religious structures as they have developed in the West and, more recently, in America. The term could just as easily be used to refer to many non-Christian religious expressions, for all religions eventually get in their own way by being religiously, rather than spiritually, oriented; parallel dysfunctions occur in Judaism, Buddhism, Islam and other religions. But for the purposes of this book, since it is the predominant religion of the part of the world I live in, I'll stick to Christianity as my main subject.

The analysis in Part Two is not intended to be an exhaustive study of any particular Christian denomination. Rather, it is intended as an overview of some of the more obvious aspects of the religion. As such, I apologize in advance for the many generalizations about Christianity as a whole that may simply not be the case in specific churches.

For example, not all Roman Catholic churches toe the Vatican's line. On a flight home from London a couple of years ago, I met an elderly Irish priest whose description of his small Catholic parish in rural Texas made me want to pack up and move out there. With sparkling good humor he told me he thought the Pope's outmoded stance on the ordination of women and birth control was the greatest obstacle facing Catholicism today. His assessment of the Roman Church: "Too rich, too powerful!" In his parish, the community literally built their church on weekends, laying the bricks with their own hands. This priest's counsel to the mostly Latino members of his church regarding church dogma: "Follow your heart." About church ritual: "I've heard better confessions drinking coffee in a truck stop than in the confessional." This man radiated so much sanity and goodwill, he inspired me with hope about the state of certain individual churches.

While I am glad there are exceptions to the general points I make here, I nevertheless feel the overview is necessary to show the *tendency* of organized religion to eventually confine rather than liberate spiritual experience. My intent is to stimulate awareness of the unconscious, unintended consequences of religious organization, and not to condemn individual churches or denominations. The term Old Church is used to indicate an archetype of organized religion as it has developed in the Christian religion over the past two thousand years, and not any specific denomination or church. When I cite individual churches by name because they exhibit some of the tendencies of the Old Church, I do so with a sincere acknowledgement of the good that any organization consciously intends wherever two or more are gathered for a spiritual purpose. I also respect the power of the unconscious to thwart that intention. I, too, have made such attempts and failed.

Some of my criticisms of church obviously stem from the personal abuse I received within it, but I believe these have been tempered by my own botched attempts to do things differently. Although organized religion must take responsibility for the inquisitions, holy wars and other evils it has brought about, church is not an inherently bad thing. The traditional church simply operates out of the distortions caused by a preoccupation with its own survival. Yet, so we do not repeat the past we must not forget or dismiss too quickly the mistakes the church has made. It is important to understand fully how the form of church has in various ways dominated the content, in effect smothering the spiritual potential which exists within it. As the church is willing to expose the beliefs which underlie these distortions to a more developed understanding, it can be forgiven for its shortcomings and encouraged to grow beyond them. It is my hope that the church, founded, not by Jesus, but by well-meaning disciples who were spiritual seekers in their own right, is ready to take a hard look in the mirror, to gain the self-knowledge which will allow it to grow to its fullest godlike expression.

I believe every soul longs for the fulfillment that only comes of spiritual experience and expression. When we see the both the inner and outer "saboteurs" that hinder that spirituality, it becomes possible to transcend them and bring them into alignment with the thrust of our growth and development. I offer my perspectives on the Old Church in this spirit, that we might understand its place in the evolution of consciousness. Guided by the light of this understanding, we need not discard its valuable elements nor be limited by its partial truths. And when we are ready to move beyond the walls of the Old Church and get out of the box containing traditional Christianity, we will find there are other forms available for pursuing an authentic spiritual experience. I call these forms the New Church. In Part Three of this book, I will offer a description of this emergent New Church that provides direct access to essential spirituality.

# A Misunderstood Intention

*Jesus never organized a church on earth,*
*nor did he authorize anyone else to do so.*
*He said to Peter, "Upon this rock*
*I will build my church."*
*He did not tell Peter that*
*he was to be head of the church,*
*with a line of popes to follow.*
*He said, "I will build my church.*

**CHARLES FILLMORE"** [1]

One of the most pervasive beliefs fostered by many Westerners arises from the common misunderstanding that Christianity, as we know it, was founded by Jesus. We take for granted that everything Christian—from the necessity of converting non-believers to the promotion of anti-abortion political agendas—is somehow connected with Jesus and the religion he started. How do we come to accept this? The same way a fish isn't conscious that it's swimming in water—it never thinks about it! Unable to make a distinction called "water," the fish lives, moves and breathes in it without really being aware of it. In much the same way, Christianity has been so much a part of our history that it remains largely undistinguished as the context in which we live. As a result, we don't generally question the traditional assumptions of Christianity we've assimilated. Instead, we remain ignorant of the fact that the religion inspired by Jesus was really created by others who were interpreters of his intention. We live as if Jesus and Christianity are the same thing when this just isn't the case.

This fact seems especially difficult for North Americans to grasp. Because its original colonies were largely settled by Christians seeking greater freedom of religious expression, Christianity has in many ways been synonymous with American culture. We are just now beginning to notice that there are other Americans who are not Christian. Until it recently became impolitic to do so, our leaders would refer to us as a Christian nation, and a whole stable of Christian Coalition politicians would return us to that state even now. As other religions now make themselves more evident, as increasing numbers of Asians, Africans and others immigrate to the United States, we want them to know *they* are minorities— different, foreign to us—for *we* are a Christian country. We live, move and breathe in a Christian atmosphere that makes it very difficult to separate not only the Church from the State, but Jesus from the religion we assume he made. We practice Christian ethics, pray Christian prayers and celebrate Christian holidays, and, without giving it much thought, associate Jesus with all of it.

This kind of enculturation takes place very early. The message of Christianity is encoded in almost all the important events of American childhood. We receive it unconsciously as children and it is reinforced daily in every aspect of our lives. Unless something happens later on and we have some reason to question it, we live that inaccurate message for the rest of our lives. This is not necessarily a bad thing, except insofar as it recedes into the unconscious and we don't know we are living a partial truth.

One of the primary ways Americans in recent times have received the Christian message is through that impossible-to-miss holiday, Christmas. Supposedly a commemoration of the birth of Jesus the Son of God, in a manger in Bethlehem, Christmas has been largely eclipsed by the secular celebration. It has become an excuse for mass consumer frenzy, one our economy has come to depend on to assure our country's prosperity. Capitalism seems to have co-opted a religious event for its own purposes. But what if this has been a friendly takeover? As we'll explore in Chapter 13, the merger of business interests with religious ones actually affirms the power of Christianity. Capitalism and Christianity join hands during the Christmas season, not as a commemoration of Jesus' birth, but to make a statement about the religion he supposedly created. The real celebration at Christmas, then, is not about the birth of Jesus but the pervasiveness of Christianity.

Christianity, the religion said to be founded by Jesus, has become the predominant religion of the Western world. While individuals might long for spiritual awakening, one like Jesus seems to have had experienced, Christianity is actually preoccupied with another agenda. If we look closely, we see that Christianity is not identical with Jesus or his teachings, as many have long presumed. Rather it is a highly complex organization, enmeshed with political and financial interests, with millions of people, entire cultures in fact, enrolled in it. And so Christmas is a prime opportunity for Christianity to display itself. Unfortunately, with all the excitement about who Christianity says Jesus is supposed to be, the real significance of his life is almost always overlooked.

In their religious creed, Christians are taught to believe in Jesus Christ, begotten, not made, the very God of God, *and* in the one, true, holy, catholic, and apostolic Church. They are asked to affirm that Jesus founded this church upon the rock of his apostle Peter. They are supposed to understand that by doing this Jesus established the apostolic lineage that comprises the Popes of the Church. In general, the Christian religion promises its adherents that they will go to heaven after they die[2] on these conditions: if they believe that 1) this creed is true; 2) Jesus died for their sins; and; 3) they are saved by baptism within the Church.

Additionally, while this creed does not say so explicitly, it is generally understood that as a Christian one must believe that Jesus was the literal Son of God from the very start of his life—why else would a host of angels have burst into song at his birth?—and that his mission was to save sinful humans through the founding of the Christian religion. The gospel tales of the auspicious beginnings of Jesus' life, the prophecies which foretold his birth, the unusual circumstances surrounding his conception—in fact, everything told about Jesus' life, death and resurrection—focuses Christian belief on his divinity from the start of his life.

As a result of this teaching, Christians end up believing in a myth, the story of a supernatural god who falls to earth and lives in human guise for thirty-three years before returning to the heaven from which he originally came. The Christian religion idealizes Jesus, turns him into a god, and reduces his life and teaching to a belief system. It then offers people a promise of redemption through the magic he is supposed to be able to work on their behalf.

A lot of Christians expressed outrage over the earthy depiction of Jesus in the film "The Last Temptation of Christ." They hold that Jesus is perfect like God, far above and beyond themselves, an idol to be worshipped, not identified with. So strong is the Christian belief that this is true, these people refused to see Jesus depicted as an ordinary person who struggled to understand his true nature, and succeeded. With such a belief, it's unthinkable that *anyone* who engages in a spiritual growth and development process might also attain a state of realization. Indeed, there is a strong tendency among Christians to believe it is blasphemous to even think of trying. In this view, the Christian savior must not be too much like one of us, not if the magic of his salvation is to work.

But wouldn't Christianity be far more compelling if it embraced the Jesus-as-human element that many Christian viewers of the film found so objectionable? What is so remarkable about a supernatural being overcoming physical laws when by definition he is not subject to them? Nothing in particular. But what about a natural man who learns to transcend the limitations of time, space and gravity? Now that is impressive! As far out as it seems, this possibility gives hope, something for everyone to aspire towards.

Under the influence of Christianity, however, humans have been loathe to aspire to transcendence; this realm belongs to Jesus alone. If it was admitted that Jesus was one of us—a human being who fulfilled his evolutionary potential—the need for the Christian religion is debatable. For historically, the church has offered itself as a mediator between God and man. If mediation is unnecessary because humans can evolve themselves to a higher spiritual plane, it's not clear what function Christianity serves.

Christianity, however, avoids dealing with Jesus as an ordinary man and instead promotes the myth that Jesus was God's emissary sent to earth to start the Christian religion. This position justifies the church's existence and no one who believes in the Church has to reckon in any personal way with the tremendous spiritual capacity Jesus demonstrated. All are effectively absolved from the task of growing spiritually.

Traditional Christianity, what I term the Old Church, was the product of Jesus' followers' reluctance to identify themselves with the possibilities he represented. Christianity came into being because Jesus' early disciples faced this challenge and simply were not ready to take it on. I believe the witnesses to Jesus' process of growth and development sincerely tried to make sense of what he told them about it. But they were like blind men trying to learn about a sunset—they heard the words Jesus spoke but never grasped the depth of their meaning. They saw the miracles he performed but could only explain them as supernatural magic. Unable to take on the challenge *of* Jesus—which was, in effect, the challenge of their own spiritual life—they instead formed a myth *about* Jesus. The myth was told and retold religiously until one day there was a religion. Christianity wasn't founded by Jesus—that was just part of the myth men made up about the religion *they* founded! When Jesus spoke of founding a church, he had something else in mind altogether. Let's look at what this might have been.

Apart from the myths about the man, and a few facts from those who wrote about him fifty or more years after his death, we know relatively little about Jesus. But words attributed to him, or inspired by him in others' writing, communicate the insight of one who is awakening spiritually. One senses that his words radiated truth at such an expanded level of understanding, which when they were fully perceived, psychological defenses were broken down, hearts opened and minds cleared. From the reported accounts of those who knew him, or knew people who knew him, simply to be near Jesus was to be profoundly affected. Healings and blessings seemed to naturally come about in his presence.

But Jesus himself never claimed to work miracles. He certainly wasn't a showoff and he never said he'd been born under anything other than ordinary circumstances. And, most important, he never reserved the divine power he accessed for himself alone. On the contrary, he made a point of telling his disciples that whatever he was doing they would also do—and "greater things than these"—if they would believe in him. This was not to be mere belief in the surface of the works Jesus displayed to them, or any myth about them, but in the depth of possibility he represented. Jesus invited his listeners to discover the principle of divinity within themselves, the one he had already realized when he declared, "The Father and I are One." Believe in *that*! he urged.

However, Jesus was not able to fully communicate this discovery—the joy of his life—to his contemporaries. Like Moses before him, and Mohammed and others after him, his spiritual experiences expanded his awareness far beyond the understanding of his companions. Demonstrations of his power simply evoked awe, admiration and eventually the worship that would actually prevent his devotees from doing themselves what Jesus had done. Language could not adequately translate the all-encompassing vision of reality he beheld and began to integrate.

Taken literally, Jesus' words reveal only the palest hint of the vast riches of spiritual truth he perceived. He longed to connect with those who had ears to hear, as records of his outbursts of frustration with his disciples' thick-headedness make painfully clear. He used metaphor and simile, spoke in parable, offered familiar examples; but only occasionally did he receive a flicker of recognition in response from those men of "little faith."

One instance occurred when Jesus queried Peter, "Who do you say that I am?" and Peter responded, "Thou art the Christ." In that moment, Peter recognized the divine principle manifest in Jesus and Jesus blessed him for that. You can imagine Jesus sighing with relief, "At last, someone knows what I am about. Someone has finally heard me, seen me." As Peter demonstrated an increasing perception of the reality about which Jesus had been teaching his disciples, Jesus acknowledged Peter's expanded level of spiritual understanding. He describes this understanding metaphorically as the rock upon which he will build his church.

But we see that Peter was not entirely rock solid in his understanding, for in the same chapter (Matthew 16) he objects to the difficult information Jesus attempts to share about his mission. Peter may be able to see the divine in Jesus, but not yet in himself, so he does not fully trust what he sees and he equivocates. Jesus calls his wavering state of mind a stumbling-block and to Peter says, "Get thee behind me, Satan."

Nevertheless, Jesus didn't give up on him—Jesus definitely wanted to get his point across. So a short time later he took Peter, along with James and John, on a field trip to a high mountain where he shows himself to them, along with Elijah and Moses, in a transfigured, radiant state. Awakening to yet another level of spiritual awareness, they were astounded. Because they had been imprinted with the ancient taboo against coming face to face with the Divine, however, they were also afraid. When Jesus instructed them to keep the vision a secret "until the Son of Man is raised from the dead," they were likely relieved at not having to explain this overwhelming experience to anyone else.

Later on, down in the valley, Peter and the rest of the disciples were in for more bewilderment. Jesus seemed to become even more obscure in his teaching and, when they wanted him to take action to avoid the doom he prophesized, he refused to save himself (and them). Instead, Jesus continued to try his best to communicate to his disciples that the Pharisees' threats needed to be carried out as a test of the possibilities of self-transcendence. After all, one of the main subjects of Jesus' life and teaching could be summed up in this statement reported by John as made by Jesus toward the end of his teaching ministry: "He who loves his life loses it, and he who hates his life in this world will keep it for eternal life."

Historically interpreted as justification for a more traditional "pie in the sky" approach to life, it can also be read as a mystic's understanding of what happens when the personality's ego attachments are transcended in the moment of God-realization. Free of a limited sense of personal self, the real Self lives unbounded by spatial and temporal restraints. Yet, since the possibility of eternal life still remained theoretical to him, Jesus saw proving its reality as his ultimate life purpose. He'd been experimenting with the technology of consciousness in his miraculous works for several years—now he realized it was time to go all the way. In this, Jesus was like the astronaut who's studied and understood every theory about space travel and finally realizes someone has to be the first pilot to actually prove those theories. Reluctant or not, there is a possibility to explore, and self-actualization obliges the one who has committed himself or herself to fulfill the human potential by doing so.

But such a thing was outrageous, literally inconceivable to Jesus' disciples. Only now, two thousand years later, with many advanced technologies commonplace, do we have a context that allows us to begin to appreciate the experiment Jesus was proposing. Given that most of us would still shudder to think of volunteering to be the first person frozen alive; we'd understand at least how it could be possible that cryogenics would work. Lacking any such context, however, it is understandable that when it was time for Jesus to test his hypothesis that life could be lived on a level prior to and beyond the physical, the disciples' ignorance ruled and betrayals abounded. They believed him foolhardy, and at least one of them thought to save Jesus from himself. Even Peter, with all the understanding faith he did have, was overcome with fear and denied Jesus.

At his Last Supper, Jesus was physically surrounded by his devotees. But, spiritually and emotionally, that meal was taken alone. Jesus was left with the realization, "I have meat to eat you know not thereof." As a consolation, he invited his disciples to remember him and to consecrate that memory. This wasn't because he needed them to worship his body and blood for what he was about to undertake, but rather he hoped that a conscious memory of him might contain a seed of awareness that would eventually find fertile ground in them. This seed might produce in abundance what Jesus knew was possible as the fruit of an evolving consciousness.

Jesus never intended to start another religion. What would he want with it? From the accounts we have of his life, Jesus was an iconoclast, shattering the tablets of the Judaic legalism prevalent within his own family's religion. He held with contempt the laws of the Sabbath when they interfered with his spiritual practice of healing. He heaped disdain, not blessings, upon those who used religious law to limit creative human expression. While Jesus enjoyed spiritual experiences in abundance, his religious observances appear to have been minimal, performed in the spirit rather than the letter of the law. There is no evidence that Jesus gathered his followers together in any building for a worship service of the type we have long associated with church. His use of the word "church" in his conversation with Peter, therefore, must have had a different meaning for him, one that Peter did not fully grasp.

Jesus didn't use the word church to mean an organized religion or a movement you could join like a club. I believe he used it to indicate individuals who, like Peter in that moment of recognition, perceived the divine principle, the Christ, coming into manifestation. The word he used was *ecclesia*, which means "called out ones." The term served as an acknowledgement of the level of spiritual awareness attained by those individuals who are called out of their limited egoic existence by a commitment to relationship with God. As he traveled his own path of spiritual awakening, Jesus reached this awareness himself. It was a precursor of the realization in which he was increasingly grounded—Spirit is embodied within all human beings, Spirit is evolved through all humans being.

Those who were close to recognizing this were "members" of church as Jesus spoke of it. However, as his own teaching admitted, many are called to this church but few are chosen. It's not that the many he refers to lack the potential, nor is it that God or some other power fails to choose them. It's that so few answer the call to spiritual awareness. Most of us don't want to take on the responsibility for living in a committed relationship with the Divine this would require.

The church, as Jesus defined it, is a spiritual experience, not an outer observance or belief system. That spiritual experience could be available, he taught, where two or more are gathered with a willingness to be inducted into a higher state of consciousness. It is unlikely, however, he really had in mind that such gatherings should promote social, political and religious agendas as Christianity has done over the past two millennia. The available evidence simply does not show Jesus to have such relatively limited aspirations. Rather, Jesus appears almost exclusively concerned with his realization process. He spent his time trying to translate his experience so others could understand their significance, and learn to transform their own consciousness.

To those who never experienced a mystical event of their own, or did not know Jesus as an ordinary man, it was understandably safer to attribute his extraordinary spiritual power to a supernatural gift that belonged exclusively to a god, than it was to accept it as the evolutionary refinement of a natural human power that could be accessed by everyone. Over time, the power generated by the original experience of Jesus' own awakening was diffused and diluted and the man and the myth about him became confused. It proved too difficult for these people, who were also the builders of the early church, to embrace the challenge of Christ to live the authentic life of a fully human/fully divine being. Instead the Old Church chose to take the well-traveled road of belief that we humans are, after all, only human, and, as such, we cannot and should not be expected to be more than this.

Rather than empowering people to achieve their wondrous capacity for self-actualization, the Old Church emphasized human shortcomings. Humans were assumed to be innately sinful. This encouraged them to depend on God as defined by the Old Church, who through its own agency, would meet the many needs dependent people have and save them from their grossly inadequate selves.

Today, Old Church institutions still foster similar limited notions of human nature. As a result, Christ, or the divine principle Jesus recognized as his true nature, remains unrealized in most people. The widely held misconception that the institutional church was founded by Jesus' intention, however, is now being challenged by individuals whose own spiritual experiences clearly contradict the authority of the Old Church. For example, a spiritually maturing woman wants to proclaim her spiritual awareness in the ministry of the priesthood. Yet when she approaches the Roman Catholic Church she still meets a rigid misogyny which prevents her from doing so. Which is more accurate, she wonders,—the authority of the Church or her realization that she is one with God? Likewise, a priest has grown in his capacity to love to the extent that he is capable of intimate relationship; however, he is denied its fullest expression in sacred, sexual partnership. Is this institutional prohibition truly the will of the Divine? Is the spirituality of a woman flawed simply because she is female? Is a man who loves God *and* another human less of a realized being? Does God really judge the sexual preference of its own manifestations? Would Jesus have done so?

The Old Church insists on its authority in such matters. Yet to have a deep experience of awakening such as Jesus did is to acknowledge the lack of jurisdiction of any outer authority in such matters. Indeed, it is futile to legislate or contain Spirit in any way. Believing in the authority of the Old Church on issues like these makes it possible, however, for the believer to rest in the assurance that there can be a right answer to life's difficult questions. To let go of such authority would seem to plunge one into a sea of uncertainty where one might drown; the believer must cling to religion, then, as to a life raft. It's true there is some risk in moving beyond belief and learning to navigate the vast seas of expanding consciousness for oneself. Ironically, however, the most treacherous spots in our inner oceans are not obstacles placed there by Satan; they are those icebergs formed of the ego's rigid attachment to what it believes is right!

From the point of view of spiritual awakening, the security of being right reinforces the very thing that obstructs us. Religion and religious righteousness, while they may intend to make us feel better about our human condition, deepen our sense of being separate from God and our spiritual self.

We often do feel better when we believe we are right, but this doesn't mean that Spirit is any less a prisoner of our ego. Religious observances simply make us feel better about being stuck in that cell. They occupy us in such a way that we do not have to face the actual limitations of being exclusively identified with the ego. Without even realizing we are deprived of a greater experience in life, we follow the rules of religion and rest secure in the knowledge that our good egos will go to heaven. This is all very attractive as long as we believe that we are our egos. Practically speaking, one function of religion has been to reinforce that fact. A religious cliché puts it this way: "God is God and you're not!" The subtext: "Just let the Church work its magic on you and you won't have to worry about a thing."

By making Jesus larger than life after his death, the Old Church made him synonymous with God. They attributed his attainments not to a real person who worked to transform his being, but to a mythical superhero, the latest addition to a pantheon of gods. The institutional Old Church, past or present, offers Jesus, not as a guide for those who struggle to discover their way on a spiritual path, but as an object of worship. By objectifying and idealizing him, it effectively absolves seekers of the responsibility, risk, and ultimate fulfillment of living as authentically as Jesus did. It deprives them of the opportunity to discover their natural capacity to grow and develop beyond what they might ever imagine possible. Because this thwarts the evolutionary impulse, the Old Church does a disservice, not only to the individuals affected, but to the consciousness of humankind as a whole.

It could be argued that the Old Church, by giving a sense of security and safety to its constituents, is acting in service to evolution. One might say that it honors the principle of survival of the fittest, with the fittest defined as those who know how to protect themselves and stay safe. Yet Jesus himself was unwilling to be safe in the way his disciples urged him to be. He repeatedly met threatening situations with faith. He was a pioneer in the realm of consciousness and this was his way of showing the kind of aliveness that becomes available once we move past the fears that confine most of us to a very narrow existence.

To some observers such as Judas, Jesus' teaching that you must lose your life in order to gain your life was pure madness. Judas is often seen as a betrayer of Jesus, but if we look closely at his character he was simply trying to save Jesus from himself and preserve the community of disciples from harm. You might say he acted in the interest of the physical survival of his species.

But perhaps Judas' remorse after he turned Jesus over to the Romans was because he suddenly realized that Jesus had been trying to tell the disciples about an evolutionary impulse of a higher order. Judas, in his attempt to save his teacher, had been serving the interest of the evolution of his species, while Jesus was serving the evolution of consciousness. Judas simply had not understood that evolution proceeds paradoxically—that what is true on one level is often contradicted by the deeper understanding of a higher level. He operated according to the best of his limited understanding and this constituted, not a wrongdoing so much as a shortcoming. Relative to the truth available to Jesus at the time (ego loss = spiritual gain), Judas acted from information derived from a partial truth (safety = survival). He really did the best he knew to do, but because it was only part of the truth, he fell short.

The founders of the burgeoning Christian religion likewise operated from an incomplete understanding of the spiritual impulse that inspired Jesus to speak of church.

As we will see in the next chapter, the apostles' attempt to find meaning in the life and teaching of Jesus while staying emotionally safe, caused them to merely skate on the surface of the depths of consciousness Jesus had plumbed. They tried to find a way to fit their amazement with Jesus together with their concerns for survival. Using Jesus' injunction to convert humankind, they formed a powerful structure that eventually allowed the church fathers to secure a good life for themselves. By claiming that it could mediate with God to assure salvation, the Old Church amassed wealth and power which continually reinforced its own authority and its constituents' dependency. As a result, over the ages the Old Church has been rife with distortion. This misplaced emphasis has led to a corruption of leadership and denied the spiritual imperative within individuals to actualize their full potential, prompting Pope John Paul II at a millennial Easter celebration to apologize, if not for the wrongdoing of the Roman Church itself, at least for the Catholic people who did wrong.

Whatever spiritual opportunities the Old Church may have helped people avoid, and whatever abuses it has wrought in the name of Jesus, on the positive side, the Old Church has consistently been a civilizing influence in the cultures it has conquered. For one thing, in the propagation of the institutional Old Church, art and craft flourished—witness any of the myriad medieval villages in Italy built around its colorfully frescoed *duomo*, not to mention the vast treasure-filled Roman basilicas.

In the less material realm, rational challenges to the magical/mythical view held by the Old Church from those who objected to its dogma have resulted in huge scientific and technological developments. This advancement, made in reaction to the Old Church, is actually responsible for creating a language and context for the kind of spiritual experience Jesus was unable to adequately describe. So, in a roundabout way, the Old Church's tendency to limit the human spirit has actually aroused it. Consciousness will find any way it can to evolve, and that's some really good news!

# The "Only Human" Fallacy

*I am larger, better than I thought,*
*I did not know I held so much goodness.*

**WALT WHITMAN**

There's an old cliché often used to justify our shortcomings: "After all, I'm only human." It certainly seems true, doesn't it? Well, yes and no! Many people struggle along in life; even when they're doing the best they can, their accomplishments seem hardly worthy of mention. But then there are others who seem, for want of a better word, more than human. Look at Gandhi, Martin Luther King, Mother Teresa—these and others like them surpass the expectation the majority holds on what it means to be human. Yet there's no denying it—these were real people made of the same flesh and blood as the rest of us!

It is a mistake, one usually made by those whose psychology has them settle for less in life, to think of humanity as so limited. In reality, our human potential embraces a wide range of possibility, and the persons named above simply demonstrate the more actualized end of a continuum. When cynicism, resignation and a variety of other factors in the human psyche impose limits on our human potential, the psyche tries to vindicate itself by acting as if "settling" is the best that can be done. This psychological racket keeps us spinning in endless vicious cycles in which we are proved, again and again, to be incapable of being more than we are currently demonstrating.

It's in the spirit of genuine inquiry, not cynicism, I am now going to explore the psychology that birthed the Old Church.

Previously I have stated a premise that basically says historical Christianity is the best offering Old Church organizers could have made within the framework of their understanding. Why is this so? What made the Old Church stop short of its potential for facilitating spiritual growth and development? It's important to look into this carefully, for it's likely these psychological factors still operate within the Old Church in its contemporary forms.

In summary, the primary influences determining the actions of the early leaders of the Old Church were threefold: One, some of those early Christians spent a significant amount of time in the presence of Jesus, a highly evolved human being. Two, when Jesus died, they suffered a profound loss of that meaningful contact. Three, their own stage of development was less evolved than that of Jesus. We will see that while the disciples were inspired by their contact with Jesus, left to themselves they were more strongly driven by their fears. Consequently, they produced a religion derived from and aimed at a stage of human development similar to their own—one that is preoccupied with issues of self-preservation and the fulfillment of deficiency needs.

Their religion, rather than showing people ways to meet God as the unknown and unknowable, attempts to control life by making it manageable within the confines of a dogmatic structure. By not facing the human ego's terror of annihilation, the Old Church feeds rather than resolves the fears of its constituents and fosters their dependency.

Relatively recent work in the field of psychology correlates levels of consciousness with social and cognitive development.[3] Individual psychologies, we see, are quite different at these various levels. For example, a migrant worker preoccupied with making ends meet has different motivations and behaviors than the corporate executive who isn't concerned with where her next meal is coming from. One fears physical hunger, perhaps starvation, while the other's greatest concern is the meaning of life. Understanding where one stands within a spectrum of consciousness, it's possible to work with states of fear and not be stopped by them. Eventually such efforts may bring about a transformation of consciousness in which fear no longer motivates strategies to control life, but builds a scaffold for a faith that allows a wider embrace of life and spiritual experience.

For most of the two millennia the Old Church has existed, a very basic fear of the loss of relationship with God has prevented people from questioning Christianity—not only its authority but the entire concept of it. The courageous souls who did so in the past were accused of heresy and persecuted by the Old Church. But now a more sophisticated psychological perspective is generally available that makes it clear that the Old Church is not *the* way to God. Traditional religion is a step—and not the only, and maybe not even a necessary, step—on an evolving path of spiritual growth and development. With tools that allow us to look at ourselves from the vantage point of evolutionary psychology, we can do what early Old Church leaders did not—examine their shortcomings for what they are. By addressing the concerns and fears of those early church leaders and the people who comprised the sheep in their flock, we may discover a way to keep in the Old Church what is most functional, and to let the rest of it go. We'll then be able to offer, in addition to respected traditional forms that remain supportive to a process of spiritual unfoldment, other avenues to the authentic spiritual experience which Jesus originally offered humanity.

In the latter part of his ministry, Jesus tried to prepare his disciples for his imminent and violent departure from their midst. But they resisted his prophecy—they did not want him to die. They held to their hope that somehow his death could be prevented. Indeed, they implored Jesus to use his powers to avoid this fate, and, failing in that, concocted schemes they believed might save Jesus in spite of himself. When the inevitable happened and their beloved Jesus was gone, his close followers were left to deal with a tremendous void in their lives. When a person dies following a prolonged illness or advanced years, the loss triggers a normal, albeit difficult, grieving process for those closest to the deceased. But the grief following the sudden death of an admired public figure, however, seems to be of a different order.

To understand how Jesus' disciples might have felt, we might stop and consider how the death of public figures in our lifetime has affected us. For example, several generations remember the shock and mourning of the entire nation when

President Kennedy was assassinated. Three days of non-stop news coverage revisited the fatal scene; reported on the suspected killer, motives, methods; and followed the horse-drawn cortege in solemn procession to Arlington Cemetery. Those images hold so much power for our nation that more than thirty-five years later, when his son died in an airplane accident, the news coverage of his death was largely a replay of his father's.

Just like Jesus' disciples, we think largely in terms of living, not dying. Even when faced with the inevitable, we avoid it—by making it more than it is! The news of Kennedy's assassination caused our whole country to reel from all sorts of fears and doubts regarding not only the security of our country, but our own personal safety. Like any death, his threatened a way of life we thought we could depend on. But instead of simply feeling that fear, we, aided by the media, wanted to make it mean something. So we idolized the victim and idealized his death as a sacrifice in the line of duty in service to us, the citizens of his country.

Eventually, though, we were forced to recognize that as charismatic a presence Kennedy had been in life—no matter how he had inspired our hopes and dreams—he could no longer carry that torch for us, no longer be our god. The eternal flame which burns by his graveside still serves as a reminder of what this man represented to us.[*] But it has been up to us, as it is the task for the survivors of any loss, to kindle sparks of life from the smoldering ashes of death's dissolution, to build a new fire. Really this is the challenge posed to us by any death, but it is exaggerated when the one who dies is well-known.

Often when a leader dies, it is tempting for followers to try and keep him alive by emulating the leader. They imagine how their leader would have responded to any situation they face, and then do that. While this impulse may come from a good intention, however, it is simply not possible to be someone else. Eventually the followers will have to develop their own path in life.

This is very commonly seen in families around the death of a parent; the child will attempt to replace the parent. The eldest son, left in charge of his siblings, tries to cook them breakfast just the way mom did. But even if he can remember exactly how mom scrambled the eggs, he will never be able to duplicate them exactly, since mom was also one of the ingredients of the recipe. If he is willing, however, to utilize the principles his mother taught him and perhaps discover some of his own, it is entirely possible that he will develop his own unique way of preparing breakfast. If he brings himself fully to the task, what he does could actually be an improvement on his mother's method.

Growth of the individual and evolution of the species are natural to all living beings. The death of a parent or a leader upon whom there has been dependency can be a kind of birth for those left behind. To the extent the leader created a context for others' living, he or she has serves as a womb in which the followers have been gestating. When the leader dies it is as if the nourishment available within the womb is depleted, triggering the onset of the labor and delivery of a new being who will carry forth the evolutionary imperative to create a more refined reality.

But did the followers of Jesus rise to the occasion of the possibility offered them by his death? Or were they only able to go as far towards it as they were psychologically prepared to go? After all, where Jesus left off would have been a huge leap for anyone to make, particularly with only a three-year mentoring period for training. No, the disciples probably didn't pick up the ball Jesus dropped in their court, and it's likely that humanity in general has taken the better part of the last two millennia to even conceive of the possibility that we can be consciously involved in our own evolution. It seems we must be getting ready for this, because the technology we've developed allows us to alter genes and clone life forms. In the not too distant future, we're told we'll be able to download the contents of our brains onto a microchip so we can extend our consciousness beyond the physical life of our body.[5] (We might call this newly evolved life form *homo siliconis.*)

Jesus, however, seemed to perceive the possibility of conscious evolution two thousand years ago. His teaching pointed to an understanding of an evolutionary process. In the parable of the seed growing itself, he outlines a progression, "First the blade, then the ear, then the full corn in the ear." (Mark 4:28) He goes on to describe how this is a manifestation of a pre-visualized possible reality: "Look up and see the fields already white for the harvest." Humanity is just beginning to understand the biology, psychology and technology that can take these statements beyond mere metaphor.

In one theory about the human capacity for transformation, Barbara Marx Hubbard[6] claims that Jesus is a template for a future human. As such he represents a self-actualized human being, one who has fulfilled his human creaturely potential and begun to utilize the power of a co-creative partnership with God, the energetic creative source. Hubbard calls human beings *godlings*— humans who are becoming aware of their godlike nature. She suggests the resurrection of Jesus from the death of his human physicality was a demonstration of what is possible, not just for one special man, but for all of humankind.

This resurrection remains as a kind of four-minute mile for our species, *homo sapiens*. Once Roger Bannister broke through whatever physical and psychological barriers had stopped men before him, others raced beyond him to achieve even greater speeds. In like manner, the breakthrough in the consciousness of one member of our species, Jesus, portends the likelihood that sooner or later there will be an evolutionary leap forward by the entire species. Hubbard anticipates that as humanity stops believing in the inevitability of physical death, it will be birthed from the "uterine" earth experience out into the larger universe as a new species which she calls *homo universalis*. Like those runners who are no longer daunted by the four-minute mile, we will no longer regard death as the obstacle we presently do. Perhaps this species will be the offspring of *homo sapiens* and *homo siliconis!*

While I find such speculation about Jesus intriguing, it's not difficult to empathize with those who dismiss it as they would any science fiction. Even in these days of instant access to just about anything via the Internet, it still seems farfetched to think about a computer walking around with "me" inside it (even though this life-extending option is predicted to be available within fifty years or less). Jesus' immediate followers had absolutely no technological savvy to even suggest such a preposterous notion. They had no context for considering the distant goal of this type of human evolution. These people lived in a simpler time; they viewed the world magically: God, the great magician in the sky, performed miracles, and the mysteries associated with such magic remained just that. For Jesus, "I and the Father are One" might have been true, but for his followers it was still "God is God, and I'm not!"

Yet, even if they didn't fully understand Jesus, being around someone with such far-out ideas, who did such wondrous things, exhilarated and inspired them. Because of the impact he had on their lives, in his absence, the disciples must have really missed him. He was not only their friend, but their teacher. You can imagine they mourned for the loss of the richness of life they felt in his presence.

But after his death, the void formed by his absence was soon filled with their questions. What just happened? What did it mean? What were all those parables Jesus told really about? What next? Jesus had promised they would experience an infusion of the Holy Spirit and they did. The disciples discovered they, too, had charismatic powers; but what should they do with them? Oh yes, they recalled, Jesus had wanted a new church established— this, at least, was a straightforward request. And so, the disciples latched onto this one bit of concrete instruction and set about the task. The result of their efforts is the early Christian church.

The Acts of the Apostles reveals the zeal with which Jesus' disciples reconciled their loss by following what they thought to be his wishes. Jesus had commissioned them, they believed, to preach about him to all nations. So they enthusiastically set about telling and retelling the story of those amazing things they had seen and heard. In so doing the apostles were able to appreciate Jesus' life in a way that was perhaps not possible for them while Jesus walked among them. And they found ears eager to hear the tales which spoke of the Messianic liberation from oppression, much longed for by Jewish people. Fresh from their inspirited contact with Jesus, his disciples attracted others to form community with them to explore the "good news" that one day would be recorded as Gospel.

From the earliest days of its founding, however, the newborn church necessarily focused on its own survival. The apostles drew nourishment from their experience of Jesus as a baby suckles at its mother's breast. The infant organization fed for as long as it could on the awareness of the one who inspired it. But as time passed and generations were distanced from the initial events which so impressed Jesus' early disciples, the church developed an autonomous existence. This turned out to have little connection with the spiritual experience that had originally inspired it.

The first days of Christianity were characterized by community gatherings of interested persons in private homes that were adapted for the occasion of worship. Their informal service, which took place on the day after the Jewish Sabbath, was to remember Jesus' death and celebrate his resurrection. The earliest liturgy consisted of witness, praise and thanksgiving loosely structured around a common meal in which all present participated. The early Christians, mostly Jews or converts to Judaism, still observed the Jewish law and continued to also worship in synagogues. So, in the beginning, no one paid much attention to the early Christians.

Over time, however, the apostles' message began to attract those outside of traditional Judaism. Their new religion drew the suspicion, ire and, eventually, persecution from both the orthodox Jews and the Romans who ruled at the time. Until then, the Jews and Romans had cooperated in respectively holding the religious and political power in the territory where Christianity first took hold. Now the status quo was challenged by this upstart movement and together they sought to put it down. Thus, while the first Christians might have been spiritually inspired, they were threatened both politically and physically.

Following the impulse of any young creature to seek protection under fearful circumstances, the infant church built psychic walls to defend itself both from without and within. Within these walls it set about to create an identity for itself, securing a place by defining itself more clearly. As a result of these efforts, the home-based church meetings changed from spontaneous, experiential celebrations into more formal rituals conducted by clergy for a passive congregation. The fellowship meal became a more ceremonial remembrance of the Last Supper. The ability to partake of this symbolic communion was restricted to those who were formal members in the community.

From the undifferentiated state in which it had been birthed, a new religion quickly developed into an increasingly delineated entity whose main focus was its own identity. What began as a sect of Judaism had, by the third century, its own set of scriptures, creeds and doctrines, a clerical hierarchy, specific methods of religious instruction, a liturgical calendar and detailed orders of service. While open to Jews, Gentiles and others, inclusion in the salvation promised by the new Christian religion was by rite of secret initiation.

To belong, one had to subscribe to belief in the message of the evangelistic apostles and formalize this through ritual baptism. This emphasis on belief in certain doctrines of faith, rather than spiritual experience, became the hallmark of the religion. The doors in the ever-thickening walls of organized Christianity began to open only to those who gave their intellectual assent to the acceptable theological belief system. Increasingly, they slammed shut in the face of those who had a mystical realization of an expanded viewpoint.

Through the two millennia of its existence, the Old Church has created and clung to rigid forms of expression, not so much by conscious design as in fulfillment of the developmental tasks set before it. There is a tendency to think of an institution such as the Old Church as a huge immovable object, as inert as a large boulder. (And this notion is often reinforced by the kind of obstacles that arise when we begin to talk about change within an institution.) But truly an institution is alive. Like other living things, it grows, moves, breathes, and reproduces itself in organismic fashion.

The apostle Paul referred to the church as the living body of Christ, and likened the members of the church to the various elements of the human body. An apt metaphor, it allows us to apply a psychological understanding of human development to the Old Church itself. We may then possibly consider its accomplishments as an institution created by and composed of human beings, from the perspective of the developmental tasks it has attempted to master. We can also discern the developmental phase the Old Church is presently in, and perhaps project scenarios for its future.

&

There are many developmental models we could choose from to examine the psychology of the Old Church. I have selected Abraham Maslow's Hierarchy of Needs because his psychology of growth and motivation begins with the most basic human needs and extends to include a state similar to that reached by Jesus. Since any analysis of the Old Church would need to include the developmental stages of all of its participants, I think this model is well-suited to apply to the development of a church inspired by Jesus but founded by his followers.

While he began his work as a behavioral psychologist, because he articulated the range of possibility for human development, Abraham Maslow is considered by many to be the father of the human potential movement. In 1954, he developed his Hierarchy of Needs when his reflection upon earlier research he'd done with monkeys caused him to conclude that not all of a monkey's needs were equally important. He observed that if one was both hungry and thirsty, the need for water proved more urgent than the need for food. This made sense considering an organism can live far longer without food than without water.

Extrapolating his observations and applying them to humans, Maslow went on to outline and prioritize five broad categories of needs. Briefly and in this order, they are: the physiological needs (for air, water, food, sex, etc.), the need for safety and security, the need for love and belonging, the need for esteem, and the need to actualize the self. In a later refinement of the hierarchy, Maslow added the need for transcendence to the category of self-actualization. The first four categories he termed *deficiency* or *D-needs,* while the last category he labeled *growth needs* or *Being-values.* Maslow asserted that the two sources of motivation in behavior that affect human development are deficiency motivation and growth motivation.

A person whose D-needs, have been fulfilled, Maslow considered healthy, while those who have not had these basic needs gratified he described as suffering from neurosis. Neurosis, Maslow claims, is a psychological equivalent to scurvy, and has its origin in the deficiency of factors necessary to sustain life. Until the basic needs are met, the life energy of the deficient neurotic is almost entirely and, often ineffectively, directed toward their fulfillment. Just about any story you'll hear on the eleven o'clock news is an account of such frustration. Homelessness, domestic violence, drug-related crimes—you don't even have to scratch the surface of these problems to find someone struggling to get D-needs met. Look in our nation's prisons and you get a picture of the stunted development that occurs when these needs are not fulfilled.

On the other hand, a person who has found fulfillment of these basic needs tends to become motivated by an urge to grow and devotes his life energy to being all that he can be.[7] At this level of development the motivation to grow extends beyond most limitations which may typically circumscribe aspects of life; neurosis can be notably absent even in the face of environmental deficits.

Viktor Frankl[8], in the remarkable account of his experience in a Nazi concentration camp, points to the power of the urge to create along the lines of Maslow's growth needs. Frankl tells how debilitated camp inmates were able to labor in freezing cold, without proper food, clothing, shelter or rest, because they were motivated to live by such Being-values as purpose, meaning, justice, truth and beauty. They found a reason to live beyond their immediate circumstance. Many of these growth-motivated individuals created a definition of themselves beyond mere physicality, and produced, as Frankl himself did, meaningful outcomes not only for themselves but for others as well. This ability to transcend the horrific conditions of their internment revealed something godlike in these individuals. They demonstrated the power and potential of human beings to move beyond the limitations imposed by physicality and co-create an unbounded spiritual reality into which they could then enter.

Maslow's Hierarchy is often pictorially represented as a pyramid, broad at its base, narrow at the top. (Figure 9.1) Such an image seems a reasonable way to show the distribution of a group through various stages of development—certainly more of the world's people are preoccupied with feeding and clothing themselves than are concerned with the philosophical verities of existence. The labels on each level of the pyramid climb it like a ladder, and it's pretty clear that life at the top is considered more desirable than on the bottom. To rise in Maslow's Hierarchy is to ascend the ladder to the peak experiences to be had on top of the heap.

The Old Church likes the ladder image too. The Old Testament story of Jacob's ladder has informed Judeo-Christian thinking about the relationship of humans to God for thousands of years. The traditional religious ideology associated with Jacob's ladder places an authoritarian God—the One—over and above its creation— the Many. From the top of this hierarchical ladder, God, the Creator dictates its divine will to the creatures far below. This belief is seldom questioned by the religious people

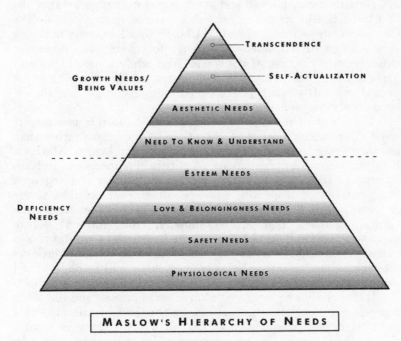

MASLOW'S HIERARCHY OF NEEDS

Figure 9.1

of the Old Church. Rather the Old Church reflects and reinforces this dominance hierarchy in its leadership structure. But herein lies one of the primary distortions of the Old Church.

The Old Church, as a religious organization, purports to be on the upper end of hierarchy—nearer to God certainly than to the masses.[9] But here's the rub. The Old Church says that it is devoted to spiritual, or Being-values, but if you look at what it does, it is actually in the business of promoting deficiency needs. People come to the Old Church looking for the fulfillment of precisely those D-needs named by Maslow on the second and third levels of the Hierarchy, namely the need for safety and security and the need for love and belonging. In return, the Old Church offers them everything from a scheme for salvation to a place they can belong.

Now that may be well and good, but in exchange for this, the Old Church asks its belongers (a.k.a. believers) to *depend* on the Church for these things. The Old Church uses hierarchy in such a way as to create a dependency that reinforces its own dominance over the needy people of the world. And while some of this may happen altruistically (motivated by love, truth, beauty, etc.), much of it doesn't. It's really just a veiled method for getting the D-needs of the organization met!

The effect of the distorted way the Old Church uses hierarchy to dominate rather than liberate is to emphasize rather than reduce the separation between God and human beings. Matthew Fox attributes the phenomena of elitism, competition, and abstraction within the traditional church to a linear striving up a Sisyphian ladder of spiritual accomplishment.[10] The ladder image as used by the church reinforces rather than resolves the fundamental dualism that has dominated and limited human perception. Indeed, this imagery is the hallmark of a mind preoccupied with concerns at the basic need level of Maslow's Hierarchy, the mind that believes everything will be okay "…if I can just make it to the top."

It is true that an increased awareness of oneself and life offers a perspective like the one that can be obtained by climbing to a high place, enlightenment does not involve the sense of separation implied by the steps up a Jacob's ladder. A discontinuity does exist between levels of being—radical shifts do occur that move us in a direction that seems far beyond a previous way of being. But this discontinuity is really an evolutionary progression in which we remain connected with the roots from which we grew.

Ken Wilber describes evolution unfolding as nested hierarchies, or holons. The real task of evolution is for the more evolved level to *transcend* and *include* the one below it. The Old Church hierarchy makes the mistake of *transcending* and *dominating* rather than including, and so do its followers.[11]

As a result many humans frequently fail to sense their interconnectedness with other species from which they may have evolved. This has created a self-destructive, exploitative dominance of humans over all the living and non-living resources of our home planet. As one grows spiritually it is possible to become inflated by lofty experiences or lose a sense of connection with the ground. The hierarchical ladder image, if used erroneously, endorses such disconnection with unfortunate results. Our human ego is tempted to think those who have reached the top of any ladder are intrinsically better than those who have not, and will try to convince others of this in order to wield power over them. But as anyone who has played "King of the Mountain" knows, the glee that one finds at the top of the heap is short-lived. It is lonely there, and our need for love and affiliation would eventually have us looking for others with whom to share our experiences. For the Old Church to include rather than dominate its members would mean to offer them the means for fulfilling their deficiency needs without making them dependent in the process.

Since the ladder image has been misused in the past, I have wondered if there isn't a more effective image than a pyramid/ladder to depict a hierarchy of growth and development. I've flipped through the ads of many contemporary publications dealing with spirituality and found a slew of symbols trying to get a point across about human potential. There are lots of circles. It's been stylish recently to think in terms of images of wholeness and a circle is a convenient shorthand for this. But while "wholeness" has a nice ring to it, conveying a sense of inclusion, it doesn't accurately evoke a sense of development as the ladder image does.

The infinity symbol also gets a lot of good press these days, communicating a sense of ongoing movement; for me, however, it again misses the sense of progressive unfoldment I'd want the new symbol to communicate. A square connotes a sense of balance, but a square will forever be just that—not too inspirational! The Christian symbol of the cross is simply too fraught with associations to make a new statement. What's left? Spirals, triangles, rectangles, parabolas—I'm sure someone could find a good use for all of them. But if I were to choose an alternative to the pyramid/ladder to describe Maslow's hierarchy, I'd pick the spiral to do the job best. (Figure 9.2)

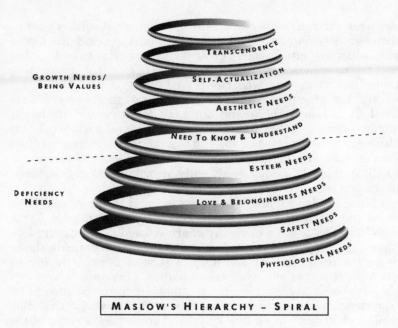

GROWTH NEEDS/
BEING VALUES

TRANSCENDENCE

SELF-ACTUALIZATION

AESTHETIC NEEDS

NEED TO KNOW & UNDERSTAND

ESTEEM NEEDS

DEFICIENCY
NEEDS

LOVE & BELONGINGNESS NEEDS

SAFETY NEEDS

PHYSIOLOGICAL NEEDS

MASLOW'S HIERARCHY - SPIRAL

Figure 9.2

A spiral hints at the wholeness of a circle, but with a greater sense of movement. In fact, if you do with an image of spiral on paper what any kid with a pair of scissors could do—you can easily transform it from a surface to a spring. Boinnnng! Your spiral moves up and down. Like a pyramid, it's broad at the base, and narrow at the top (or is it the other way around?); however, because it lacks a ladder's rungs, this spiral conveys more continuity within the evolutionary progression than the ladder imagery does. It hints at recurring cycles, providing an added dimension to the pyramid/ladder imager, since over the course of a lifetime, we do actually seem to circle round very similar sets of circumstances, with the opportunity to grow each time we visit one of them.

As we learn to make more enlightened choices which allow us to get our needs met by others or discover how to meet our own needs, we spiral, rather than climb, inward to our depths and upward to the next evolutionary level. Each turn of the spiral brings us into closer contact with our most essential godlike self. As we are irresistibly drawn to the source of all power in evolutionary fashion, we gain access to a broader perspective, wisdom and power. But this is not a power to be held over or against another; it is only useful as it empowers others as they journey toward the same center in themselves.

Looking at Maslow's Hierarchy of Needs in this way, Jesus' life and teaching would represent a human being moving deep into the center of an upward spiral of fulfillment. Jean Houston refers to this type of person as "the possible human" in her book by the same title. The possible human is a completely self-actualizing person who lives at a consistently high level of enjoyment and performance in life; one who recognizes, realizes and expresses the godlike qualities of his beingness. As an example of this level of human beingness, Jesus' greatest need was to realize and express principles of goodness, truth, freedom and other meaningful ideals. He was ultimately unconcerned with issues of his own physical survival.

The newly birthed church, on the other hand, was, as we have shown, very concerned with sustaining itself. The church was created by people who were less evolved than Jesus and whose needs were different than his. In terms of the spiral symbol, they existed on the lower, outer edge of the upward spiral. Immersed in dualistic ways of viewing reality, and preoccupied with their own deficiency needs, the church organism was like a caterpillar groping about the ground from which the hierarchical spiral grew. It had a lot of work to do to get ready for the long evolutionary journey to the center where one day its actualized potential might be realized as a butterfly.

The primary goal of the Old Church in the past two thousand years has remained fixed on the fulfillment of basic needs. The false belief in the limited capacity of humanity also remains fixed. We can easily see how this happened. The primary concern of the Old Church was to establish and maintain its organism with the institutional equivalents of air, food, water, shelter, sleep and sex. To find air to breathe, the church had to leave the womb in which it was dependent on Jesus' spiritual energy and understanding, and also cut the cords which tied it to Jewish tradition. To get nourishment, the church developed its own ideology which could feed it spiritually, and raised funds to feed it materially. The church took shelter wherever it could, using home-churches until it had the means to build proper church-homes. The church slept in the comfort of the New Testament promise, and reproduced by means of evangelical efforts of its members.

With the elements of survival obtained, the church's next task was to secure what it had accumulated. This it accomplished through the development of a complex infrastructure of leadership, dogma and liturgy. One example of this: When it became apparent that the heirs of married priests might lay claim to the church's landholdings and deplete its treasure chest, clerical celibacy conveniently became church law. Members of the church were also trained to defend their faith. Initially this was to protect it from those outside the church who persecuted the Christians. But eventually it served to keep it safe from those inside who would challenge the authority of the church on matters of doctrine or spiritual practice.

The church fulfilled its basic needs for love and belongingness by marketing itself as the club most important to join—the promise of a heavenly reward over the threat of everlasting damnation being sufficiently attractive to motivate a lot of people to sign on with the new religion.

A large percentage of the world's population today acknowledges and/or embraces Christianity. Significant work toward the fulfillment of the last basic need, the need for self-esteem, has been accomplished. Still the institutional church remains confined to the box it built to provide shelter and protect it from harm. The Old Church has yet to move beyond its concerns with its own existence and so continues to offer followers religious structures that are only suited for the lower, outer end of the hierarchical spiral. It has not made any provision for the spiritual development that might take one to the riskier, more fulfilling spiritual experiences at its higher, more central core. As a result, the lowly, worm-of-the-dust perspective of most early church members persists in the unconscious minds of those who participate in the current version Old Church. There, the fallacy of "we're only human" is more readily believed than the reality being demonstrated by advancing technology that we can be something more than we dare to imagine.

As long as there is a need to find safety in limitation, the Old Church ways will persist. The dogmatic approach which is fundamental to maintaining the religious "box" structure, however, has become anathema to contemporary seekers who have any degree of intellectual and emotional development. The insistence of Old Church hierarchy that people remain immature in their spirituality is like the attempt parents make to keep a teenager at home instead of letting her date. Even when such a decision is ostensibly for the young person's own good, it thwarts an adolescent's developmental impulse to grow beyond the confines of the parental home. As long as the church restricts religious belief and practice and insists that humans settle for less than what they can be, self-actualizing individuals will need to leave the church home and the doctrines that define it.

When I heard the echoes of Nietzsche's "God is dead" proclamation in the late 1960s, I was at once scared and relieved. The child in me longed for the Santa Claus-God of my childhood, for the baby Jesus of Christmas morning, for the assurances the stained glass and incense and High Mass the Old Church gave me. Yet the adult I was becoming intuitively knew that these were images of God, not the real thing. The real spirit of God was to be found elsewhere, in unknown territory. Jesus had said the kingdom of God was within, although I did not truly hear those words until I felt the urge to explore my own inner frontier in search of God. Like many others of my generation I sensed that if God was yet alive, I would not find It in the traditional church, so preoccupied with itself. I began, as so many others of my generation, to investigate the depths of my own self—at first by myself, then within an informal community, then in a church.

Ironically, an important part of this exploration for me has been this return to the church form as a minister. The impulse to organize spirituality into religious form is common for human beings, and it was for me as well. But rather than serving the D-needs of the Old Church, I see my role as helping to evolve the form of church into something that more accurately translates Being-values, one that opens the way for a spiritual experience so the unpredictable, uncontainable spirit of God has the freedom to express itself in a community of "called-out" ones.

# The Distortion of the Word

*The worst thing about preachers is
they think they've got to say something
whether anything can be said or not.*

**WENDELL BERRY**

Anyone who has had a true spiritual experience inevitably runs into difficulty telling others about it. There are so many things we humans have the capacity to describe; but a mystical event is literally beyond words. One's identity shifts from the contents of consciousness to consciousness itself. In this state, one *is* the infinite space from which all words form—and there are no words big enough to contain this space. Later, every attempt to talk about what happened tends to diminish the experience, for words are spoken by a part of us that is so much smaller than what is spoken about. Nonetheless, because it is what we humans do, we are inclined to speak of our spiritual experiences. Jesuit priest Anthony de Mello describes the confusion that often results in "The Song of the Bird:"

> The disciples were full of questions about God.
> Said the master, "God is the Unknown and the Unknowable. Every statement about him, every answer to your questions, is a distortion of the truth."
> The disciples were bewildered. "Then why do you speak of him at all?"
> "Why does the bird sing?" said the master.[12]

The mystical experience, like a dream or a symphony, cannot adequately be captured in words. While it is possible to talk about the fact that something amazing, wonderful, or out of this world occurred, the words formulated after the fact can only do what language always does, symbolically represent the event—they can never replace it. Yet we humans, equipped as we are with a symbol-forming brain and a pair of vocal chords that love to vibrate, get so caught up in our conversations we often confuse the words we speak about an event with the thing itself. We become more concerned that our explanations of events are logically consistent than that they accurately translate the reality of an experience.

The words we speak can never be the whole truth of our experience—they are always once removed from it. As long as we are clear words are not identical with experience, we won't make the mistake of making words more important than the experience. Religions, however, frequently fall into this trap, and this is certainly the case when it comes to the Old Church and its use of language.

In fact, one could say that religion *is* the attempt to contain primary spiritual experiences in words, concepts, beliefs and dogmas. The container the Christian religion uses is what we know of as church, and what I have been calling the Old Church. As children we are taught to believe that a church is "God's house." But I maintain that the Old Church is not so much a House of God as it is a House of Words *about* God. That is, if you go to this house, you are less likely to have a direct experience of God than you are to hear a lot of words about God. At times, those words may inform and inspire someone to seek an experience something like what the words attempt to describe. More often, particularly for those who long for a mystical realization of the Divine, words are a distraction and a distortion.

The best words can do is evoke an image of a sensory experience that connects the person speaking them with the person receiving them. In the process of thinking about something, I am both speaker and receiver, calling upon my own memory of past experiences for reference. For instance, in using the word "lemon," I generalize the experience of many lemons I've encountered into the mental image of a "new" lemon. Sometimes my mouth salivates in the way it would if I were eating a real lemon now, even though I am not. If I am in conversation with someone else who has eaten a lemon before, I could probably induce a similar physiological response in them by using words descriptive of the texture, smell, color and taste of lemons I recall. But my words do not necessarily refer to any specific lemon that either my friend or I may have actually experienced. Those words have been organized by the brain into concepts, systems of belief formed from previous experiences we've had, or that we've extrapolated from conversations with others. Conceptualization removes us even further from the primary experience.

If we have conceptualized something thoroughly, we might believe we have just as well have experienced it when in fact we have not. I once convinced myself of this. For many years the film "It's a Wonderful Life" was repeatedly shown on television throughout the Christmas season, but for various reasons I had never seen the film. I did, however, see many TV commercials for it. From these ads, I became familiar with the setting, story line, characters, actors and outcome of the movie. Concluding it was just sentimental trash, I was secretly proud that I'd avoided seeing it despite all the viewing opportunities the holidays afforded (I counted seventeen showings one year!). For years I insisted that I already knew enough about it that I didn't actually need to see it. Then someone gave me a videotape of it, and I finally agreed to watch.

I sobbed from beginning to end. What I had arrogantly believed *about* the film and my experience *of* it were quite different. The real thing was far richer and more challenging than what I'd imagined. My concept about the film kept it tidy in a box on the shelf; the actual viewing of it, however, spilled its contents into my heart, inviting me to surrender to the sometimes messy but powerful emotion of love. The experience of the film affected me in a way my beliefs about it never had. As a result, I was changed. Afterwards, I wondered why I hadn't wanted to see that film in the first place—it opened me to a powerful experience of God!

But we humans can be masters of avoidance. We protect ourselves from direct experiences with our arrogance ("Been there, done that!"), cynicism ("Who cares about that?"), clutching ("Change? Things are just fine the way they are!"), and any number of other strategies for staying in control. (Notice how the avoidance almost always expresses itself in words!) It's far less threatening to who we think we are (the ego in charge) to talk *about* experiences than it is to *have* experiences. To come into an experience of something is to be exposed to an unmediated power—and this power, or what I shall call God, originates in sources we cannot contain with words and produces outcomes that cannot be controlled by words.

Dealing with the power of the Divine has been a challenge to humans ever since the first bolt of lightning struck earth. We intuitively sense this power can transform us and we are ambivalent about that. So even though some part of us may long for contact with God, another part of us will also go to great lengths to avoid it. One of our many selves admires divine power and is attracted to the possibilities it offers, while another fears it and its capacity for upsetting the status quo.

Consider God as the power of love. I know a man whose every conversation for the ten years I've known him centers around his desire to meet the right woman to marry. But every time he meets someone who is attracted to him, he finds a reason that she's not the one for him. Like so many others, he longs for love; yet he also fears what he will have to do for love, or what love will do to him. So he defends against love when it is offered.

Even though we may fear the power of God in its many expressions, we also tend to be somewhat jealous of it. We want that control for ourselves, and so we wield the limited amount of personal power we have over those who may not have as much. As a result we ignore what real power we might have if we shared power with the gods and others. But this too is really an avoidance strategy. To our ego, the self of us who is accustomed to thinking of him or herself as "only human," unbridled spiritual power can be overwhelming. This power is like a wild horse the ego finds beautiful to behold from afar but is afraid might trample us if we get too close. It's too much for us mere mortals, or so our ego has informed us. After all, this power might change our world and the ego along with it.

The ancients believed it wrong to look upon the face of God, for in such an intimate encounter they would die. The timid among them substituted rituals of appeasement and worship for a direct encounter with the Divine, while those with more courage took tentative steps forward into the arena of the gods in hopes of harnessing the power found there. Thus were religion and science born, each attempting to deal with a potentially overwhelming power in its own way. The religion of the Old Church resorted to concepts and practices which would hold unknown phenomena at bay, while science sought to understand the unknown by entering into it by way of experimentation.

As a result, Christianity has proceeded for two thousand years relatively uninformed by science. Ironically, Jesus was a scientist. Like Star Trek pioneers, Jesus had boldly gone where no one had gone before, but there was no language adequate to describe it. He attempted to talk about his spiritual discoveries but was largely unsuccessful in his communication. When Jesus recognized that his disciples basically had no ears for the words of his teaching, he offered them something far better— demonstrations! He let the scientific evidence speak for itself.

The miracles Jesus performed were exhibitions of the spiritual power he'd been able to access through his own adventures in the realm beyond words. He invited his disciples to witness events such as the transfiguring of his own body along with Elijah and Moses, and he is said to have resurrected from death not only the body of his friend Lazarus, but his own. If Jesus lived today he might have been able to get his message across more easily. Every day on television kids see people de-materialize and re-materialize. So the idea of resurrection is not only not a big deal for them, it is almost a matter of fact, a feat that is likely to be accomplished technologically one day. But the disciples were two thousand years away from Star Trek; they had no such framework for understanding the phenomena surrounding Jesus and their own similar experiences.

In the absence of an understanding of what Jesus was about or how they might be like him, the disciples did what religious humans do when confronted with the awe-inspiring, fear-stimulating aspect of reality. Whereas more scientific persons might have attempted to replicate Jesus' findings, the disciples made him into a god. As such he was a object of worship, not research. It is interesting that in Christian mythology, the one apostle who seemed unafraid to explore the phenomena of the risen Christ by poking around in the spiritual body was chided as a non-believer. The doubt which made Thomas infamous led him to a first-hand experience that left no room for skepticism. Like Thomas, the curious scientist is not satisfied by religious concepts and theories. But the religionist is more content when he is able to wrap up confusing experiences into a belief system, with any mysterious loose ends tucked into a neat bundle. So we often see the Old Church marching around carrying something like this on the end of a big stick. It waves its dogmas and creeds about like a flag and calls them faith.

Many subscribe to a religion (from the Latin *re-ligere*, to bind together again) because they believe it is a kind of glue that is necessary to keep them in relation to God. But as much as religion keeps them bound to a belief system, they actually stay distant from the experience of God. By the time Jesus' life was recorded, every word uttered by him or about him (for a few years anyway) was declared to be the Word of God, Holy Scripture. The scripture writers reduced Jesus—a living, breathing, sentient being having a remarkable awakening—to his spiritual capacities. They reduced him to a word, albeit The Word. Old Church Christianity, among other things, is a lot of words about this Word which obscure the real significance of Jesus' experience.

The following humorous story was scrawled on the wall of a major university:

> And Jesus said unto them: "Who do you say I am ?"
> And they replied, "You are the eschatological manifestation of the ground of our being; the kermygma in which we find the ultimate meaning of our interpersonal relationship."
> And Jesus said, "What?"[13]

Where would Jesus find a place for himself in contemporary Christianity? The language of the Old Church about Jesus that still pervades it would seem to raise some doubts that he would find one at all!

Old Church theology attempts to explain the spiritually mysterious in a way that sends everyone scurrying for the dictionary. The key to power in a religious system lies not in accessing or appreciating the Divine but in being able to say the right words about It. Stephen Gaskin, leader of a hippie spiritual community in Tennessee called The Farm, once described the Sermon on the Mount as "tripping instructions" for humanity. If that is so, Old Church theology says it is more important to be able to define the terms in the guide book than to actually make the journey. And so it is that we miss the point entirely, unless something in the investigation of all those words triggers a memory of a primal spiritual experience many people have had as children. Sometimes the concepts, like the thought of a lemon, will start the juices of our longing for the real "real thing" flowing once more. Until that happens it is likely we are sadly and ignorantly settling for a lot less than what is possible.

Unfortunately, we live in a culture that encourages us to have *more* experiences of a lesser quality than fewer, more meaningful ones. I recall when I was in grammar school there was once a contest to see who could read the most books over summer vacation. To prove we'd read the book, we were required to write a book report. As soon as I'd read a few books, I figured out how to write a convincing report just from reading the jacket liner notes. Although I thought myself quite clever at the time, I stopped reading the inside of the books, even though I loved to read. I won the contest, but I really had no idea what those books were really about, not to mention that I missed the pleasure of the stories they told.

Likewise, it is possible to know all about Christianity, all about Jesus, even all about the themes of his teaching, and never approach the heart of the Christ experience which Jesus claimed, on the basis of his experience, we all could have. In medieval times, when some Christians who were tired of the excesses of the church sought a more personal spiritual connection with God, images of the suffering Jesus emerged in religious art. One of the most powerful of these mystical illustrations portrays the Sacred Heart of Jesus. The adult Jesus is shown parting the folds of his clothing to reveal his pierced heart; he points to this as though inviting us to touch it.

I'd probably looked at this image more than a hundred times in my life without fully grasping the meaning of this gesture, until one day I had an experience of my own suffering Christ.

It was around the Christmas holiday, when like so many others, I felt pushed and pulled in a million directions. Not only were there special church services to prepare for, but there were also my family's celebration and personal observances I wanted to make time for, as well as more party invitations than I knew what to do with. Totally overwhelmed, I slumped into a helpless feeling of not being able to give anybody what they wanted. As I explored this with my therapist, however, I discovered an aspect of myself that had not collapsed. Part of me knew all I could give anyone was the truth of my deepest, most essential self, which I know as Christ expressing as me.

My frustration and fatigue came from my attempts to give from a more superficial level of myself. I thought I had to give what others expected of me, according to a whole set of shoulds I carried around in my head, including the ones from the invisible ministerial rule book. I believed I needed to give not only the right Christmas presents, but all the right words to heal all the pain people carry with them from the unhealed trauma of childhood holidays. But then, recalling Jesus' words, "Not as the world gives do I give unto you," I began to weep. I sensed into the great suffering of this enlightened, loving being who wanted nothing more for people than that they should realize that the greatest gift had already been given to them, even though it was a gift that was largely misunderstood, ignored or refused. I realized that as a minister all I really had to offer anyone was an experience of their own divine nature, which I knew was the only thing that could make the healing difference.

In the image of the Sacred Heart, Jesus attempts to show people the way, not to his heart, but to their own, so they might discover for themselves the kingdom that he'd been telling them was inside them all along. Again and again he points to the heart as a path to the vulnerable, compassionate truth. He points to the heart of the matter, to essence. Yet the Old Church fixates on the finger that points to the heart and worships it. Jesus' greatest disappointment must have been that we did not realize what he was pointing to, that we prefer the control a finger represents to the unknowable, uncontrollable, passionate God present within our own heart. So we remain safe and sad in our separation from what is most deeply and essentially us!

Mystics have sometimes described their union with God as a living flame burning in the heart. The Desert Fathers, monks who lived as ascetics just about two hundred years after the Council of Nicea created an orthodox Christianity, deliberately offered themselves to the "furnace of transformation"[14] in hopes of entering mystical union. Like scientists seeking to recreate conditions similar to those which apparently helped prepare Jesus for his awakening,[15] they made themselves available for a direct experience of God, while others with less tolerance for the heat continued to build the church.

Instead of burning in the transformational fire, the Old Church tamed the flame of spiritual experience and reduced the passion it engenders to a controlled burn. As the Christian religion organized, the development of theological belief systems, editing of scriptural writings, and increasingly rigid membership requirements directed attention away from the real experience of God available to all humanity, focusing it instead on symbolic representations of the experience of one man, Jesus.

Why would the Old Church-makers do this? Perhaps because the truly spiritual experience can be terribly unpredictable and inconvenient to whatever neat world we've been able to manage. A spiritual event can easily be viewed as a disruption to a so-called normal life. Historically, people have been quick to control the spiritual experience with words, concepts, beliefs and dogmas to avoid the discomfort of such disruptions. Religious symbols pay tribute to the idea of real spirituality but are poor substitutes for it. The symbols themselves are structured to convince us that when we are religious we are having the best spiritual experience possible; but this is like believing a Coca Cola™ is the real thing because the advertisement says so. Coke isn't orange juice —it is what it is!—and although it may have some pleasing qualities, the only real thing about it is it's Coke-ness.

Likewise, religion is religion, but it is not spiritual experience. But Old Church religion often tells us that it is. The rituals, the worship, the offering of symbolic gestures—this is what the Old Church tells us will cement our relationship with God and secure a desirable place for us in the hereafter. All the hierarchical, scriptural, theological and architectural constructs which compose the Old Church effectively create a diversion. And the seeker's attention is drawn away from the experience of this moment at hand, the here and now, where and when, as Jesus discovered, the kingdom of God could be found.

When I have asked workshop participants to pictorially represent the church they attended when as children, most people draw some variation on a square building with a tall steeple attached. If they depict the interior of the building, typically it is with rows of pews and a male minister standing at the pulpit. Frequently there aren't any people, or if there are, they are lined up like bowling pins in the pews. I have never seen any drawing where there was any attempt to indicate God other than in the religious symbol of the cross. When I have asked the same people to make a picture which depicts a spiritual experience they've had, they generally draw scenes from nature with a lot of sunshine, trees and flowers, and with people, often with hands joined in a circle. Not a single person among the hundred or so who have done this exercise has located the experience they describe as "spiritual" within a traditional church setting.

As a symbol of authentic spirituality the Old Church is no substitute for the real thing. Wearing a red ribbon as a remembrance of persons with AIDS is a gesture; as such it is demonstrably different from the hands-on care of someone who is dying from the disease. The symbolic is significantly different from the real. Our fear of the potentially disruptive "real thing" continuously drives us to the safety of the symbolic realm.

While we may attain a measure of safety, however, we remain incomplete in the realization of our full potential. Armed with words and other symbols on our religious quest, we seek and find, not the truth, but immunity from the truth and the threat to our ordinary egoic sense of self that a numinous event might pose. Just as antibiotics ingested throughout a lifetime may render a body more susceptible to infection later in life, protection against spiritual experiences is not helpful in the long run. It simply postpones the inevitable, and the harder one tries to avoid the growth such experience brings, the more devastating and disruptive it may be to one's sense of well-being when it occurs.

Rudolf Steiner noted how the high fevers of childhood diseases seem to mark openings in consciousness for children. Understanding the necessity and naturalness of such difficult physical initiations to both the physical and spiritual growth processes, Steiner encouraged parents not to inhibit these openings with medical treatments. While growth of this sort is challenging, sometimes dangerous, the excessive safety of immaturity is not benign over the long term. Thwarted evolution eventually leads to self-destruction.

It is vital for those who would have a direct experience of the Divine to investigate the reality behind the symbols, to drop religiosity in favor of a more empirical approach to spirituality. If the Old Church insists on controlling spiritual experience as it has for two millennia, and persists in maintaining the rigidity which prevents spiritual experience for most people, I have no doubt this House of Words will collapse. While this may be disconcerting, when it does occur we all will have the opportunity to find beneath all the dogmas and creeds a vast reservoir of silence. And in the silence, God itself.

In the silence of one of the most profound of my own mystical experiences, words began to speak themselves. These words indicated the possibility of a different kind of language, a sacred language, which could directly translate the spiritual into words. I felt these words more than hearing them: "Blessed be the silence. Blessed be the words that issue forth from the silence." Perhaps, like the song of the bird, the blessed words spoken by Jesus and other great masters will be received, not as catechism to be memorized, but as direct emanations of the divine vibration, to be enjoyed rather than subscribed to. As Father de Mello comments upon the little parable quoted earlier, the bird sings "not because it has a statement, but because it has a song." In this sacred language,

> The words of the scholar are to be understood. The words of the master are not to be understood. They are to be listened to as one listens to the wind in the trees and the sound of the river and the song of the bird. They will awaken something within the heart that is beyond all knowledge.[16]

# The Perpetuation of Spiritual Immaturity

*...but when I became an adult,*
*I put away childish things.*

**1 CORINTHIANS 13: 11**

T hrough the ages, religion has promoted the phenomenon described by transformational catalyst Richard Moss as the "parental dynamic." When life is lived out of the parental dynamic, as has been the case in most civilized cultural systems to date, our immaturity is unconsciously perpetuated. Moss writes:

> The parental dynamic filters reality in an unconscious parent-child fashion. This begins as an infant gradually develops a personal consciousness and distinguishes itself from the parents. Our very sense of reality carries a hidden authority over us, and the seemingly external situation we are in (the medical world, the therapeutic world, the religious world) is held in consciousness as a parent is looked to for safety, answers and self-substantiation. By so doing we define ourselves in a circumscribed pattern as a kind of child that by its very nature never has authority fully to be. The child vis-a-vis parent is always being defined, never genuinely defining, and thus will never have authority over the so-called problem.[17]

The "problem" common to contemporary human beings is a fundamental alienation of the individual self from the universal Self. We continue to struggle to reconnect our individual awareness with the Something More from which we intuitively sense we have been cut off. As a species, our human evolution has reflected a journey of almost complete unconsciousness of that split to our current painfully acute awareness from which it is becoming ever more difficult to hide. The pangs of this increasing spiritual hunger call us to respond to our problem as never before.

In a less conscious stage of evolution this problem had not yet been perceived. In the infancy of our species, humans were more like other animals, clumped together in tribes, instinctually governed by "herd psychology,"[18] and programmed for the survival of the fittest of the collective. The concept of individuality is a relatively recent event in human development. As recently as two thousand years ago, Jesus introduced a teaching regarding the importance of the "one sheep" apart from the flock—this represented an entirely new psychological outlook for humanity. Individualism was a radical departure from the social conformity which had secured the human tribes until the agricultural revolution and subsequent technological advances made humans apparently less dependent on one another for physical survival. The original teaching that inspired Christianity laid waste to the religious legal systems which denied the individual and also to the family systems which claimed the attention of people that more rightfully belonged to God.

According to this teaching of Jesus, devotion to God included the difficult work involved in growing up spiritually. To become psychologically differentiated from one's tribe meant leaving father, mother, sister, brother, even spouse, behind. It meant perceiving as enemies those of one's own household because they would keep one bound into roles which limited potential for self-awareness. It implied that by claiming a new kind of relationship with reality, no longer living as a child defined by the family, one could become an author expressing the life impulse in creative, uncircumscribed relationships with others.

But Jesus taught in the context of a culture still entrenched in the parental dynamic. His own metaphors refer to a parent and child relationship between God and himself. He did not have the language (or perhaps lacked the experience at the time he was teaching) to describe a kind of spiritual relationship of Creator with creature that did not refer to family. His words in the Garden of Gethsemane, "My God, my God why hast thou forsaken me?" reflect his own crisis: the awareness of his own aloneness, the absence of a hand-holding parent to secure passage through the dark night of self-actualized becoming. The "Father" to whom he ultimately surrenders his spirit is far more vast than any personalized daddy the cozy familial images of traditional Christianity conjure up for the faithful to believe in.

Given the rest of Jesus' testimony regarding the necessity of leaving the family form behind, I believe the inconsistent reference to family in his own spiritual experience is evidence of how the parental dynamic in our psyche continually pulls us back into a less evolved space. We are convinced we will be more secure there, even as the evolutionary impulse urges us to leave it behind. The dialectical tension of this tug of war has yet to be resolved. What Stephen Mitchell, author of *The Gospel According to Jesus*, refers to as the "centrifugal force of the family," continues to suck the church into its vortex. Despite Jesus' teachings, the Christian Church formed itself as another version of family for the believers who came after him.

Jesus himself lived out his purpose as an individual alongside other individuals who were ostensibly doing the same. Alignment of their various individual purposes with a larger purpose made them a community. Within the community each had a task to accomplish—personally and for the good of the whole. Each of the disciples was respected, if not admired, for the contribution they made, even Judas, who carried out the difficult task of betrayal. Jesus rejected the notion that he was master and the others servants to him—he called them friends. He was visionary, teacher, healer, leader but he was not father to his community, nor is there evidence he created dependent parent/child relationships with them.

The Christian Church, however, distorted the community context in which Jesus lived by falling back on the parental dynamic. Perhaps insecure with their relatively unactualized selves, early Old Church founders compensated by relying on the old family model. By establishing a parental outer authority, the religious organizers avoided their lack of confidence in an inner authority. In so doing they effectively disempowered anyone who claimed to have such an inner authority. By the time the Christian church was a few centuries old it had become a new kind of family, complete with priests and monks who were called *Father* and *Brother*, and nuns known as *Mother* and *Sister*.

The "children" in this new family were taught how to be good children, which in the context of salvation required them to obey the commandments of God and the Church. In one of the earliest myths that form the Judeo–Christian scripture, we learn that Adam and Eve were bad children because they disobeyed Daddy God, so they had to leave their Paradise home. But Daddy God wanted to give people another chance not to disobey so he sent his son Jesus to die on the cross so we would have another chance to be with Daddy God. If the children were good and obeyed all the rules and did everything right, they would get what they had always wanted, the perfect love of Daddy in heaven for all eternity. If they were bad and disobedient, they would go to hell and burn forever and never ever see Daddy God again. One of the rules, however, is that the children must always remain children.

Adam and Eve made the mistake of trying to grow up. They dared to learn for themselves about the world in which they lived. That made Daddy God mad because only Daddy God can be a grown up. "So, children," the Old Church informed her people, "whatever you do, don't ever grow up. Don't ever become responsible for yourself. Don't try to find Daddy God without us. You need us. We will take care of you. Just do as we say and we will make sure you get to heaven." For two thousand years the Children of God have nodded and bowed to the Fathers and Mothers in the traditional church who dutifully discipline them so they will be good and acceptable.

Haven't we all looked for a formula for salvation? A quick fix for the stubborn problems life presents? Logical answers to the puzzling koans of human existence? This is exactly what we have longed for and what Old Church has tried to provide. Acting from childlike dependency, we asked for and got a kind of church that is similar to the newspaper magazine section where the solutions to the puzzles are published. Or the 900 number you can call for three crossword clues for seventy-five cents. All the answers are in the Bible, we are told. Or in the Catechism. Or in the sermon, if we would only listen more closely.   "Just do what you are told!" "If you heard it in church, it must be right." It's in a foreign language? Don't worry about understanding what you hear, concentrate on doing what is right and good. Just fill in any blanks with the information you're given in church.

I recall the dismay of one of the first counselees who contacted me as I began my ministry in Nassau. She came to me with a dilemma regarding an unplanned pregnancy. She explained the situation and what she saw as her options. Then she asked me to tell her the right thing she should do. I responded by telling her I didn't believe there was any *one* right thing, but I would help her explore what was the right thing *for her* to do. She, however, insisted I did know the right thing and demanded that I tell her what it was. I reiterated my position. She was truly mystified and angry with me. It was the first time she had encountered a clergy person who would not make the distinction of right and wrong for her. In her eyes it was my job to have knowledge of absolute right and wrong for all people and all situations, and I was clearly not doing my job by withholding this from her. She emphasized this point by telling me that another pastor she consulted had not hesitated to tell her what to do, even though she was not willing to do what he said. I told her I felt I'd do her soul a great disservice if I pretended to know the answer to the difficulty that lay before her. I invited her to pray with me for guidance from God directly that she would discover for herself the action to take. She refused and left in a huff, seemingly unwilling to take responsibility for her decision.

When we ask ourselves to grow up spiritually we threaten the sense of security belonging to the church family has provided. No matter that we are called to individuate, the fact that we may need to leave our church home in order to do so is likely to set off alarms in both parent and child.

Rumblings from the "kids" should make churches question how much longer they can bank on traditional notions of filial devotion. As the nuclear family breaks down in the secular world, and gun-toting children join the ranks of terrorists, church families would do well to notice that, in certain cases, the kids are getting the goods on their clerical "parents" and seeking to equalize relationships within the religious setting. The parental disapproval which has previously bound people to their religion has become less threatening as individuals increasingly take the

risk of self-responsibility. The Pope's ban on birth control for
Catholics continues, for instance, while many individuals within
the Catholic church make conscience-based decisions for themselves about what is appropriate for their spiritual practice.
Reactionary church hierarchies are finding threats of excommu-
nication or other punishment less effective today as "disobedient"
children grow up out of the need to find their safety within the
religious system.

Since the pre-millennial decades from the 1960s on, the veil
of the parental dynamic has begun to part and we are starting
to see with new eyes the spiritual causes of our own unhappiness. We have learned, for example, that an estimated ninety-
seven percent of families in the United States have been affected, directly or indirectly, by the disease of alcoholism. If we
regard, as Dr. Carl Jung suggested, that alcoholism and other
addictive disorders, are diseases of the human spirit, this country suffers from a lot of spiritual disease. A testimony to the
ineffectiveness of church religion to address this problem is the
fact that participation in the spiritual recovery program Alco-
holics Anonymous and related groups has increased dramatically
since 1975.

As Americans have become more aware of the dysfunction in
the themselves and in their families, they've also begun to notice
and name the dysfunction in their churches families. They've revealed the sexual abuses within the church that wounded their
spirits. They've called attention to the financial abuses of church
leaders.

They have also left their church "families" in droves in the
last twenty-five years, embittered about religion and God. Join-
ing the ranks of the unchurched, they have nursed their spiritual
wounds in therapy, Twelve Step groups, Eastern-style meditation or any number of workshops and seminars provided through
non-religious spiritual centers. Many people have found these to
be satisfying alternatives to church participation. Within the context of these non-church spiritual settings, some people have
begun to discover ways to explore spirituality that may allow
them to move beyond the parental dynamic altogether. Others
who felt wounded in the church and their family of origin remain
alienated from any notion of spirituality, and still struggle to find

meaning exclusively within the material aspects of career, family and entertainment.

The price of spiritual freedom is the kind of responsibility only a spiritually mature individual can assume. Paul's teaching about the necessity of putting away childish things reinforces Jesus' own experience of breaking free from the parental dynamic, and the wisdom of other spiritual traditions as well. Stephen Mitchell, tells of his experience:

> A couple of months after I began studying with my old Zen Master, he said to me, "You have three jobs here. Your first job is to kill the Buddha." I had read that phrase in the old Zen teachings, and I knew what it meant—to let go of any concepts of a separate, superior, enlightened being outside myself. Then he said, "Your second job is to kill your parents."
>
> "What does that mean?" I asked.
>
> "As long as there is anything you want from your parents," he said, "or anything about them that upsets you, they will be an obstacle in your mind. 'Killing your parents' means accepting them just as they are. They enter your mind like an image reflected on the water. No ripples."
>
> "It sounds very difficult."
>
> "Only if you think it is," he said.
>
> Then he said, "Your third job is to kill me."[19]

To the extent institutional Christianity requires those behaviors which emphasize the parental dynamic, it will continue to attract those people who continue to take comfort in their spiritual immaturity. Many of those who choose to grow up in their spirituality have found the traditional church a hindrance. If they haven't already done so, they will find it necessary to kill those aspects of the religious organization that deny the full creative expression of the self-actualized, individuated human being.

The current strategy of church marketing is to provide slick media-rich worship entertainment[20] to draw in the reluctant unchurched "seeker." But spiritually mature persons will discern that preachers in blue jeans with Christian rock bands livening up their worship services are only attempting to put a new patch on an old piece of cloth. That cloth, which is the entire matrix that forms the parental dynamic of dependence, submission, and obedience to a god-like structure outside of us, is, in Richard Moss's words "the main veil circumscribing consciousness."

This veil must unravel if consciousness is to expand; that is, if we are to have the kind of spiritual experience that Jesus himself had and invited us to share. By continuing to empower the illusion through which we know ourselves as real, i.e., a system which insists that we can never fully grow up, we assure that we never will. On the other hand, if we can allow the veil of religious parentalism to fall away, we may finally come to realize our full inner authority and spirituality.

As religion unravels, the societal fears hidden by the veil of the religious parental dynamic must be faced. These fears center around the belief that a rigid fundamentalism, like a strict parent, is necessary to keep evil at bay and the social and ethical fabric from being destroyed. In examining the premise of this belief it is important to consider that the widespread crime and violence in our culture often attributed to a lack of religious/family values, may in fact be the projected shadow of a child attempting to meet idealized standards of goodness promoted by the Church, rather than the feared expression of an unchecked evil force at large in our society.

The solution to societal chaos is not more religious rigidity but an increased spiritual responsibility. If, as is necessary in the process of maturation, we can be conscious of and take responsibility for our capacity for doing evil as well as good, we will not need to repress or project our more destructive, lower self, aspects. Instead, we may be able to acknowledge and realign this lower self with our deeper and more essential self's desire to be cooperative and harmonious within a community that loves and accepts us as we are, because that is what genuinely feels best. We will not act "good" in order to please the institutional parent, but to express an intrinsically pleasing essence, which in turn is a pleasure for all.

# A Misuse of Power

*Of all that was done in the past,*
*you eat the fruit,*
*either rotten or ripe.*

**T.S. ELIOT**

As creatures on this earth, most of us sense the presence of a power greater than ourselves. We intuitively feel this Something More connects us to life, and that without it, we would lose our life, or at least any life that would be worth living. Because we instinctively favor life over death, we lean toward this Something More with the longing we have for life itself. And, paradoxically, we also retreat from it with awe-inspired fear.

Not everyone has defined this Something More; for some the longing for it has never been acknowledged. But many others throughout the ages have tended not only to name, but to formalize through religious practices their relationship with this Something More.

For instance, the ancient hunters thought about their Something More as totem animals. They used an image or relic of a wooly mammoth or large cat to help them find and kill their supper. Early agrarians, whose crops depended on the right weather conditions, gave to their sense of Something More the form of fertility goddess. The proper sacrifice to her would bring the favor of the rain-god or sun-god, whichever was needed; on the downside, if the goddess wasn't pleased with the sacrifice, there could be a flood or a drought. The pagans of Greece and Rome made their Something More into a whole pantheon of gods people could worship and/or pay off. Having a good relationship with these more powerful beings meant you could ask the gods to bestow their particular quality on you, and you could use it to get the best of your enemies and make your life easier. Judaism and, later, Christianity called this Something More something quite definite—God. People could now look to Something More for more than mere survival; as the Almighty and Ultimate, God would provide a sense of justice, righteousness and meaning for life on this earth.

So, what much Western religious thought has referred to as God is really what began in us humans as simply a vague sense that there is Something More to life than meets the eye. The Eastern religions might speak of God, but they don't cloak it in anthropomorphism the way we do in the West. In Eastern thought, God is synonymous with a state of Pure Being, not with any particular Being. But in the Old Church that developed from Western ways of seeing things, God is conceived of as a version of a human, albeit a mighty, powerful, and longer-lasting one. This God of the Old Church is thought to be the Creator of all, that is, in the sense that He made, or caused to be made, everything in existence. The Old Church teaches that God, by definition, is one without beginning or end, existed before, and is therefore separate from and dominant over, everything else it created, i.e., its creatures.

Traditionally, one purpose of the Old Church has been to bridge the distance between God and these creatures (us!). While supposedly mediating this relationship, however, the Old Church over-emphasized what it deemed the proper order in this relationship, that is, of Creator *over and above* its creatures. It reinforced a sense of separation between God and humans in such a way as to justify the ongoing need for its mediation services. The Old Church, according to its own conception of the relationship of God and His creatures, was required to regulate the spiritual life of humanity. And because it saw itself mediating or standing in for God, the Old Church assumed it too had a duty to dominate that life. As a consequence the Old Church has replaced a possible authentic, direct relationship to Something More with a disempowering substitute—itself.

In the Judeo-Christian tradition, we are taught that humans are made in the image and after the likeness of God. On that basis we have every reason to aspire to a certain creativity of our own. But we quickly learn from the allegorical story of The Fall in the Garden of Eden that we are never to forget the penalty for expressing our natural creative power. The first humans are shamed and then expelled from Paradise for their "disobedience" to the divine dictate. What could be a more powerful reminder of who is really in control?

Our simultaneous longing for and fear of this shaming, punishing God is very confusing. We don't know whether to love or to hate God. And it's not just God, who now seems so distant from us, that we worry about—but ourselves. In our fallen state, we doubt we are worthy of a closer union. Like a child with an abusive parent, we creatures don't know whether to run toward or away from our own Creator who, we are told, cares for us and yet whose wrath we must endure. The threat of annihilation paralyzes us. We are unable to walk away from the painful aspects of a relationship with God, just as we are hesitant to fully embrace the potentially pleasurable ones.

Left with no apparent choice but to submit, we give up our creative striving and settle for trying to be good enough to please the Powerful One in the limited circumstances provided us outside the Garden gates. If we are good enough (i.e., if we deny ourselves properly), our placating self wistfully hopes to one day reenter that Garden. The more creative part of us, meanwhile, secretly resents having ever been excluded from it in the first place. By threatening to deprive us of the fulfillment of our deepest spiritual longings, religion colludes with our fear of God. It feeds on our shame and encourages us to abandon our self-esteem and creative power while giving ourselves over to that which presumes to intercede for us with the Supreme Being—the Old Church.

The organizational structure of the Judeo-Christian religions developed from a dominance theology which emphasizes the power of stronger elements over weaker ones. While in this theology the stronger element is God and the weaker one humanity, the early religious dominance hierarchy of the Church reflected its own cultural norms. These placed men in the position of power over women and children, and constituted what Riane Eisler[21] has called *androcracy*, the man-ruled society.

Eisler prefers the term androcracy to the more familiar *patriarchy* as a descriptor of the dominator social structure of the past five thousand years. First, she feels it does not so readily call up *matriarchy* as an opposite form (matriarchies had their own oppressive tendencies, she notes); and, next, she postulates that beyond either of these systems another might possibly exist. She calls this new form *gylany*, a partnership-based model of relationship in which both genders are linked equally with one another. Extrapolating her theory to the spiritual realm, one might envision the possibility of a relationship between God and humankind in which creatures enjoyed a co-creative partnership with the Creator.[22] For now, however, the dominance paradigm makes such egalitarian thinking seem, if not blasphemous, laughable.[23]

Although Jesus included both women and men in his ministry, the traditional Christian church still subscribes to a man-ruled structure. It justifies this by falling back on its claim that Jesus did not specifically commission any women as ministers. Pope John Paul II's insistence on prohibiting women from the priesthood is strong evidence that androcracy still rules within the Catholic Church. While Protestant churches in the last twenty years have been more open to the ordination of women, there are indications that the contribution of women is not yet completely embraced. For example, the "Re-Imagining God" conference held in 1994 in Minneapolis created quite a stir in mainstream Protestant churches. The message to those women who might challenge the Old Church—don't mess with our images of God! As recently as 2000, the Southern Baptist Convention made an official statement that while it accepts women ministers in the role of preacher, it does not deem them suitable to be church pastors. So when it comes down to it, even the more inclusive churches resist recognizing the feminine principle as equal to the masculine.

In the Judeo-Christian androcratic religious structures, God, addressed with masculine gender descriptors, could only be approached by men. Females were expected to merely look on. The religious dominance hierarchy that places God, the perfect One, on top of the spiritual ladder which reaches to heaven, situates men on the rungs immediately beneath Him. Women and children are placed beneath Them. As defined by the androcratic structure, success within the religious organization occurs when all the weaker elements are conquered by the stronger elements. When this perfection is attained, the gates to heaven are opened and full relationship with God is possible.

In the androcratic system women represent an inferior aspect of humanity. A woman can distract a man, seduce him and otherwise corrupt him and keep him from doing what's right, just as Eve did to Adam. She must be kept in her place (as it would be impractical for the survival of the species to eliminate her altogether!).

A woman is also judged inferior because she is identified with the earthiness of childbearing. The Old Church implicitly rejects the earth in favor of heaven, which is considered the place at the very top of the ladder, up in the clouds, where God sits on His throne. In androcratic religious thinking, transcendence is synonymous with dominance over earthy functions, which necessarily involve the body with its bothersome sensuality and sexuality. Thus, in the Old Church, virginity and celibacy are the highest expression of the religious vocation.

Frequently, such a rejection of earthy qualities distorts spirituality. Celibacy for either gender is often a denial of the life force—witness the celibate Shaker communities that literally died out for lack of procreation. But in the Roman Church, even when a woman takes a vow of chastity she is still not allowed in the priesthood. For the kind of sexual purity the androcratic religion requires for its priests is believed impossible for a woman. Her physiological make-up is naturally attuned to earth cycles of sexual reproduction—how could she be truly spiritual?

Yet, the double standard frequently applies. It is well known (though not openly admitted) that many avowed male celibates are actually not. For men it seems the mask, if not the reality, of dominance over the sensual aspects of life is most important for retaining power under the androcratic system. For a woman it seems the best way she can prove her holiness is to give up not only her sexuality, but life itself. Historically, the most revered women in the Old Church have been virgin martyrs.

My own experience of being treated differently as a female in the Old Church has impacted my entire life, and I know I am not alone in this. I want to share more of my story here to illustrate how the androcratic dominance structure of the Old Church is hidden in its priests, and how this does harm.

Raised in the Catholic church of the '50s and '60s, I wished to be one of the holiest ones—a saint. I loved God and wanted to be pleasing to Him. I knew people were rarely martyred for their faith any longer, but I conjured scenarios of persecution of Catholics by the Communists. During the Cuban missile crisis I rehearsed what I would do if the Communists invaded my hometown. I prayed that I would be strong enough to defend my faith if they tortured me.

It seems ironic now that the only abuse I received in relation to my Catholicism was at the hands of the parish priest. Like other children who are sexually abused in the Old Church, my desire to be pleasing to God was used by a "celibate" male clergy to his own advantage. Children often become victims of abuse because they cannot effectively say no to the advances of an adult. In the case of religious sexual abuse it is not only an adult who must be refused, but apparently God as well.

For me this was an excruciating dilemma, for I felt at once special and tainted. I was having my first exciting, sexual feelings with the man I felt was the closest to God of anyone I had ever known. Yet because of his age, size and position, I intuitively knew there was something wrong about it. At eleven years old I was coerced into an intimate relationship I did not ask for, but did not know how to avoid. Neither did my classmates. There were other girls in my seventh grade class caught in the same trap. We would make fun of the priest behind his back, even as we obediently submitted to him when he backed us into the corner of the room he had partitioned off from his office for his sexual adventures.

The abuse went on for almost a year, until one girl told her parents. I was mortified when my mother confronted me with what the girl reported and asked if that had ever happened to me. She told me I was wrong to have let him do what he did, and not to ever let it happen again. Later, she told me that a group of parents complained to the Order to which the priest belonged, and were requested by the Order to keep the incident quiet. He was not disciplined, nor was he removed from the parish. He left, I later learned from the priest himself, when one girl's father threatened to kill him. Almost thirty years later, when I visited my old parish to find out what had happened my molester, I was told by the current pastor of the church that I should consider letting the matter drop. I should forgive the priest who had been already punished enough by his sins. Nonetheless I persisted and found the man in residence at a nearby monastery. In a meeting I requested the abbot to arrange, I confronted him.

I had been to this monastery once before, on a field trip that had taken place at the time of the abuse. I was struck this time by how large the abbey loomed over me as I drove down the shady lane to meet with Father B. Thoughts racing with anxiety, I suddenly recalled one of the fond names Catholics have for their religion—Holy Mother Church! I felt the confusion of any child who has been an incest victim. How could the Mother have let this happen? Why did she not protect me? Why had the only way open for me to enter the church been through the back door—as the Other Woman?

When I met the priest, he clearly remembered me but denied doing anything wrong to me. I reminded him that he had kissed me with his tongue. But, he argued with complete innocence, those deep-throated kisses he had forced on me were simply his way of expressing affection. It took me an hour and a half of recounting to him the ways in which his behavior had adversely affected my life both spiritually and sexually to elicit any response resembling remorse from him.

When at last he admitted a small measure of regret, it struck me he really didn't think he had done anything very wrong. "At least," he protested, "I'm not like those priests you read about in the newspapers." I asked him in what way was he different from them. With all sincerity he replied, "Well, I never did touch any little boys."

He as much as said he was just a normal, heterosexual male expressing his prerogative in an androcratic system to do what he pleased with a female. Because he did not have intercourse with me, he had not broken his vow of celibacy, at least not technically. He had played by the rules, more or less, and his mask of virtue remained intact as he pursued a life of monastic prayer.

I left the meeting with compassion for this man. In his desire to be pure enough for the church, he had allowed his own sexuality to be repressed and distorted. He had unconsciously become an ordained instrument for the abuse of power the Old Church wields.

I also felt a deep sadness. I recalled my own desire as a child to be of service to God, and how I had been refused for all but service to this man. I had once confused him with God, but now saw him as a pitiful pawn of an institution which entitles men at the expense of women. As a result, the Old Church was also cutting itself off from the feminine aspect of all of creation, again limiting itself to only half the truth.

As I drove away from the monastery, the abbey church looked a great deal smaller. It had been a risky encounter and friends I told about it later remarked how gutsy I had been to set it up in the first place. And I had surprised myself that I was able to expose the Old Church of my childhood. As much as anyone, I would have liked the assurances I believed my compliance might have brought me. Being true to myself, however, was more important.

Confronting my abuser was like pulling back the curtain which conceals the power structure that allows such abuse to occur. It made this structure conscious and not so threatening as before. Afterwards, I felt like Dorothy when she realized the truth about the Wizard of Oz. The charlatan professor was well-intentioned, good-hearted and misguided, but he was actually powerless to do anything more than make smoke, noise and empty promises. He was powerful only because of the power given to him by those who feared him and wanted something from him. Likewise, religions based on fear play on the suspicion of their subscribers that their faith is not perfect enough to procure a relationship with God.

The wizard-professor used self-improvement gimmicks available to any pop psychologist to trick Dorothy's friends into feeling more intelligent, courageous and loving. Likewise, the Old Church offers prescriptions for salvation, giving those who have faith in it the equivalent of tin hearts, badges of courage and certificates of intelligence. But for Dorothy, whose request expressed a deeply authentic spiritual longing to return "home," the professor wasn't able to do a thing but sheepishly escape, leaving her unfulfilled. Only the good witch, who had been Dorothy's guardian from the start of her adventure, was able to help her get what she wanted. And she did this by reminding Dorothy of the power she'd possessed all along to bring herself home.

We all have such an intuition of our own possibilities, although we rarely hear about them in the Old Church. Instead we are told that the things we need for our salvation will come from the Church. We have been taught the sacraments of religion have not just the symbolic but the real power for achieving salvation for all of us fallen humans. Yet much of this is a kind of religious placebo. While the placebo effect is known to work wonders, it only works because we believe *it* works. Tell someone they are receiving a placebo drug, for instance, and the effect often disappears. The religious placebo effect wears off as people realize that all the Old Church provides them with is a ritualized substitute for the spiritual experience of reunion with God. And this experience is readily available in any awakened moment without assistance from any outside agent!

Religion is ineffective for facilitating spiritual realization because people outgrow the magic the religious institution offers. They begin to see through the smokescreen that hides the inner workings of the Old Church. Suddenly the high-minded, open-hearted idealized family that's been the fantasy of what a consecrated organization should be falls apart. Instead, there's just another organization caught up in the economic and political realities of the culture from which it derives. This one, however, desperately strives to maintain the illusion that "God is in charge."

Church politics can be so bitter they gag those who have a taste for spiritual sweetness, leaving those who feed on power to run the organizations. Like the Pharisees Jesus knew well, these power-driven leaders know how to look good while getting the job done. Those who do not play the game well—preferring a spiritual resolution to a political one—are seen as weak leaders. Meanwhile, those who do play well, become part of the elite who set the tone for religious trends. Thus the church pastor who is authentic in sharing weakness as well as strength with the congregation becomes the prey for the power-hungry elder who claims the minister is not spiritual enough to lead. On the other hand, the religious leader who asserts his holiness in a Pope-like fashion—infallible and immovable—is rarely challenged. The latter will probably have a church that is run like a tight ship, while the former's organization may be loose enough to have some room in which genuine spiritual experience may be had.

There is tremendous pressure on church leaders to hold a pose of holiness so they can maintain a place in the religious power structure. Many ministers succumb to the seduction of the Pharisee's way—they bend to their desire to please either the people who fill the offering basket on Sunday and their denominational superiors, or to fulfill the image of the ideal servant of God almost everyone, including clergy, carries in their mind.

A priest friend once described to me the horror his new office assistant, recently hired from within his Lutheran congregation, expressed one day in a staff meeting. The first part of the meeting included a personal sharing session, and when it was my friend's turn, he honestly told the group how he was feeling about some personal difficulties in his family life. This new employee was shocked he had troubles of his own. He was not what she had imagined him to be, she said, and as much as demanded that he change his life and feelings to suit the persona she was accustomed to seeing in the pulpit. It's no wonder most ministers reserve expression of their real feelings to a precious few, and quiver with fear of betrayal by some of these. Often they prefer to wear a mask of acceptability than risk discovery of their human traits.

There is a high price to be paid for such perfectionism. Many clergy experience a painful disconnection from their source of spiritual nourishment as they carry on the exhausting church business of trying to be all things to all people for the glory of God.

The senior minister of a large progressive church in the Midwest recognized this phenomenon and had an impressive, albeit confusing way of dealing with it. Whenever a new associate minister was hired into this dynamic ministry, he or she was sent to a posh codependency treatment center, all expenses paid. However, when the twenty-eight days of treatment ended, the hiree went to work on an 24/7 schedule. The implied expectation placed upon the new minister was that it was possible to work an seventy-hour week if one just knew enough about how not to be codependent. Such quick-fix techniques rarely do more than provide a satisfying illusion of addressing this deep spiritual malaise, so all participants are free to continue in dangerously addictive patterns of behavior.

Sadly, this senior minister died of brain cancer, yet the pattern he established continued. He was replaced by a man, an adult child of an alcoholic, who within a year had assumed the winning formula of his predecessor, right down to the cut of his expensive suits and the ability to shed a heartfelt tear at a moment's notice. He worked the 24/7 schedule himself, and continued to send his assistants to the treatment center. When it was discovered he was having an affair with a church secretary, his wife, also a minister in the church, left him and he was fired.

Beyond the point of genuine interest and inspiration, the excessive work that goes into shepherding a flock is frequently performed to gain approval and validation, not only from those being helped, but also by those onlookers whose high opinion may be an assurance of tenure for the pastor. Many clergy report they are so preoccupied with the administrative and pastoral demands of their job that they devote only five percent of their time to spiritual practices such as introspective prayer and meditation. Some clergy I know suffer from this sacrifice but justify it in terms of the welfare of their ministry. Others find it a useless kind of suffering and give up ministry altogether in favor of greater opportunity to deepen their spiritual connection. Personally, if I didn't feel called to find a way to transform church for both clergy and laity, I would have traded this difficult occupation long ago for one which did not so consistently tempt me to co-opt my spirituality.

Addictive codependency and perfectionism attempt to compensate for a self believed to be inadequate and powerless. Addiction promotes the delusion that there is some amount of stuff from the outside which will give a feeling of adequacy or control. But the entire universe does not contain enough stuff to fill the black hole of spiritual emptiness caused by the belief we are separate from our Source. The Something More for which we have longed is already ours.

Self-realization is the non-fiction equivalent of clicking our ruby red heels together and repeating three times, "There's no place like home." Then we are all like Dorothy, waking up from a dream to discover we've never left home in the first place. This happens when we not only affirm but actually *feel* the immanent power that transcends the power we have attributed to outside sources, when we realize that our "fall" from divine grace is but the illusion of a mind cut off from the awareness of oneness with God.

We are saved from suffering, not by religious magic, but by our recollection of this truth. The need for intercession by an organized hierarchy is eliminated when we recognize that the only church that exists in real terms is the one that is established in the sanctuary of our deepest and most essential self. The only leadership of this church is our own higher self, connected inextricably with the Source of all that is. Rather than demanding we give our power over to outside mediators who may abuse our perceived dependency upon them, our own higher self connects us with the power that exists within us and invites us to be the freely creative beings we were born to be.

Historically, many of those who long to know God have allowed themselves to be bound by religious structures which promised deliverance from ignorance and alienation. But these dogmatic theologies, combined with rigid canonical law, oppress the true free nature of spiritual self-discovery and, thus, the traditional Old Church enslaves many who seek to be freed. Today, however, those binding ties are unraveling. Larger numbers of people are enrolling in the "invisible church," a term coined by sociologist Thomas Luckmann and elaborated on by Martin Marty.

> Many people find meaning without belonging, religion without community. They pick and choose among the offerings of the bookstore, the television set, the magazine rack, the dormitory, and the promptings of their heart. They are free to be eclectic.... The invisible religion is invisible because it is private, personal, not regularly institutionalized, not monitored by priests or contained in organizations. *As such it lacks specific social power.* Personal religion is chosen by millions as an alternative to religionlessness or godlessness. They must be getting something out of it.[24]
>
> [Emphasis mine]

Marty's statement regarding social power reveals much of religion's hidden agenda. Under the guise of a mission for the reconciliation of Creator and creature, religion has used the power of its supposed alliance with God to bring its own order to society. Traditionally, organized religion has rallied to the cry, "If God is with me, who can be against me?" Implicit in this are threatening consequences for those who would oppose the church and its brand of socialization. Political expressions that refer to contemporary Christians as the "moral majority" and "religious right" recall the pharisaical smugness Jesus once deplored. "Good" Christians feel empowered by their religious convictions to condemn those who would perform abortions (and some murdering extremists have taken this righteous entitlement even further). This is not to deny that much real good is done by people who are part of religious organizations. But most of this good work is social work, not spiritual work.

Examples of spiritual work comes from such great beings such as Mahatma Gandhi , Martin Luther King, Jr. and Mother Teresa. Although each eventually surrendered their lives to their calling, they were able to express their spiritual lives in a social context without destroying themselves spiritually. The power of these persons to effect change in the world was not political power, but authentic spiritual power, born of some degree of self-realization. It is significant that in their work they never threatened loss of God's love for those who did not choose to follow the path they invited others to travel, nor did they do the greatest part of their work in the context of a church or other formal religious setting. Their efforts serve as an inspiration for those who would seek a new kind of organization which allows spiritual, rather than religious, power to lead the way.

Churches appear to be changing. There is more talk of making scriptural language more gender-inclusive. Many churches have instituted "come as you are" services, and it's not unusual to call the church pastor by his (and, more frequently, her) first name. Church has become more fun, even entertaining. As high church clerics in their golden-threaded vestment robes are replaced by preachers in blue jeans, and as we tap our feet to choirs of rock 'n' roll angels, we are tempted to think this more casual version of church is less concerned with being powerful in traditional ways. But I am not so sure this is the case.

The Old Church got into really big business in the latter part of the twentieth century and is presently dishing up a postmodern religiosity in new megachurches the way a fast food franchise serves up a precooked burger—and with a similar profit margin. Right-wing political organizations like the Christian Coalition have seeded their delegates in more than 60,000 Christian churches in the U.S. and virtually fill the campaign coffers of conservative candidates from the offering plate. The ancient themes of Old Church oppression play on, though they may be more difficult to hear over the cacophony of jargon hype and the motivating sales talk of contemporary church leaders.

And what of God? It's easy to forget that the obvious and not-so obvious abuses of power within the Old Church past and present have all been in the name of God. Has God required this, as tradition would have us believe? Or have we been hexed by a spell cast upon us by early androcratic religionists? Is it possible, as Riane Eisler suggests, for us humans to co-exist in partnership with one another, sharing power with one another, even in religious settings? And is it further possible, as I have suggested, that we might ultimately, as self-realized beings, be empowered sufficiently to realize that all humans can share co-creative power with God? As we hold these questions open, our discovery will reveal the evolving truths which may answer them. Meanwhile, let us be clear it has been the Old Church, not God, that demands submission to its power.

# 13

# Churchianity:
# The Big Business of Religion

> *Go ye therefore, and*
> *make disciples of all the nations,*
> *baptizing them into the name of*
> *the Father and of the Son and of the Holy Ghost:*
> *teaching them to observe all the things*
> *whatsoever I commanded you.*

MATTHEW 28:19,20

The Yoido Full Gospel Church in Seoul, South Korea, holds seven services each week, with twenty-five thousand in attendance; additional worshipers watching in satellite auditoriums via closed circuit television bring the total to six hundred thousand people each week! In the United States, church attendance figures are more modest but still significant. The Willow Creek Community Church, a non-denominational megachurch in a suburb of Chicago, boasts three weekend services at the fifteen-million dollar facility on their 131-acre campus which are attended by fifteen thousand "seekers," those not yet fully assimilated into the believer community. Another six thousand "believers" worship at midweek evening services. Second Baptist Church of Houston has grown in the last fifteen years from a congregation of five hundred "on a good week" to more than twenty-two thousand on any given week.

The Gospels of Mark, Matthew and Luke each include a narrative describing the forty days following the resurrection of Jesus. During this time, Jesus is reported to have sent his followers to evangelize the world, declaring his Great Commission in the words quoted above. Through the ages, Christians have taken these words as a literal command to undertake a mission which will not be complete until all peoples of the earth have been converted to the Christian religion. Surely, the megachurches in Seoul, Willow Creek and Houston are filled with good Christians who are getting the job done!

According to the Old Church, a "good" Christian is one who can sell the Christian message to others. The good Christian witnesses to unbelievers in such a way that causes them to change their mind, to see the light of the Christian way. "Born-again" Christians, like the Jesus People who in the 1970s evangelized in public places, are impressively perseverant in their efforts. They are so completely convinced of the damnation of the non-Christian and so earnestly enrolled in their belief that there is only "one way" to be saved, it seems they must lose sleep over the ones that get away. A Christian believer's sales pitch can be remarkably compelling, especially for the fearful, the uncertain and others who may be vulnerable to threats of an eternity in hell. And as Christians who bought the same line as they now sell (and perhaps need to justify their purchase), they are particularly effective in closing the deal that saves a soul for Jesus.

But as sincere as their pitch may be, it seems these believers' prime motivator, the Great Commission, may not have come from Jesus at all. In recent translations of the Gospel which eliminate any portion of New Testament text that was added by the early church, the Great Commission has been excluded. Yet, from the earliest days of the church recorded in the Acts of the Apostles, the success of the Christian mission has been measured by the numbers of unbelievers converted to the faith. Wars, inquisitions and persecutions were all justified to some extent by the notion that Jesus authorized this "You'd better believe or else" strategy.

Since this is so highly inconsistent with Jesus' teaching of love and tolerance, the Great Commission appears rather to be the wishful thinking of the founding fathers. In their increasing distance from the source of their inspiration, these Old Church leaders served less from the generosity of the truth Jesus taught than from an increasingly self-serving distortion. Just like the bird in the hand, numbers of converts who could be counted (along with the coins they brought to church coffers) were more immediately and tangibly satisfying than the Kingdom of God. No matter how close Jesus declared it to be, the spiritual promise that Jesus offered was damnably elusive even for men with the most pious intentions. Once again Jesus' spiritual teaching was set aside and replaced with one that was more accessible to ordinary people. After all, everyone knows how the numbers game works—the one with the most wins!

What we have called Christianity for the last two millennia is actually *Churchianity*—the institutionalized effort to build bigger, better churches in which to corral the ever-increasing numbers of converts who enable church leaders to stay ahead in the numbers game. Churchianity, which is governed more by the laws of market economics than by spiritual law, has been, and remains today, big business. Institutional churches offer salvation to those who will conform their beliefs and behavior to religious doctrine in the same way retail stores promise fulfillment to their consumers who conform to the dictates of Madison Avenue. For the price of unquestioning belief, God-in-a-box churches will serve up protection from self-doubt and insecurity, provide a surrogate family, and most important, prescribe a way of life that comes complete with endorsements of political platforms.

In the competition for business, Churchianity's various outlets vie for the attention of consumer-believers so they will bring their tithes to the collection plate. From the earliest days of Christianity, different factions that came to be known as Orthodox Christianity and Roman Catholicism insisted their brand of religion was the one true Church. Each claimed for themselves the apostolic succession that would justify positions of honor and financial tribute. This battle for recognition concluded in the 1100s with a schism between the Christianities of East and West. When the Church of Rome emerged as the self-proclaimed winner over the Christian Orthodoxy based in Constantinople, it insisted that all true Christian believers belonged to their congregations. (It went on to declare as heretics all who disagreed with that assertion, or had other ideas of what it meant to be a Christian—they were in service to the devil and needed to be eliminated). In the 1500s, however, the Protestant Reformation spawned the development of other alternatives, denominations of Christianity that were to become successful competitors with Roman Catholicism in the religious marketplace.

Denominational loyalty was relatively fixed for centuries thereafter. Church growth was tied to family growth, with successive generations of believers carrying the religious traditions of their ancestors forward without question. Larger numbers of believers, however, entered organized religion as the world was explored and conquered in the name of both church and state. The zeal of co-sponsored missionaries targeted and converted heathen markets, swelling the enrollment figures of state-sanctioned denominations.

Civic and church life have been closely tied, if not inseparable, for much of Christian history. So pervasive was the presence of some kind of Christian church in every aspect of Western civilization, that until well into the 19th century exclusion from the politically correct religious fellowship was tantamount to ostracism from society altogether. Outcasts from the prevailing state religion of England escaped prison to settle North America. They quested for greater freedom of religious expression (even though the "free" religious expression of groups such as the Puritans tended to bind the individual with social dictums as restrictive as those left behind in Europe). Exclusion and persecution of religious non-conformists by the community was not uncommon here either. However, when the United States was formed with a constitutional separation of church and state, as well as a guarantee of freedom of religion, seeds were planted that would yield a proliferation of religious expressions. As these new forms came into existence, each of the new sects developed their own imperatives for making more Christians.

Once the frontier was settled and a stable population base established, the number of churches in a town increased and the competition between denominations resumed. Church clubbiness, the social desirability of associating within one fellowship rather than another, became a factor in determining the growth of one denomination over another. Thus, to be a Methodist came to mean not only to subscribe to John Wesley's brand of Christian theology, but to also belong to the congregation that worships at the First Methodist Church, the imposing brick church with the towering steeple on the corner of Main Street and Broadway. Being the largest church building in the city, its size implies something quite favorable about the people who meet inside it (unlike the poor No-Name Gospel Church across the tracks that cannot afford a building at all).

Certainly, many individuals were sincere in the practice of their religion. The increasing materialism of an American working and middle-class culture, however, showed that what Americans were religious about was shifting. Church involvement was more about socialization than transformation. One belonged to a church not out of a deep longing for spiritual experience, but because it was what was expected by the family and the community.

As American settlers struggled to procure a place in the rugged territory of the frontier, they were intent on securing it; and, once having secured their place on earth, they now wanted to maintain and improve it. Participation in the church became a vehicle for assuring the favor of both God and neighbor in these efforts. For a forward-thinking, community-minded individual, church was the right thing to do, the right place to go, the right place to be seen. A good citizen could be recognized by this persona of religious righteousness, seen by all as a "good" Christian, no matter what actual beliefs, attitudes and intentions were hidden beneath the mask; his material prosperity would also signal the community that he was blessed, a member of the Christian "elect." To obtain this all he needed to do was attend the church he inherited from his father.

In the cities, flooded by immigrants during the same midnineteenth to early twentieth century period, religious affiliations also grounded the community life of various ethnic groups, serving their social as well as spiritual needs. Identification with the church of one's country helped the Europeans who came to America maintain their language and culture within the melting pot. Immigrants belonged to a church, not only for religious reasons, but so they could continue to belong to each other. Again, religious affiliations were handed down within the family.

Thus the churches of various denominations in the United States grew as families grew. Churchianity thrived as an unquestioned institution of American life until the mid-1960s. Against the backdrop of the Vietnam War, however, young people of this period began to reject traditional social and political institutions as meaningless and destructive, and they searched for alternatives. The spiritual vacuum of the Establishment was filled with much experimentation in the realm of consciousness alteration and expansion. Non-Christian Eastern religions became interesting to many, as did herbs and drugs that could apparently induce a spiritual state. A sexual revolution opened the doors to an expression of sexuality that appalled the religious world. The passions of many in this generation were spiritually motivated, though with the exception of those who became involved with religious cults, they were largely not religious in the institutional sense. These seekers were not church-goers—they married in gardens not churches, if they married at all. Church was something that belonged to family, and the family as an institution was also rejected.

Even though many counterculture ideas and practices were eventually co-opted and redirected by Madison Avenue to serve the purposes of the growing techno-industrial business world, the social systems within the United States changed. Particularly due to changes in the structure of the family, contemporary Churchianity can no longer depend upon the denominational loyalty that sustained it into the mid-twentieth century. With a high divorce rate, the family system is no longer stable enough to assure that religious affiliation will pass through the generations as a legacy.

In fact, the whole notion of legacy is increasingly in question. With our environment at risk, we increasingly have a "live for today" type of culture that promotes comfort at the expense of continuity, even of our own species. Secular culture, with its multitude of media entertainment options offers virtually unlimited distraction from spiritual discontent, and there are a vast assortment of opportunities offered for material success (easily attainable, in fantasy if not in reality, according to the same media that entertains us). The result has been a decline in church attendance and panic within the denominations to maintain their market share.

Still the complexity of our culture has many people confused, overwhelmed and desperate for a central organizing factor in their lives. The conditions are ideal for the new wave of Churchianity. As we enter the twenty-first century, the main churches gaining congregants are those largely non-denominational churches and megachurches whose message is fundamental and methods are evangelistic. Relying almost exclusively on the directive of the Great Commission, this new version of an old imperative has set out to save the souls of unbelievers (and further its own unspoken ends). Churchianity capitalizes on the desire people have for a more secure social position in an era of economic instability. By setting standards of religious *rightness* that bolster a sense of personal *righteousness* in a time when a wide range of lifestyle options are available, Churchianity attracts those who are intent upon finding one completely unambiguous way of life.

Martin E. Marty calls contemporary religion "a consumer item for a nation of spiritual window-shoppers." What is the hottest item on the shelf? The religious idea that there can be a "right" way and that it can be *my* way. The promise of this kind of emotional security will seduce almost any safety seeker into belief, since, psychologically, we have been trying to prove ourselves to be right, to be *alright*, ever since we were children. A state of divinely endorsed, socially accepted, and institutionalized rightness, is the adaptive child's equivalent of heaven on earth. We'd give not only our eye teeth but our intelligence and conscience to get this kind of security. And we can! Just down the road at the local Churchianity-store.

The contemporary church sells religious rightness—promoted, packaged, and accompanied by the Bible, that inerrant guide to right and wrong. The more religious consumers buy this product the more Churchianity can grow. And Churchianity includes, as previously implied, the economic and political systems that sustain and are sustained by the big business of church. So as shoppers buy the message of their church and their sense of religious rightness grows, we increasingly hear moral issues debated in legal settings, we find religious political candidates claiming moral superiority over secular opponents, and we see catalogs filled with items such as Bible banks, Jesus erasers and bracelets, Christian gold coins, yo-yo's, balloons, rulers, stickers, coloring books, and puzzles—all items that attach a religious significance to material goods—produced by a national novelty toy company.

Everywhere we turn today, those convicted with the belief that "God is might and might makes right" impress (or oppress) us with the necessity of being on God's side, the right side. Drop a dime for Jesus in the campaign fund of your Christian Coalition candidate. Better yet, use the convenient automatic payroll deduction plan. The message of the Religious Right is that the assurance of things hoped for (safety, security, control) is insured by faith in those who will legislate morality and keep a gun in the hand of those who may need it to protect their "rights." Full participation in the ethics of the Religious Right entitles one to membership in the not-so-silent Moral Majority, which assumes itself to be nothing less than the chosen people of God in whose name all lost sheep *will* be brought into the fold, all souls *will* be saved, or else be damned.

Playing to the uneasy feeling many people experience around the dissolution of the family structure—their fear that something has gone terribly awry—the Religious Right seeks to right the apparent wrong. The religio-political pleas for a return to "family values," are markedly inconsistent, however. Just look at legislative actions from the same Rightist quarters that purport to reform the welfare system and otherwise legislate morality.

For example, it has been argued that unwed mothers somehow profit from their dependency on government welfare programs, and the only way to teach them a different lesson is to withdraw any financial assistance and make these mothers work for living. This would be a simple solution if there was affordable, reliable child care available to these mothers, as well as training and education for jobs that will pay more than minimum wage. But since these conditions do not typically exist, the single welfare mother struggles in an impossible double bind which inevitably impacts her child.

The moralist of the Religious Right assumes that pulling the financial rug out from under single (i.e., immoral) mothers will cause them to abandon immoral behavior in favor of a more righteous life. The legislated morality that would deny financial assistance from the government to mothers and children may indeed serve to prevent some out-of-wedlock pregnancies, but, if so, it is at the cruel cost of the neglect of children already born. Additionally, the laws proposed to eliminate abortions guarantee an increase in the number of births of unwanted children who will be ready targets for the abuse of ill-equipped, frustrated mothers and, in later life, prime candidates for the prisons, already full to capacity.

What is the unconscious intent that underlies the political agenda of the Christian Right? Will we one day remove the mask of Christian brotherly love of the Religious Right and find a powerful political machine ready to exert fascistic control over the disenfranchised "minorities," creating a kind of volunteer slavery in the name of Jesus? Dependent mothers and children (as well as gays, people of color, and others) will need to turn somewhere for succor. Let it be the church, Churchianity implies.

In fact, if in the spirit of "love your neighbor as yourself," the resources of Churchianity were freely and widely extended to those in need, outreach efforts might be truly effective in relieving the burden the government has carried for many years. Unfortunately, there is a price implicitly attached to the support a church might offer to a needy person—belief (and concomitant dependency on the system of belief) in the way, truth and life of the Old Church. The Old Church extends assistance only with a call to redemption, whether or not redemption has been requested. In one system an aid recipient may trade self-esteem for a welfare check, but in the other she risks losing her selfhood, taking on the judgement of others that the cause of her predicament is a sinfulness that must be redeemed.

Moral censure and the covert threat of damnation by the Divine inspire a repentance in the "sinner" that, with a bit of coaching, easily manifests as another Right vote in the ballot box. Meanwhile, that former welfare mom can have a nice domestic job at minimum wage in one of the homes of the legislator she helped elect, while her child is ....hmm, where is that child? No matter. Somehow the divine (white is right?) order is reestablished. The world can rest easy, and on the Sabbath, worship at the church that makes it all possible.

～

If religion is a consumer item, then churches are its retail outlets. As churches must attract shoppers, the ability of a small church (automatically assumed to be an insignificant, undesirable franchise simply because of the head count) to grow into a large one depends more on the entrepreneurial and managerial skills of its ministerial leadership than on ministerial spiritual awareness.

Robert Schuller, known to millions of Americans who've watched his national television program, "The Hour of Power," is also the founding minister of the Garden Grove Community Church in California. He shares the secrets of building a large ministry in the programs of the Robert H. Schuller Institute for Successful Church Leadership. He recommends to church leaders who wish to grow larger churches that they follow the "Seven Principles of Successful Retailing" which have made suburban shopping center developers "one of the phenomenal successes of American business in the twentieth century." He describes the Crystal Cathedral, the church he grew from humble beginnings on the site of a drive-in movie theater, as "a twenty-acre shopping center for Jesus Christ."[25]

Schuller no doubt epitomizes the successful contemporary church leader. His sound-bite sermons are easy listening—he likens them to billboard advertising. Speaking what Calvin Miller, author of *Marketplace Preaching*, calls "shopping mall English," he delivers an upbeat, motivational and heartfelt message designed to give people "exciting and inspiring good news." The fundamental principle of good churchmanship, according to Schuller is "find a hurt and heal it;" but only by always being positive and never controversial. I wonder if Jesus returned today if he would recognize his own radical teachings couched in the ad-man's language. Would he have been willing to take one step inside the discount warehouse of worship? What would he make of this big-business Churchianity that markets a product that bears so little resemblance to the remarkable spiritual experience that awakened him?

The marketing principles which have made Schuller's church a commercial success serve as the foundational structure of the American megachurch, whose intent is to evangelize and convert large numbers of people. Aimed at the unchurched who are disenchanted or bored with traditional liturgical forms, the megachurch focuses on entertainment and excitement. The author of a *Common Boundary* article researching the Second Baptist Church in Houston comments on how they answered the phone each of the dozen times he called:

> "*Exciiting* Second!"   Maybe it was just the Texas twang with the *i* drawn out an extra beat, but the words invariably assuaged the skepticism they simultaneously triggered.

Church marketing directors know there is something contagious about a fun, energetic church. As a culture we largely want to escape from our pain by having fun, and media images entice us to associate with others who look like they're having the good time we'd like to have.

A church I have visited locally has the reputation for being such a place, and also a great singles' meeting place. It reminds me a lot of the teen club I joined in high school. Everyone went there after sporting events; it was a chance to hang out with the cheerleaders and football heroes. Although I occasionally had fun being a part of the "scene," I rarely made significant contact with anyone there, and often left feeling lonely and empty. Likewise, if a church simply entertains people so they will join ranks and push the numbers up, the deep longing for spiritual communion is left unfulfilled. This kind of manufactured fun also masks the real spirit of joy that comes of working through a difficult spiritual issue or of achieving a breakthrough of understanding—the sorts of overcoming that warrant genuine celebration rather than the rah-rah "witness" of one of Churchianity's cheerleaders.

Exciting, entertaining, and altogether as attractive as other media shows, the contemporary megachurches (and those that aspire to be) get caught up in and promote exactly those practices which diminish the already depleted spirituality of our culture. Reeling from sensory, informational and stress overload we need less, not more, stimulation, especially in our attempts to connect spiritually, but we are clearly addicted to whatever techno-industrial products arrive on the popular scene. And driven by the demands of the marketplace, the imperative of Churchianity's mission, and no small amount of personal ambition, church leaders, who resemble corporate executives more than spiritual leaders in both their professional and personal lives, continue to give consumers what marketing surveys say they want.

As the Third Millennium dawns, polls show Americans are returning to church. Some of these had millennial apocalyptic concerns and wanted to be in the right place at the right time to take advantage of a prophesied Rapture. Others are baby-boomers and their successors who are looking for a religious structure in which to raise their children. Yet others are seeking a deeper meaning for their lives in a time when the culture is largely devoid of it. What are they finding? Basically the same old-time,

Old Church religion that's always been in the mainstream denominations, as well as some new-time fundamental varieties that
use contemporary techniques to promote a "back to the good old
days" religion. These prodigal churchgoers are still offered salvation in exchange for belief in a setting where they might take
sanctuary from the chaos of contemporary life. But most of them
will stay in the church only until they get bored or distracted,
which, because of the addictive attraction of other weekend activities, they inevitably will.

We are a religion-soaked but restless nation. Religious consumers shop churches to find the one that will allay the vague,
nagging discontents of their postmodern souls. Roaming like
teenagers at a mall amongst the various forms of traditional religion, they stop for a while in one and when the novelty wears
off, they're off to see what's new in the religious marketplace.
Those who genuinely, although most often unconsciously, seek
spiritual experience will ultimately find their ventures into the
commercial religion marketplace like looking in a discount jew-
elry outlet store for the pearl of great price. While it may be filled
with lots of glitz and glitter—good imitations and the best intentions—the real thing simply can't be found there. Despite
impassioned performances that would convince otherwise, the
big-business church of Churchianity is spiritually empty. Motivated by spiritual materialism, sustained by appearances rather
than substance, it worships success, not spirit. The numbers, not
the numinous, guide its practices.

I appreciate this indictment of Old Church Christianity may
seem unfair and cynical, especially to anyone who has had an
authentic spiritual experience within the context of their local
church. I would argue, however, that whatever good may have
come out of traditional Christianity is in spite of, not because of,
its stated mission to convert the world. By claiming the One Way
to redemption, Christianity has suppressed the diversity of exploration and expression that results from the individuation of a
spiritually growing person. Through implicit denial of the validity
of other paths to spiritual realization, Christianity disenfranchises
those spiritual seekers who would create a uniquely suitable path to
God. With its emphasis on righteousness, or what I have called
religious rightness, Christianity soothes the insecurities of the human existence by promoting and perpetuating narrow thinking

and spiritual immaturity. The final result is that Christianity ignores its own inspirational source, Jesus. It disregards the fact that Jesus shunned the smugness of the organized religion rites of his own day in favor of a fresh direct approach to the divine. It neglects to take seriously the spiritual possibility Jesus realized and invited us to do likewise.

To know our oneness with God, we must be able to observe the ways in which we do not act as one, and make distinctions that might help humanity bring its aspirations into alignment with its practices. A major distinction I have intended to make here is that a "one way" religion is not the same as a "oneness" religion. Churchianity/Christianity has traditionally offered one way, a way that has blessed those eligible for positions of theological authority with worldly power and privilege, while abusing the sincere loyalty of those who would believe them and depend upon them. This has been an error that today calls out for correction.

I believe the *ecclesia*, the "called out ones" who will gather as a new kind of church will be those who seek not so much to right the wrongs of the Old Church, as to see them for what they are —partial truth distortions of a positive intent. This new church will forgive the Old Church by knowing a more complete truth about those who created and perpetuated it. It will be able to withdraw the power given previously to the Old Church, and redirect this energy into new channels of creative, essential spirituality.

In this process comes the redemption of the human efforts to build a church and the possibility of doing things differently. What has been lost or neglected in the Old Church can be recovered in a New Church. The final section of this book will address the experience of my attempt to translate my own Great Commission into a new kind of church that would be such a "oneness" church. Not a "one way" church, but another way. If we can think of church as being not some immovable institution but as an evolving life form, then this New Church is not so much a rejection of the Old Church as it is a completion of some of its partial truths. This New Church represents, then, not the last word for what a church can be, but another turn in the spiral of actualization that is unfolding itself as a more complete expression of the church Jesus intended to create.

# PART THREE
# The New Church:
# Revealing the Spirit

*Where two or more are gathered in my name,*
*there am I in the midst of them.*

MATTHEW 18:20

The church I founded, Unity-Midtown, meets in a lovely historical landmark building in Atlanta called The Academy of Medicine. From the parking lot, a foot path winds through a garden filled with flowers of the season, beneath a gracious magnolia tree and past a towering cottonwood tree growing to one side of the grassy lawn, to the wide front steps. Massive white columns support the gracious portico, and a pair of large wooden doors open into the black and white marble-tiled rotunda. There, hanging directly below a domed skylight, is a crystal chandelier that originally made its home on the set of "Gone With the Wind."

Through another set of doors is the auditorium where Unity-Midtown's services are held. The ceiling of the room is shaped and decorated like a large Victorian Easter egg, painted coral with white frosting. Sunlight pours in through tall windows along the length of curved walls. A medium-sized stage is unadorned except for a small lectern, several chairs and a round table with candles set in the position of the four cardinal directions. The rest of the auditorium is filled with rows of plush seats covered in deep rust-colored velveteen. It is an elegant, yet intimate space, with an acoustical sweet spot that makes it possible for a whisper to be heard anywhere in the room.

The Academy of Medicine also houses several stately conference rooms, a medical library, and a small room containing a museum collection of old medical instruments. When we first considered holding services in this building, I was amused that after all my attempts to get away from the medical profession I found myself once again within the hallowed halls of medicine. The Caduceus symbols which embellish the ceiling of the rotunda not only recalled the building's early days in the '40s when it was originally a professional club for Atlanta physicians, but also served to inspire me that this church, among other things, could possibly be a healing ministry.

Indeed, many of the people who walked through the doors of Unity-Midtown seemed to be looking for a kind of spiritual hospital. Many of them had not been in any kind of church for twenty years or more. They were often guarded and wary. They felt wounded in the churches they attended with their families, and *any* church was a reminder of the past shame, guilt and condemnation they'd accumulated in a religious setting.

A large number of Unity-Midtown's first congregants were gay. Preachers had told them the Bible forbade homosexuality and condemned homosexuals. Since this interpretation made it impossible for them to be themselves, they chose to leave their childhood religions rather than live a lie. This was rarely a decision made lightly. Many believed they were forsaking God when they left their church—they had been told as much by parents and preachers. As a result these men and women typically become self-sufficient outside of any religious structure—they felt they'd been abused by religion and wanted no more of it. However, since this new church they'd found offered them love and acceptance no matter who they were, or what they believed or practiced, many felt they could return to an active relationship with God. They began to speak of themselves as "recovering Catholics" or "recovering Southern Baptists."

As the church grew, people other than gays began to attend. These were mostly intelligent, educated, middle-class people who had become disenchanted with traditional religions. Most proclaimed an aversion to the hypocrisy of the churches they had attended as children. Others felt they had outgrown narrow, dogmatic teachings that no longer seemed relevant to their lives. More than a few had been, like me, sexually abused in a religious setting. While this made for a diverse congregation, each person seemed to share a desire to explore the spiritual side of life and all of them were extremely suspicious of traditional religious forms.

I empathized with them. I knew firsthand the negative attributes of organized religion. I constantly struggled to reconcile my calling to be an agent of spiritual awakening with my job as a minister in a church I both loved and hated. The anger about church that I shared with my congregants seemed justified by our experiences, yet, on the positive side, it also motivated me to try to do things differently. I very much wanted to create a new kind of church for the twenty-first century. However, the more I tried to do some different things in my church, and actually had some successes, the greater I felt the inertia the traditional church form seemed to exert.

Everything I introduced that was in any way a reaction to traditional church seemed to meet with tremendous resistance from someone in the congregation—either it was too much innovation or too little. After a particularly powerful service, where the music and speaking and interaction with the congregation were truly inspired and satisfying to me, I'd get a call from someone who'd walked out halfway through because we'd left out the congregational song. Others would tell me they didn't come to church more often because they hated group singing. I was aware of how confined a psychological space I was trying to work in—congregants said they wanted things different but it seemed this was true only as long as the change didn't affect them! I just couldn't get it right. And I came to a stark realization that I had no idea how to get out of what increasingly felt like a prison. My apparent helplessness enraged me even more and I looked once again to the church I loved/hated to blame. I wanted to leave, but something else called me to stay. Stay I did, only to discover that something larger than myself—the evolutionary impulse—was already at work to bring about the changes I desired.

Part Three describes the New Church. I begin by describing an evolutionary "wave" that is bringing new forms of religious expression into being. I summarize the consecration or intent of the New Church, addressing in a general way each of the points raised in the critique of the Old Church from the perspective of the alternative the New Church offers. Then, I discuss levels of church form as seen from an evolutionary perspective, with a description of the psychological needs that are served at each level, and what growth tasks need to be completed before graduating to the next level. Next, I provide some general guidelines that may be helpful for bringing the New Church to life in an already existing church, or in a new situation. As part of this, I give some examples of my experience in creating the New Church that existed in conjunction with Unity-Midtown.

Finally, I share what an actual participant has to say about her experience with the work of the New Church. For me, this testimony about how the quality of lives has been transformed affirms my decision to start (and complete) this book and the church it describes. The sincerity, innocence, wisdom and power of those who have in some way participated in the New Church experiment, have evoked whatever is best in me. For this, I am grateful.

# 14

# The Evolutionary Wave

*Evolution is not a force but a process;*
*not a cause but a law.*

**JOHN, VISCOUNT MORLEY OF BLACKBURN**

An evolution is taking place in the realm of spirituality. Religion, especially as it has been traditionally expressed in Western Christianity, has been a container which has defined how we approach our spirituality— it is a kind of box that has confined our spiritual experience. The more we learn about why this box was built and how it is maintained, the more obvious it becomes that we have been limited by it. As we acknowledge this box has served a purpose, albeit one that increasing numbers are outgrowing, we can begin to open to a more expansive understanding of what might promote spiritual unfoldment at the levels beyond the Old Church. We can begin to describe new church forms that will include yet transcend traditional religion.

Traditional forms of Christianity remain intact because there has been a taboo against questioning them. Just as my gay congregants felt they would lose their relationship with God if they left the church, fear of castigation has kept many people from ever asking if other forms are available. Historically, the Church has had its ways of keeping would-be reformers quiet—torture being the least of them! Over time, however, evolution tends to overrule these fears; for while individuals may be sacrificed, their ideas live on. Humanity's unfolding consciousness demands more room in which to expand than traditional religious forms currently allow.

As lovely a meeting place as the Academy of Medicine is for Unity-Midtown Church, the time came for me when, as its spiritual leader, I realized the limitations of its alluring architecture and what this symbolized. Over the years I noticed this also seemed true of certain congregants; they appeared to thrive in the church for one or two years but would then hit a wall of some sort and leave. Of course, this was not a literal wall, and certainly not, strictly speaking, a function of the building design. But the physical structure did represent a limit to the kind of spiritual experience that could happen in traditional settings, and for those who got to a point in their development that there was a call for a deeper experience, there was no physical or energetic space in the context of the church in which this could happen.

I came to realize that for humans to be fully actualized, the invisible walls of the church-box that has contained and defined our spiritual experiences must be made conscious and seen for what they are. If those walls are still needed, we can at least be more aware of their design and purpose. If not, they can be dismantled so that we can grow beyond their psychological bounds and fulfill more of our human/divine potential.

It is one of the theses of this book that religious forms are in place to serve persons at a certain stage of development, and they will continue to do so until they are spiritually ready for some other form. As they exit the form they have outgrown, however, it often happens that onetime ardent churchgoers are confused about why they are leaving. Some will say the minister's sermons have gotten boring, or that they no longer like the kind of songs they are asked to sing. Others will bemoan the loss of the good old days when there was a more active outreach ministry or when there were doughnuts served with the coffee, or when so and so led the choir, or before the carpet color was changed. Not knowing how to explain the emptiness they now feel in a situation that once held a great deal of meaning for them, they may grab for something to blame, something that can be used as an excuse to leave.

And yet, seen from a perspective that *anticipates* an evolving spirituality, people who are growing spiritually *should* outgrow religious forms—no excuses needed or called for! Would you demand an apology from a child who stops crawling because she's learned how to walk? Would you suppress this new-found freedom? Of course not! Even though it was once the infant's most significant accomplishment, a toddler eventually stops crawling when walking becomes possible. This graduation occurs naturally in the course of human growth and development.

Leaving a context in which one has learned and grown is a sign of maturity, like a bird that's grown up enough to fly away from the nest. But taking that first flight from the nest can be frightening—it looks like a long way down! Often, a mother bird stops feeding her baby and calls to it from a tree branch away from the nest to encourage it to fly. Hungry, the young bird is more motivated to leave the comfortable but limiting nest. In the absence of this incentive to grow, it would fail to enjoy the freedom and responsibilities of an adult bird. If the baby bird never leaves the nest, at best, the parents are going to have to keep feeding it for the rest of its life. At worst it will simply die.

In a traditional church we often worry about those who leave. But perhaps we should really be worrying about those who stay when they're ready to go. Like a nest, traditional religious settings are appropriate only as long as they serve the spiritual growth of individuals. Beyond that there is a risk of stunted development or stagnation. As we have seen, however, one of the limitations of Old Church style of religion is that it tends to place more emphasis on keeping the nest full than on setting birds free. It tends to chastise birds who are ready to leave the nest by making them feel guilty. As a result when they eventually do fly away, it's often with a bad feeling about the nest and its keepers. Even when we might have some negativity towards it, we have to remember that the traditional church, like the nest, serves a vital purpose. It's staying too long that's the problem.

Traditional religious forms, as well as some transitional forms that have emerged in the last hundred years, offer a context for doing spiritual work only at a certain stage of development which will be described fully in this section. This stage cannot be skipped, but it shouldn't be prolonged. As long as traditional church serves a person by meeting the needs of this stage of development, then that is where they need to be. The physical and organizational structure of this kind of church, even when it appears restrictive or repressive, is just right for this stage. But, when the needs of that stage have been satisfied or transcended, then other forms that invite a higher level of spiritual maturity are more appropriate. In other words, it's time to leave the nest! The work of this level is complete and there is no need to stay within the old forms. In fact, it is imperative to move out of those religious confines because they will begin to thwart the impulse to spiritual awakening.

Like many people, I left the nest of traditional religion as an act of defiance. But I see now that this doesn't have to be the case. I could have viewed my exit, not so much as a rebellion against traditional church, as a kind of graduation to another level of possible understanding and empowerment. But I was not encouraged to see it this way, and I did not realize this on my own for a long time. Instead, my path was to put a lot of energy into righting the wrongs I felt the Church had done to me and others. Eventually, however, I was exhausted by my efforts and realized that it is not my job to condemn historical Christianity, but to understand that it has a place in the evolutionary scheme of things. The church has merit in being the kind of religious expression that it is, *and* the ways and means of traditional Christianity are shortsighted when represented as being complete in themselves.

Instead of taking the relative shortcomings of the church personally, I am now able to see them as partial truths in an ongoing evolution of spiritual expression. My intentions have now shifted. I no longer want to fix traditional religion, but to place it in perspective. I want to honor the purpose it serves, while showing that its function is limited. Further I want to suggest some new forms of church that would help people when they are ready to leave the traditional church nest.

As it did for me and others I have ministered to over the past ten years, seeing the Church as an evolving rather than a static structure, allows understanding and forgiveness of its shortcomings. Just as the leeches used in more primitive forms of medicine stung those they tried to heal, one must respect the church's conscious intention to do what is best, even when its wars and persecution caused suffering. Unconsciousness, even when well-intentioned, brings pain to individuals. Hopefully, a more enlightened perspective honors the positive contribution traditional religion has made to spiritual unfoldment *and*, through greater awareness, offers the Church an opportunity to make amends for the past by refusing to create that kind of suffering again in the future. But before any recovery effort can begin, we first have to admit that there is a problem—as I've shown in Part Two, the holy church is not all it's cracked up to be. There have been problems with it since its inception and hopefully now we have some insight into their causes.

As much as western culture has been enmeshed with the Christian religion, it's easy to forget that the form of religious expression we call "church" has been evolving since humans first conceived of it. People all over the world—Hindus and Buddhists, Greeks and Romans, Baal worshippers, Jews and many others—gathered together for religious ritual and celebration long before Christianity came to be identified as *the* church. The forms of religious expression used by people throughout the ages have changed as religious understanding has changed. The development of Christianity itself actually represents such a shift.

Since as a culture we are so closely identified with the Christian church, however, it is sometimes difficult to have the kind of perspective on it that we might if we were looking at a religion that belonged to some other culture. Add to this the fact that the Old Church form of Christianity insists that its form is synonymous with the unchanging nature of God. Still, we have to acknowledge that even the Old Church has undergone significant changes over the past two millennia. The Great Schism with Eastern Orthodoxy is one prominent marker in the development of Christianity. The Protestant Reformation is another. In more recent times, the Vatican II council convened by Pope John XXIII signified church renewal for the modern era.

Yet, even with this evidence of some change within the institution, Old Church ideas continue to dominate the Christian church. Although the contemporary version of the Old Church updates its presentation, in substance, its ideology remains unchanged. The Old Church continues to operate in service to those who are at the same level of human development it always has.

A truly transformative shift in the church inspired by Jesus Christ calls for a deeper change than we have heretofore seen in Christianity. It requires that the church find a way to serve people who are developing beyond the one in which only the more basic deficiency needs are met. To do this, forms of expression that do not necessarily resemble any of those used in the traditional church liturgy must be created. These new forms should not be merely variations on a theme, or innovative ways of doing traditional services, but a radical reorientation of theory and procedure; that is, a significant shift in the whole way the Christian church is conceived of.

When I considered pioneering the church that became Unity-Midtown, I had a clear intention to serve this re-visioning process, although it was not clear to me exactly what that meant. In starting a church in Atlanta, I knew only that my primary passion was to experiment with creating a prototype for a New Church. It took eight years to finally discover a truly workable format.

"Expect the unexpected!" was our battle cry as my congregants and I struggled with entrenched ideas about what a church was supposed to be. With equal parts relief and befuddlement I'd often hear someone say, "This certainly isn't like any other church I've ever been to." In all fairness to those who came to Unity-Midtown, many of them were just looking for a church home, not the radical departure from that in which they found themselves. They didn't necessarily embrace the notion of a new church, nor were they particularly conscious of wanting one. When some of them discovered how conservative they actually were in relation to the vision I had of what a church could be, they actively resisted my leadership.

This provided me with the kind of second force that is so important in any creative process; in the act of meeting their resistance, I was forced to commit to the possibility for a new church. It was not comfortable for me, however—I was bothered it upset people that I felt I could no longer do church in the old way. But like Martin Luther, all I could say is, "Here I stand, I can do no other." Except it might be more accurate for me to have said, "Here I swim, I can do no other." For it was as if the evolutionary impulse had washed over me and I was caught up in its wave. The view I glimpsed from the crest excited me because I caught a vision of a church designed to facilitate spiritual experience rather than religious adherence. In the trough of this evolutionary wave, however, I felt swamped, overwhelmed by the enormity of the effort I saw it would take to bring about this new kind of church.

How could I consciously serve the evolution of the church? How could I create this new church when I myself couldn't even describe what it really was? Intuitively I seemed to know such a thing existed *in potentia*, but it was not easy to articulate what I sensed. So, in the early days all I was able to do was to point to the Old Church and say "not that!" I did the best I could to provide experiences that showed rather than told of this New Church, even though my efforts were often met with the inertia exerted by the archetype of the Old Church, both in my congregants (many of them loved the novelty of the services I created for them, but insisted on keeping certain traditional trappings) and in myself.

At the start of this experimental church, the only thing that made sense at the time was to gather a group of people together and begin. An announcement was made in another Unity church in Atlanta that I was pioneering a church in Midtown, and a group of nine people I didn't know met with me a couple of weeks later. We had two other organizational meetings during which we discovered a place to hold services and set a date for doing so.

There were nineteen people present, including myself and a guest musician, on that Sunday in October, 1990, when we began. The talk I gave at the first service of Unity-Midtown Church was entitled "In the beginning ... God." I spoke about feeling empty; there were no words for what I saw as a possibility before me. But, I told them, I sensed the presence of a longing—a longing in the Holy Spirit to find new forms through which to express itself—and I intended to place my life in this church in service to that. I knew that as we entered the twenty-first century there was something more a church could be. I told them about my dream, and about the research I wanted to do to bring about this envisioned new church. I told them I honestly had no idea how to go about this, except to start where we were and see what happened.

All I knew about starting a New Church was God – the Unknowable One that couldn't be known except by experience—and everything I thought I knew about what didn't work in the Old Church. I had no idea how to express a realization of God as a church, although that was my aim. I had been trained to do church as a Unity minister, however, and that gave me a tangible, though compromised, place to start. I had to face the fact that as far as church-making went, the only model I had was the Old Church, albeit the liberal Unity version of Old Church (what I now think of as Transitional Church).

It was clear to me from the beginning—as soon as organizing church activities became the priority—that if the Old Church had God captured within its structure, I was going to have to figure out how to get it out of the box while to some extent I myself was still stuck inside of it. This bootstrapping was not going to be easy! There were so many things to *do*: supplies to purchase, volunteers to enroll, a space to maintain, a church to build! While I never lost sight of my vision to create a church where people could *be*, that is, have a direct experience of God, a lot of activity suddenly seemed to take precedence over whatever spiritual practice might lead to that.

Nobody else involved in the church seemed to mind. They seemed to like making a church that belonged to them. Creating a bookstore, for instance, was great fun for a couple of women who offered a section filled with lesbian-feminist literature. (The featured selection on the book table one week was a brightly covered text called *Lesbian Passion*. A nine-year-old boy was enjoying it quite a bit when his mother grabbed it from him and thrust it in my face. What was a book like *that* doing in a church?) Organizing potluck lunches for after the service, forming a gospel choir, and putting together myriad other things that went along with doing church, occupied most of the time and attention of the participants. The spiritual "stuff" got left to me, and was mostly relegated to what took place in the hour on Sunday morning.

I used that time to bring an experience of God directly into the hearts of the people who were there. I used humor, psychodrama, music, as well as deep meditations, prolonged chanting, honest sharing—whatever I could—to help diffuse the taboos many of us had about what could happen in a church service. Often, something quite powerful and moving would occur—the energy of the group would shift into high gear as the participants' consciousness altered—and we would frequently leave the service in awe. Sometimes, as we gathered in a circle for the closing song, a round of applause would spontaneously arise. I was always amazed.

And then disappointed. For it seemed that as soon as people left the auditorium where the service was held they'd immediately switch into social mode and act as if the Presence we'd all just tasted was suddenly much less interesting than the coffee and donuts that were available on the refreshment table.

The effect of this on me was that I felt very much alone in the midst of what at times seemed like a monster I'd help to create. It was jarring to me to have such profound experiences with the group, and then to feel I had to act in almost complete denial of that. Unity-Midtown, it seemed, was not so different from other churches after all my intention that it should be so. Much of my critique of the Old Church developed out of my attempt to understand what I was up against at Unity-Midtown. I saw that in spite of my best intentions, the church, and the people in it, seemed to be under the influence of something far more powerful than I was able to change by simply saying so. I could sense there was a strong attachment to a particular definition of church, and that continued to translate into an equally strong resistance to the kind of spiritual experience I proposed the New Church could offer.

In the early days of the Unity-Midtown I began to identify with Jesus a great deal of the time. I empathized with his attempts to lead his disciples on a path to self-realization that they couldn't really comprehend. I imagined how discouraged he must have been as his words were misinterpreted and misunderstood. I came to see that my dislike of Christianity had nothing to do with Jesus Christ. I realized that all along he had a vision of a kind of church that was perhaps not dissimilar to my own. I felt even more certain that my work was to help bring Jesus' vision into manifestation.

So, I realized it would not be enough to just say the New Church is "not that." I had to discover the positive contribution the New Church had to make as a development beyond the Old Church. What would this New Church need to offer that the Old Church seemed to have bungled? What would I need to understand that would free me from the vise-like grip the Old Church seemed to have on me and others? These are some of the questions for which there were no quick and easy answers. Over the years, however, I have had some insight into these matters.

I have come to realize there will never be a final solution to the problems raised by religious/spiritual organizations. There can only be contributions to an ever-evolving, more complete understanding of what best serves the purpose of spiritual awakening. I began my critique of the Old Church by saying that it offers only a partial truth, and that is true. But I have to admit that my own attempt to address the points of that critique with the positive contribution of the New Church will also fall short of the whole truth. That's simply how evolution works.

The best we can do is be compassionate from whatever point of greater understanding we might have, and forgive the shortcomings of what's gone before, humbly realizing that those who come after us will be in a position to do the same for us. Also, it's important to recognize that whatever understanding we have today would not have been possible without the contribution of what went before it. So, in my personal experience, this would mean that I would not be who I am today without the influence of my Catholic upbringing. In a larger sphere, there could be no New Church without all the efforts made by the Old Church.

In the best of all possible worlds, the Old Church has its place. And so I have no desire to eradicate the Old Church, but to offer access to more consciousness about the nature of the Old Church. With such information, people can be aware they have a choice about whether it is still appropriate for them to be a part of it or time to explore another form.

The New Church offers a response, not a reaction, to the Old Church; this is in the form of assertion, not fact. These assertions beg to be tested more thoroughly than I have done in my singular research project. This, then, is an invitation to others to see for themselves.

While the story I share here is simply my experience, I know I am not alone in the conclusions I've drawn about the need for a New Church form—Matthew Fox and John Shelby Spong are only two of the most well known clergy who have called for this. They know that something other than the Old Church is valuable and necessary. Many lay people as well are leaving the traditional forms in search of meaning and support in their process of spiritual awakening. Many more will leave once they become aware they have permission to do so. These people and others who've never had much active involvement with the Old Church will find the New Church a viable next step for supporting their soul's quest to know itself.

I know the New Church form I describe in greater detail further along in this section works. It works in the sense that is provides a context for inviting people into a deeper relationship with their own spiritual essence. It works in that it calls individuals to face their fears and meet them with faith. It works in that it is a simple form that can be sustained with minimal organizational hassle. It works because it doesn't make a lot of effort to do something that will impress, or make a lot of promises about results—it simply offers the Spirit of God a clear space in which to be experienced.

I also know that it is not an easy thing for a lot of folks to move from Old Church to New Church. There are a certain number of people whose spiritual process is actually best served by *not* making the move to New Church. In the next chapters I will discuss a Transitional Church form I believe is helpful for those who are uncertain, or not quite ready to leave traditional religious observances behind.

From the many conversations I've had with members of my church over the years, and from my experience of their reaction to some of the ideas I've had, I realize that the subject under discussion—the possibility of a New Church—is a very threatening one to individuals who have been even minimally involved with the Old Church. Scholars can rip away at the Old Church and theorize about improvements all they want from the relative distance of their academic classroom, and at times, I've wished for that freedom. However, as the spiritual leader of a group of people I work with on a regular basis, people who have opened their hearts and souls to me, whose lives I know, to introduce these new ideas and offer new experiences as New Church has meant exposure to the anguish of the attachment many people have to the old forms of church and to their conditioned ideas of who they think they are. I have been deeply moved by the suffering we humans endure to hold on to some semblance of control in a universe that will not be controlled. For this reason I have been unwilling to be the instrument of innovation just for the sake of doing something new. Each step I have taken to create the New Church has been made as consciously and deliberately as possible, with an acute awareness of the impact this change will have in real people's lives.

Ultimately, however, I have not held back. An evolutionary wave is washing over the entire structure of what we have known as church. It is doing so in the service of something much larger than my desire to see a reform in the Old Church that seemed to cause so much harm in my own personal life. The church is changing as part of a larger movement of the conscious evolution of our entire species. I believe this is a good thing. A difficult thing, yes, but something we humans have been called toward since our inception. We have been evolving Spirit into manifestation for millions of years—now we are coming to consciously realize that we are not what we think we are, but so much more. The New Church serves this impulse to awaken to our innate potential, our own essential spirituality. And my life is in service to that.

15

# A Return to the Source

*If you bring forth what is within you,*
*what you bring forth will save you.*
*If you do not bring forth what is within you,*
*what you do not bring forth will destroy you.*

**GOSPEL ACCORDING TO THOMAS**

In this chapter I will address the ways in which the New Church attempts to correct the six major distortions the Old Church brought about in disseminating Jesus' message, as discussed in Chapters 8 to 13. In addressing these problems point by point, I am offering a view of Jesus' life and teaching that is largely based on a psychological and spiritual understanding which has developed over the last two thousand years. In this way, I hope the partial truths Old Church leaders espouse might find a greater completion in the updated interpretation of Jesus' intention that the New Church offers.

## A. Jesus' Original Intent

Jesus was primarily a teacher of spiritual awakening. Like any masterful teacher he taught by his presence, by his example, and by his words. His presence radiated his awareness of his Oneness with God and was attractive to many. His life was a dramatic and powerful demonstration of a life worth living. His words originated from a level of consciousness in contact with the Divine.

Unfortunately, this level was far beyond that of his listeners, and the words spoken by Jesus were difficult for them to fully comprehend. With the spiritual understanding we have today, however, the truth he was teaching is not so obscure. Looking back it is clear that the aim of Jesus' teaching about spiritual awakening was to introduce the idea of the kind of development that is possible within each human being. Jesus was showing and telling his students Self- or God-realization—the experience of Oneness with God—was available to them. For certain of his more developed disciples, he aimed to actually induct them into a direct experience of that state by inviting them to transform their consciousness or level of being.

Jesus was a master of the psychology of transformation. From his own awakening experience he was aware of how psychological structures obscured the realized state. He had learned these internal obstacles ("the enemies of our own household") needed to be seen clearly in order for them to no longer be a stumbling block to conscious realization.

Jesus provided a context for transmitting this spiritual psychology within the community that was drawn to him. We might call this a community of his teaching. Or, to reflect the nature of the consecration behind such a context, we might refer to it as a Community of the Teaching. In the wisdom traditions of the East, a Community of the Teaching presented the primary vehicle for bringing forth the esoteric knowledge contained in the perennial philosophy. Disciples gathered around a Master for spiritual teaching, using a monastery, mystery school, or other intentional environment as a venue for their study. Within this Community, not only ideas, but methods and practices, were developed, along with a commitment to relationship with the Teacher and other students. The Community served as a classroom and a laboratory for spiritual awakening.

When referring to his Community of the Teaching, Jesus spoke of the *ecclesia*, the "called out ones." It's commonly believed that only certain people have a spiritual calling; after all, Jesus himself said, "Many are called but few are chosen." But in practice, many are called but few allow themselves to be chosen. These *ecclesia* heard his invitation, and by responding to it, selected themselves to participate with him in the Teaching. They freely submitted themselves to Jesus' leadership and teaching, and to their own transformation. Out of their own transformational process would develop their capacity to, in turn, lead others in a Community of the Teaching.

Jesus realized that the Community of the Teaching forming around him would last only as long as he did, yet he anticipated that the Teaching ("my church") would live beyond him. He saw the potential that some of the *ecclesia* might develop into teachers as part of his lineage. The Apostle Peter was apparently one of Jesus' more advanced students; the qualities Jesus saw developing in Peter led him to acknowledge that one day, in Jesus' absence, Peter might begin to form his own Community of the Teaching. We have seen how Peter and his fellow disciples attempted this, but were waylaid by their own fears and lack of spiritual experience. Jesus perhaps underestimated these factors when he passed the torch of the Teaching on to them, for the "Community of the Teaching" was subsumed in an "Organization of Dogma."

The New Church is a true Community of the Teaching, created in the spirit of what Jesus originally intended. Its sole purpose is to serve the transformation of awareness and the evolution of consciousness. It does so in a simple manner by accessing the spiritual power available in the presence of several elements. Jesus described these essential components of a Community of the Teaching when he taught, "Wherever two or more are gathered in my name, there am I in the midst of them."

The main element of the New Church consists of a gathering of two or more people who share a spiritual longing to attain the State of Being Jesus himself realized. As they consecrate themselves to their longing, this desire is purified and deepened, until the self who longs for awakening awakens to the Self who has no longing. In this mystical moment, the Presence of the Christ, or divine principle of all human beings, is present. Complete, whole and perfect in this now moment—the kingdom of God is at hand, within the awareness of this Presence.

Jesus' description of the New Church implies a place to gather. Is it an actual place, such as a building? Or is it an energetic or virtual space? Could it not be all of these? As long as the consecration is deep enough, and the commitment to be in relationship with God is strong enough, the physical space is secondary. In my own experience, having a large enough space for people to sit in a circle, dance around and rest supine on the floor is an environmental prerequisite for my Community of the Teaching. But I can also appreciate that under other circumstances the New Church could happen via the Internet, or by other means of communication in which physical presence might not be so important. As the Sufi poet Kabir says, "It is the intensity of the longing that does the work."

The other element implicit in Jesus' statement has to do with a facilitator. Jesus became friends with his disciples, but in the context of his Community of the Teaching, he definitely stood as their teacher and spiritual leader. In later sections of this chapter, I'll discuss more about the kind of leadership such a facilitator provides. For now, let it suffice for me to suggest that this is a necessary ingredient of the New Church.

The New Church, then, is very simple: two or more people filled with spiritual longing, a consecration to the possibility of Something More, a place (actual or virtual) to gather, and a spiritual teacher/leader. I believe this is a far more accurate translation of Jesus' original impulse to create a church than what the Old Church has become. It is more congruent with what we know of Jesus' ambitions, and more resonant with the spirit of awakening.

Therein lies the difficulty. This idea of church is so simple, it puts us face to face with our resistance to God. Sitting in the intimate circle of the New Church, there is nothing to do but be as you are. The ego is readily exposed and it feels as if one has been undressed. It's not hard to understand why Jesus' disciples made the church more complicated and distracting than he intended it to be—anything to avoid that exposure! Jesus tried to communicate his spiritual experience, and it was so threatening to those around him that they nailed him to a cross. Even as we long for it, we humans are terribly afraid of God's honest truth in us.

The beauty of the simplicity of the New Church is this: when we are ready to face the amazing truth of our own divine potential, we'll find there are no hoops to jump through in order to be saved, no rigid rules to follow so we can be right; in fact, there's no right way to go—nothing to defend or protect against at all. There's only an invitation to fall into the abyss of God's unending love and live there forever—here and now!

## B. What It Means to Be Human

The Old Church teaches that we are only human. Our true nature is sinful, and we need to be saved from ourselves. One day, if we do what we are told, we will be redeemed from our sinfulness and live with God in heaven. Jesus was more than human, so he can help us get back to God. He had to suffer a horrible death in order to save us, so we should feel grateful and guilty it was him and not us.

But Jesus himself did not believe what the Old Church teaches.

Instead, he offered humanity the possibility of realizing the full range of human potential. He did so by making his life an example of self-actualization. We don't know much about the years Jesus lived as an adolescent and young adult. Some suggest he traveled to India where studied with spiritual masters. Whether this can be proved or not, it makes sense Jesus perhaps received training in spiritual practices. Or maybe, as it sometimes happens, he had an awakening experience without a lot of preparation. It doesn't matter how it happened—it's more important that whatever happened to Jesus, he came through the experience with the knowledge, "These things that I do, greater things than these shall you also do." In other words, he perceived the capacity of every human being to become something more than what most have been conditioned to believe.

His ministry seemed to be one demonstration after another of how we can do what we typically think we can't. I love the story of Jesus and his interaction with the man at the pool at Bethesda. (John 5:2-9) This crippled man has been waiting for the opportunity to get in the pool's healing waters at the moment they are "troubled" by an angel. Jesus learns, however, that for thirty-eight years the man has avoided getting close enough to enter the pool when the time is right. We assume has plenty of good reasons—too many people crowding the place, the ailment that brought him there in the first place—which are all seemingly insurmountable obstacles. Yet, even the most reasonable and sympathetic person can see that none of these excuses could hold up for thirty-eight years!

Jesus uses his brilliant laser approach to cut through to the heart of the matter. "Do you really want to be healed?" he asks the man. The man considers for a moment. Then Jesus continues: "If you really want it, you can have it!" That's faith! Jesus' faith in our potential must be matched by our own. When it is, we can do and be what we never would have imagined possible.

The Old Church resembles the old rooster in the tale of the eagle in the chicken yard. According to the story an eagle was hatched from an egg that somehow was dropped into a chicken yard. He grew up surrounded by chickens who only knew how to flap their wings well enough fly a few feet at a time. Like them, he spent his days pecking at the ground trying to find insects and grains to eat. One day the eagle looks up and sees a majestic creature soaring far above the chicken yard. "What kind of magnificent being is that? What bliss it would be to fly free like that!" the eagle cried. "Oh," the rooster replied, "that's an eagle. We can't fly like that—we're only chickens! Our place is here, in the chicken yard." And so the eagle resumed his pecking alongside the others.

The New Church offers a different kind of faith to its constituents. It is not afraid for them to discover their potential and fly away to a greater freedom. It has no need to keep people in the chicken yard when it is their destiny to fly free. In fact, the New Church teaches people about that destiny and shows them how to manifest it.

The New Church perspective of human growth and development affirms that humans are self-evolving organisms. That is, people have the innate capacity to unfold a higher level of understanding and to embody that understanding in their life. Rather than seeing a person as a worm in the dust who must be scooped up out of the dirt and saved by an outside agent (the Old Church view), the New Church sees the same person at the onset of their spiritual path as a caterpillar. The caterpillar puts in a certain amount of time living a worm-like existence. But life has more in store for the caterpillar than eating leaves, and it enters a period of metamorphosis. The transformation requires the caterpillar to enter a cocoon in which its form completely changes into a kind of formless mush; after a time, however, a new form takes shape and a completely new being emerges as a butterfly who has an entirely different order of life available to it than when it was a caterpillar.

The New Church not only teaches about this possible transformation, but it also serves as a context of support while the transformation is taking place. Especially at the level of the Transitional Church, the New Church's teaching communicates acceptance of an individual's process of spiritual awakening, and challenges the individual to embrace that process and live it through to the point of Self-realization. It doesn't force anyone to grow, but it is committed to the potential for growth that everyone has. It refuses to foster unhealthy dependencies or cultivate denial of what is really so.

In the early days of my work at Unity-Midtown, I wrote a consecration statement read at almost every service:

> Unity-Midtown is consecrated to being a safe, healing place in which you will find love and acceptance for you just as you are; and a creative, alive place in which you will be challenged to become all that you can be, by realizing all that you are, as you travel your spiritual path.

As the church was forming, I focused on the first part of this statement. People loved the notion of a sanctuary from the world where they might find unconditional love and acceptance. Some people, however, complained I wasn't spiritual enough, or nice enough, or whatever enough—they didn't feel as loved and accepted as they thought they should. Then it dawned on me that my congregants expected that this unconditional love and acceptance was going to come from *me*! They were operating from the Old Church model that says such things come from outside the self, through the instrument of the Church. My intention had never been to do that; I simply wanted to give people the permission to love and accept themselves as they are, not to do it for them! The New Church offers people the possibility of finding unconditional love and acceptance for themselves, within themselves, through a direct experience of God.

I soon realized this is a level of responsibility a lot of churchgoing people are reluctant to assume. For some it feels wrong, or blasphemous to do so; for others, it's just too much effort. The people who the New Church serves best are those who are willing to be responsible for their experience in life. They tend not to want to see themselves as victims, and would rather be an active participant in their lives than a passive one. These are people who are more likely to embrace the challenge described in the second half of the Consecration Statement. They want to get on with actualizing themselves, and are willing to be facilitated in doing so. Other people tend to feel wronged even by the suggestion that there is a greater fulfillment available to them as a human being, because it invalidates their current condition. The New Church tends not to be helpful to these people.

There is a difference between invalidating peoples' experience and refusing to indulge their belief that their experience is the only one available to them. The New Church takes a compassionate stand for what is possible for humanity, even when that does not coincide with an individual's personal opinion that what is possible for humanity is impossible for them. The major healing the New Church offers is precisely in this realm of freeing people from their limiting beliefs.

In earlier days I spoke about the New Church service as being a venue for the practice of spiritual psychotherapy. That turned a lot of people off who thought psychotherapy was for really sick and crazy people. So, I modified my terminology to describe what I do in a New Church service as exploring the psychology of transformation. But the work is exactly the same— exposing psychic structures that have bound up our life energy, loosening the ties that bind them, and channeling the energy that is freed up into creative, embodied expression. The New Church provides the context for doing the work and for celebrating the liberation that often results from doing so. Beyond that it is simply a space for Spirit to evolve itself to the next level of being. And that has nothing to do with being "only human."

## C.  Word as Presence

One of the ways the Old Church has fallen short of its potential lies in its tendency to replace spiritual experience with words about that experience. It has reduced experience to words, and then made the concepts formed of those words into a belief system, making belief in that system a prerequisite for salvation. This is certainly one of the primary distortions wrought by traditional Christianity.

But could any church avoid using words in this way? Could the New Church actually be something other than a bunch of concepts and precepts? How would the New Church reintroduce spiritual experience as being more important than belief systems?

I have struggled with each of these questions for years. Again, there are no easy answers for the New Church. In the face of how expedient it is to use words about, rather than have, the experience of spiritual things, the fact remains they are not the same thing. There are words, and there are the experiences they attempt to describe.

The Old Church complicates things by making the words more important than what they describe. As a child, to become a full member of the Catholic Church you participate in the ritual of First Communion. To prepare for this momentous event, you must memorize Catechism questions and answers. There is no discussion of what it means—the only important thing is getting the wording exactly right!

The New Church, however, will flat out tell you that words don't make the difference. Words will always be inadequate to the task of describing the essentially indescribable, concepts will never approach the reality, and beliefs will not save you. Words make up a part of the New Church because they are an integral part of how people communicate with each other. But it is what we intend with the words we use—the consciousness that motivates their use—that is more important than what any of the words actually are.

Imagine the consecrated space of the New Church gathering. Visualize a group of twenty to forty people comfortably seated in a circle, in chairs, or perhaps on carpets with cushions on the floor. There's already been forty-five minutes or so spent with some kind of energetic exercise—stretching, dancing, spontaneous creative movement—followed by deep relaxation. Then twenty minutes or more of silent meditation. Now, there is an open space for the people in the group to share what is present for them.

Ideally, the words spoken in the context of a New Church service are an expression of the speaker's deepest and most essential self that arises in the moment of the speaking. Perhaps it's an intimation of what he or she connected with during the experience of the exercise or the meditation. Perhaps it's a creative expression, or a poem about the dance. As the speaker, you would just open your mouth and speak without concern for what you were about to say. You would speak of what was true for you *in the moment as you spoke*. You wouldn't worry if what you said made sense. Maybe you would allow yourself to be a mouthpiece for some deep, creative intelligence that wanted to speak through you.

In actual practice, however, you'd get a real mixed bag, and this too is part of the authentic experience the New Church provides. As the space opens for sharing, immediately you'll hear someone get into their head about the meaning of life, or the proper way to meditate. Someone else will try to impress the group with a selection they picked to read sometime during the week. And what you notice is that whenever something is contrived, you become acutely aware of that fact!

Because a New Church gathering is consecrated to consciousness, it simply doesn't matter if the right thing is said, or if what is said is done in the right way. It becomes as plain as the nose on your face—to you and anyone else who happens to be paying attention—if you're trying to hide or control or flatter, or run any number of strategies to impress the group. There's no judgement about this—just the ongoing opportunity to notice what's so as the ego runs the show. The words the ego uses have a certain quality to them—a false ring, a forcing current, slick salesmanship—and the New Church service offers the occasion to see what the ego is up to. And one of the intents of a New Church service is just that—to reveal the ego as a part of one's experience against the backdrop of a more whole, or larger Self, so the reality and potentials of this context of greater awareness might be accessed.

As I describe this New Church service, I am aware that most forms of the Old Church limit the amount and kind of speaking that can take place in a church service. The thought of speaking out in a church service terrifies many people. Before I began my ministerial training, I thought only people with religious credentials had the authority to speak about spiritual matters. In developing the New Church, however, I realized how one-sided it was for me, the minister, to be the only voice heard on Sunday mornings. Gradually I introduced opportunities for others to share within the service. People were scheduled to come to the platform and read a selection from Unity's "Daily Word" meditation magazine, and then to take a minute or two to comment on what it meant to them. Later on, we used wireless microphones to allow people to share from their auditorium seats as part of a dialogue with me about the topic for my talk. In every case, the informal sharing on the part of these congregants enlivened the service, bringing something real and energetic to what could otherwise be a repetitious order of service. I never knew what would come out of someone's mouth, and so I had to really listen in order to be able to respond, or not, according to what was most appropriate.

As we moved from theatre-style seating to church-in-the-round, the sharing became more intimate, and probably too intense for a lot of people (judging by the dramatic drop in attendance at this point). After all, this was a public gathering, not a workshop. But, by and large, including ordinary people's observations and emotional reactions as part of even the more traditional version of the New Church (what I've named Transitional Church) is an innovation worth keeping. The practice of including spontaneous sharing could be easily adapted to any more traditional service, with the effect of immediately bringing more life, energy and Spirit into the experience of the moment.

If words are motivated by a desire for greater consciousness, and if there is an invitation to be spontaneous and unselfconscious in speaking them, the words themselves become a powerful tool for bringing a person present to the moment. The act of speaking transforms a passive observer into a participant, and reminds him or her of the capacity to author experience, to be the authority in one's own life. With such an endorsement of inner authority, the New Church will make it possible for individuals to avoid wielding words as the weapon of an outer authority, nor use them to convert or condemn those with different perspectives.

Ultimately, the silent radiance of an inner spiritual realization, like the one Jesus emanated, will impact far more powerfully than any words.

## D. Encouragement of Spiritual Maturity

The Old Church views individuals through the lens of a parental dynamic. The Old Church serves the parental function, while its members play out the role of children. The children in this Old Church family are discouraged from growing up spiritually.

Instead, they attempt to recreate an ideal family within the church "home," trying to find in the church family the perfect, unconditional love they didn't get from their family. Church members remain in a childish, dependent stage of development in which they devote their energies to pleasing the parental authority. The Old Church emphasizes obedience rather than creativity, thus thwarting individuation and self-actualization. Although the individuals within the church fail to grow up, the Old Church expands, because its members lack sufficient maturity to leave it.

By contrast, the New Church sees human beings as the potential for both human and divine expression. The New Church itself is an expression of the evolutionary impulse—it *is* that impulse in action! It encourages the process of evolution, and, consequently, the growth and development of the people who participate in it.

So, the main thrust of the New Church is to energize and propel individuals into a trajectory leading to spiritual awakening. Beyond those years when a child is physically dependent on her parents, there is no reason to foster dependency. The New Church is for people who want to mature spiritually. It serves best those who have no interest in remaining a "child" of God— people who will participate in the New Church rather than simply attend it.

For that reason a certain amount of preparation is necessary to bring people to the point that they will benefit from what the New Church offers. If they come to the New Church without this preparation, they tend to experience the invitation to transform their lives as an unreasonable request; they resist change and resent the agent who brings it. One must be ready to let go of seeing oneself as a victim of life circumstances and people, and willing to assume the responsibilities of growing up.

To this end, the New Church considers psychotherapy to be an invaluable aid to the maturation process, and an effective preparation for the deeper spiritual practices offered by the New Church. Any type of therapy that addresses inner child healing work will support an individual in working through dependency issues. Even more valuable are psychotherapeutic models such as the Pathwork, a system based on the lectures of Eva Pierrakos, that are designed to help an individual work through issues that arise at each stage of development, from the egoic to the transpersonal.

In preparing a prospective New Church participant to consciously enter a process of spiritual growth, it helps to provide them with a cognitive understanding of the psychology of transformation. When one is emotionally and mentally ready, the individual will find it easier to take responsibility for his or her experience. The challenge to the ego inherent in the process of discovering and dissolving its defenses will be allowed rather than resisted.

Since the participants in the New Church are willing to move out of dependent relationships and take responsibility for their spiritual development, there is no need for the New Church to act as a parental authority. What the New Church does offer, however, is the guidance and assistance of a Teacher, who serves as spiritual authority for each New Church gathering of two or more.

The New Church, a Community of the Teaching is attracted to and forms around a Teacher who is consecrated to bringing forth the Teaching at the level of his or her understanding of it. As Jesus said, "My sheep will hear my voice." When students are ready, they will be attracted to a Teacher's being, because he or she *is* the incarnation of the Teaching at the level which the student can receive it. The Teacher's authority is a *not* a function of organizational credentials, but of the depth of awareness the Teacher can access.

Every New Church needs such a spiritually attractive, consecrated Teacher to concentrate the attention of the New Church community and bring it into a deeper relationship with the Teaching.

I've consulted with several Unity churches over the past ten years who were considering an alternative church format. One in particular sticks out in my mind. This small church had formed out of a book discussion group, and had been holding Sunday services for several years. It had never had a spiritual leader. The congregants liked having a different guest speaker come in every week to give them a lesson. But then the Board of Directors grew tired of scheduling these guests, and so the church decided to hire a minister—however, not as a spiritual leader, but as an administrator. The Board reasoned that they wanted to avoid having only one person's perspective presented each week, but I believe that this group really wanted to avoid committing to the spiritual growth a relationship with a spiritual teacher would entail.

It is precisely within the context of a relationship with a Teacher, however, that most growth will occur. Jesus said to his community, "Whoever is near to me is near to the fire." The fire of transformation burns hottest in relationship with the Teacher, and there is a strong possibility for awakening here. One of the gifts a consecrated Teacher brings to the community is the availability for a committed, long-term relationship—you might call it a spiritual partnership. The roles of Teacher and Student are clearly defined in this relationship. In such a partnership, my own Teacher, Richard Moss, says, the Teacher learns by teaching, and the Student teaches by learning.

Other important relationships form between community members, and the whole dynamic of the New Church Community of the Teaching provides grist for the transformational mill. In this way, the New Church serves not only as a classroom but also as a laboratory. The lesson and the practice all encourage the participants to transcend and include less developed aspects of self, to allow for the fullness of human potential to unfold.

I want to emphasize, however, that the New Church Community is not intended to be an ideal family, nor is the Teacher a glorified parent, or the other Students siblings. This is not to say that unconscious expectations of this sort won't be projected onto the New Church. So rather than trying to fulfill these expectations, the New Church, is dedicated to making them conscious. With greater consciousness, comes a greater capacity to be self-responsible. With greater self-responsibility comes greater maturity. With greater maturity comes the ability to creatively participate in the conscious evolution of humanity.

## E.   The Power Within

The Old Church is designed to dominate its members and control their lives both spiritually and otherwise. It effectively plays on the insecurities people have about human existence, with their ultimate fear being that if they are not saved by the

Old Church they will go to hell for eternity. The Old Church emphasizes only the survival end of the continuum of human experience, and makes people afraid to experiment to know who they might be if they were more actualized. The Old Church thrives because people are cowed by fear into dependent relationships with those who are willing to hold the power of authority over them. Of course, the fault cannot be found exclusively with the Old Church. There were and are a lot of people willing for it to be so; they cast their vote for the Old Church power structure by their unwillingness to be an authority for themselves.

The New Church, on the other hand, is not motivated by fear or dependency born of fear. It is a context, not for controlling fear, but for meeting fear with faith. We have seen how Jesus refused to use political means to avoid his fate, preferring to meet it head on. The New Church operates in a similar fashion. It doesn't need or want to be powerful in any outer sense; rather, it invites participants to draw on a source of power within themselves. That power has the capacity to transform our experience of the circumstances of life at the deepest level; In doing so, it reveals what is brightest and most beautiful within us and opens the way for us to express this in our daily life.

The New Church, while it has no interest in dominating its participants with a rigid political hierarchy, does not abdicate the responsibility of leadership. Rather, the New Church uses leadership to empower its people through the vehicle of consecrated spiritual teaching and leadership.

For the New Church to offer spiritual empowerment, there must be a leader who is consecrated to bringing forth the innate spiritual power in the participants. This means the leader must be committed to something more than the personal likes and dislikes of either the congregation or themselves. In most cases the leader of the New Church will be the same person as the Teacher; the "something more" will be the Teaching.

A lot of people, Americans especially, balk at the notion of non-democratic leadership. I did too. Democracy, or even better, consensus rule, seemed the antidote to the abuses perpetrated by the Old Church hierarchy. So, when I first conceived of the New Church, I envisioned a kind of leaderless church, where everyone participated in making decisions about everything. But in my actual work at Unity-Midtown, I soon discovered that not everyone had sufficient interest in doing this, nor were they committed and motivated enough to generate a leaderless church. Neither was everyone experienced enough to make a conscious contribution to the discussion, particularly about matters concerning spiritual practices. I learned that a leaderless church, or one with a weak leader who looks to the congregation for guidance, flounders at the level of consciousness of the least developed participants—the ones who are least ready for transformation—and decisions made in this way tend to function more like a popularity contest than anything else. Co-dependency thrives in such an environment, and real spiritual work grinds to a halt.

On the surface, the New Church's solution goes against the grain of the democratic process. The leader of a New Church is less likely to be someone chosen by a congregation by popular vote and more likely someone, who in the manner of the judges of the Old Testament, arises in response to the call of a New Church gathering, or whose Being, in the way of Jesus, simply calls people to them.

In either case, when a prospective Leader offers his or her services, if the offer is sincere and well-intended, and the vision he or she holds finds resonance, there may be a good match with a group of Followers. Effective spiritual leadership—the type that is not threatened by the empowerment of those who follow —requires a level of spiritual experience and awareness that hasn't been realized by many people. The "matching" of a Leader with a Following is often not a rational process. There are also safeguards built in to this way of filling a void in leadership, since the people of any congregation always retain the right to "vote" with their feet, and often do so in confirmation or rejection of a candidate who responds to a call.

For similar reasons, traditional methods of assigning credentials to a potential Leader may not hold up. Truly spiritual leadership cannot be ordained by any organizational hierarchy. In spiritual terms, it is the holoarchy, or Great Chain of Being, that ordains true spiritual leaders, and the New Church simply recognizes this ordination. Spiritual leaders become ordained, then, not according to gender or other doctrinal standards, but purely on the basis of their level of being. One who has received this inner ordination is recognized, not by what they say or do so much as by who they are. Spiritual leaders of this sort can be trained, but the training curriculum for effective leadership must primarily focus on personal and spiritual growth rather than on the development of administrative skills.

If an ordained spiritual leader of the New Church acts in ways that are not congruent with who they are, isn't there a potential for the power to be abused?

Certainly there are consequences for any unconscious act. The New Church, however, claims that we exist within a common ground of Being that empowers us to be co-creators of every experience in life. We are incapable of being victims. So, the kind of abuse of power that occurs in the Old Church is not such an issue in the New Church, because there is simply no one present in the New Church who can be abused.

New Church participants, by definition, are not children who need to be taken care of. They are spiritually maturing adults who take responsibility for their experiences in life. They are willing to look within any circumstance and see what they have contributed to it. They are unlikely, in the first place, to allow themselves to be victimized. If something inappropriate takes place, however, they are empowered to simply say no to it. They stand entirely at choice when it comes to being damaged by the unconscious acts of a leader; in fact, they may grow tremendously in working through an apparently abusive situation[26].

The New Church, as a gathering of two or more, is a context for committed relationship between its leaders and participants. The spiritual partnership of Teacher and Student translates into a similar intimacy between Leader and Follower. The responsibility a leader holds in that relationship does not preclude friendship with the members of the community. But this is a transpersonal friendship—one not so much based in personal liking so much as it is in the common consecration to the more universal purpose of spiritual awakening. When sufficient spiritual empowerment occurs, followers in the New Church may become leaders in their own right. When there is a call to do so, the New Church supports new leaders and the Community of the Teaching they attract.

In short, the New Church supports and facilitates the natural unfoldment of human potential. Trust and faith in Life itself empower the possible human to be all that he or she already is.

## F.   Small Business Church

Old Church, or Churchianity, has made a big business out of religion. It markets the religious message with the same intensity as Madison Avenue sells everything else in America. Ostensibly, this is to serve the Great Commission—to convert the world into Christian believers. By building more, bigger, better churches, however, Churchianity seems more concerned with saturating world civilization with its culture than with evolving the spiritual consciousness of the people on this planet.

The New Church shows little interest in this spiritual materialism. It is, in the words of Kabir, "one soul meeting another" for the purpose of spiritual awakening. Because the New Church is based on the intimacy of "two or more," any one New Church group need only be as large as allows for sharing between participants. An association of New Churches might accommodate a number of groups under its umbrella, but even such an association, to be an effective spiritual organization, needs to be small enough to foster a close relationships between the members.

If the Old Church measures its success by the number of people in its churches, or the amount of money in its collection plate, or the size of its church buildings, how does the New Church know it is getting its job done?

We may never know. Spiritual work is invisible work. A change in level of being may not always be observable; the fruits produced by the tree of realization may not always be seen by the sensual eye. These facts aside, we have to wonder who asks the question in the first place? Does God really care if the New Church (or the Old Church, for that matter) is doing a good job? Aren't such concerns more the kind of thing the ego is interested in? If so, the ego is constantly disappointed by the New Church.

The New Church is not so much about getting something done as it is about being in the process of whatever life offers in the moment. It simply offers individuals the invitation to be present to what is happening right here, right now. It has nowhere

it wants to go, nothing it wants to do. Nor does it have any specific agenda for its participants.

If it wants people to do anything, the New Church says, "Be
who you really are." It says this both to individual participants,
and to groups of "two or more." The New Church is not a
movement that needs to be promoted. It is a context in which
several elements exist that promote movement from one level of
being to another, higher one. Self-inquiry, committed transpersonal relationship, spiritual experience—the New Church offers
itself as an energetic and/or physical space in which these things
may occur.

What's an ego to make of all of this? Not much! But that's
the point. Any church that Jesus would have founded would not
have held much interest for the ego. Or for contemporary
church-builders. The ego's sole interest in the New Church
would be to formulate a strategy to co-opt the simplicity of its
purpose and form. To do just what was done to Jesus' original
impulse to turn it into a political and business operation. To
dogmatize the Teaching, to hold on to participants rather than
letting them grow and develop.

It would be arrogant to insist that the New Church is imper-
vious to these kinds of distortions. And it would be foolish to
imagine that the New Church knows how to magically deal with
its susceptibility. Yet, without idealizing the New Church, perhaps one can realistically hope that with some conscious
awareness of the pitfalls that the organization of spiritual practice creates, some of the larger mistakes made by the Old Church
might be avoided. Of course, others will be made, which over
time will be criticized by others with a greater understanding.
Such is the nature of evolution. It is not wrong to make a mistake. It's only a mistake not to learn from it. And even this may
be redeemed by the consciousness brought to bear by any conse-
quent suffering.

The intent, however, with which the New Church emerges
onto the American religious scene, is to serve spiritual needs, not
material ones. The New Church acknowledges the strong tendency in people to look for the most immediate comforting
resolution to any of their needs, and offers support in not identifying with any dependency on outside agents, including itself.
The perpetuation of the New Church is not of particular interest

to the New Church. It serves and is sustained by those who benefit from participating in the Community of the Teaching.

In other words, any particular New Church does not need to be permanent in order to be effective. In fact, the New Church is like a good therapist; at some point, if the work is really effective, it outgrows its usefulness. Energy typically devoted in the Old Church to sustaining the organization becomes available for other purposes. A specific New Church group is not so much something to belong to as it is something that *is*, as long as the various elements agree to co-exist. And when they don't, it doesn't.

In general practice, a group will be sustained as long as there is a spiritual teacher/leader as a committed presence at the center of the community. Just as when the Students are ready the Teacher appears, when the Teacher dies or leaves, it may be appropriate for that group to dissolve. A new Teacher may arise from within its ranks to assume leadership. But the organic nature of the New Church presumes that this will in fact be an entirely new expression or Community of the Teaching; any desire to recreate the way it used to be is best worked through as part of a grieving process that will allow a new creation to come forth. It is understood that the Teaching finds its way into expression in a unique way through each Teacher. The Community that forms around each Teacher is also unique. There is a constant shift in the group dynamic as the Teacher grows, as community members grow, as membership within the group changes—all these factor into the transformation of individuals within the Community.

Because the New Church is not stable in the way of the Old Church "institution," it doesn't lend itself to the kind of socialization tasks that the Old Church served. Nor does it actively promote a political agenda in the sense of making a platform or endorsing candidates. The New Church impacts culture, but it does so as a by-product of its work. The New Church doesn't set out to establish a moral or ethical standard of conduct for its participants—it is only interested in increasing consciousness. Of course, with greater awareness it may prove that, as a minister friend once said, if we know better, we will do better.

The New Church represents an emerging development in religious organization. As an evolutionary product of what Ken

Wilber has referred to as a "dialectic of progress," the New Church undertakes a deeper level of spiritual work than the Old Church. Evolution, Wilber tells us, produces greater depth and less span. The New Church transcends and includes the Old Church. Therefore there will always be more people involved in the Old Church, and fewer in the New Church. As a culture, we tend to confuse bigger with better, but it is more true from an evolutionary perspective, at least, to realize that the church with less span (fewer members) actually has more depth and greater consciousness. The small numbers of the New Church keep it from capturing the "market share" or dominating the political scene. But, remember, the New Church has no interest in these.

The intimate relationship within small groups of "two or more" creates the possibility of the Many realizing they are One and a part of an ever-expanding All. This epiphany is at the heart of all human longing. The New Church simply arises to help people fulfill this longing directly. In its time the New Church will fall away, for the same purpose.

# 16

# A Curriculum for
# Transformation

*Humanity*
*Create with me*
*A place for us*
*To human be.*
*This heals me*
*And heals thee*
*And we become*
*Humanity.*

**BENJAMIN BREWER,**
**New Church Participant**

The New Church is more than a knee-jerk reaction to the
Old Church. It is part of the evolutionary development of
religious expression. Table 16.1 summarizes my view of
the Western church. It describes church evolving through three
distinct phases: first the Old Church, which tends to serve people
who seek fulfillment of very basic needs; next, the Transitional
Church, attractive to individuals who have outgrown the Old
Church and whose survival and security needs have been met,
and who seek the empowerment that will prepare them for self-
actualization; and, last, the New Church, which provides the opportunity for transformational experiences for those who have
moved almost completely into the realm of Being-values.

Each phase of church has a particular motivating quality and
a specific intent, both conscious and unconscious, for what it offers. Each targets an audience at a different stage of human
development. Each is outgrown as its participants experience the
evolutionary impulse to advance to the next psychological stage

## Table 16.1  An Evolutionary Model of Church

|  | Old Church | Transitional Church | New Church |
|---|---|---|---|
| **History** | 0–2000 C.E. Jesus' teaching interpreted by his disciples. Within 200–300 years of Jesus' death church hierarchy ritualizes and formalizes church doctrine and dogma. Protestant Reformation makes adjustments to Catholic abuses but maintains basic Christian fear-based theology and salvation/redemption model.. | Late 19th Century. Metaphysical Christianity develops in America. New Thought churches (e.g. Unity, Religious Science) Continues to use traditional church services formats, and familiar religious observances, while including empowering content and more participatory organizational structure. | Late 20th century. Emerges from human potential movement, exploration of altered states of consciousness, 12 Step recovery movement, and disillusionment with traditional religious authority and organized religion. Initially finds expression within some Transitional Church settings, and also in separate venues. |
| **Positive Intent** | To provide means for salvation of fallen humanity, thus relieving a primary insecurity of existence. | To empower and encourage people to assume greater levels of self-responsibility in co-creation of life experiences. | To create context for direct experience of God in the spirit of Jesus' teaching, "Where two or more are gathered in my name, there am I in the midst of them.." |
| **Pitfalls** | Sustained dependency of constituents in order to maintain power structure of religious organization. | Possible use of spiritual principles merely to maintain level of ego comfort. | Potential discrediting of more traditional forms and creation of a spiritual elite. |

|  | Old Church | Transitional Church | New Church |
|---|---|---|---|
| **Primary Motivation to Participate** | Fear that deficiency needs will not be met.<br><br>"Save me." | Spiritual longing arising from need for love, acceptance, and esteem.<br><br>"I want to love and be loved." | Faith in the ever-expanding potential of humankind and a desire to fulfill that potential.<br><br>"I choose to be all that I was created to be." |
| **Method** | Parental dynamic offers safety to dependent members. | Creates a "healthy" church family model to counteract "dysfunctional" family Old Church | Offers an intimate space for transformation through self-inquiry, committed relationship, and spiritual experience. |
| **Structure** | Dominance hierarchy. | Selection of church leaders by quasi-democratic process. | Small groups of two or more who contract with a spiritual teacher. |
| **Leadership** | Authoritarian: Priest or Minister | Nurturing: Priest or Minister | Facilitative: Spiritual Teacher |
| **Short-comings** | May limit or postpone spiritual experience and expression of members by keeping them dependent on the Old Church. | This bridge to transformation may be mistaken for the destination, causing participants not to move to next level when appropriate. | Significant commitment and self-responsibility makes it not readily accessible to the masses.. Operates outside of egoic references, so results are largely intangible to outside observers. |
| **Impulse to Evolve** | Feeling of confinement, abuse, and/or disbelief. . | Longing for something more, a sense of emptiness or loss of meaning. | Dissolution of ordinary sense of self into the experience of Oneness. |

of development. We see that each phase of Church has its short-comings, and that to a large extent, the phase that succeeds it attempts to resolve these.

Seeing church as a process unfolding itself in an evolutionary fashion has the benefit of helping us detach from the notion that there is only one way a church can or should be. Realizing that church can and should express differently at each stage, it be-comes easier to align with evolution rather than fight it. If one can identify the stage of development a person is growing into, one can easily see which phase of church is best suited to support their growth. Then, instead of insisting that all people should find satisfaction in just going to church, regardless of what that church offers, individuals' spiritual needs can be met at the ap-propriate level.

This applies to the clergy as well. One benefit to burned out ministers and other church leaders is that this way of looking at church also makes it very clear that the leadership task is differ-ent in the different phases. This allows clergy to actualize more of their ministerial potential as their spiritual awareness expands. No leader needs to stay in the pulpit preaching to people at an entry-level of development when they are capable of facilitating constituents at a more developed stage. When the capacity to teach at a higher level has increased, clergy need to be encouraged to move into a new, more challenging and fulfilling situation for themselves in the phase that is more appropriate to them.

We discussed the Old Church at great length in Part Two, so I'd now like to devote attention to the Transitional Church. To do that I need to introduce a framework describing the nature of the Transitional Church and how it relates to the New Church. But first, let me share the process of realization that led me to formulate this structure.

From the start of my pioneering effort at Unity-Midtown I in-tended to create a New Church; however, as I've recounted, I had no idea when I began what that was. I started with a very flexible order of service, introduced some rituals adapted from other spiri-tual traditions such as lighting candles to the four cardinal directions, and invited the congregation to dialogue with me in the place of a sermon. I encouraged participation and interaction in many parts of the service—sometimes everyone danced, other times people bowed to each other in silence. I often improvised in the service according to my inspiration in the moment.

As far-out as some of things I tried were, in retrospect, I see the result of my efforts, for the most part, was actually a Transitional Church. Until the end of the New Church "experiment," I had no words to describe the kind of church that emerged, and it wasn't until the last year of my tenure as spiritual leader that I finally realized there was a difference between the New Church I envisioned and the Transitional Church I'd created. When I did realize this, I then understood why all my attempts to do transformational work in the context of a Transitional Church failed to be effective with most people. Even though I intuitively felt I was doing some of my most powerful teaching and facilitation, only a few people actually "got" what I was offering. I initially made the mistake of thinking people were simply being willful or dense in their resistance, or that I was simply not capable of giving them more of what they seemed to want. But then, informed by Ken Wilber's writing and a deeper study of Maslow's Hierarchy of Needs, it came to me that what I was facilitating was simply not appropriate to the level on which I was teaching, but belonged to another level altogether.

With this realization I was able to more readily conceive of an evolutionary unfoldment of church, and to see that what I call the New Church is but the most recent expression of progress in the religious organizational realm. Thinking along these lines I developed a Curriculum for Transformation, which summarizes the type of spiritual work practices and programs that would take someone across the Transitional Church bridge to the New Church (Table 16.2).

The Curriculum for Transformation zooms in on church evolution to specifically outline the stages in the transformative process. Looking at the progression from one stage to the next, it becomes apparent that movement through the Curriculum presumes engagement with, and a certain level of mastery of, the levels that precede it. Another level always supercedes the one before it, until one finally realizes God/ Self, and even this realization is presumed to be an infinitely expanding one. The Curriculum for Transformation implicitly allows for the fact that mystical realization may also occur spontaneously at any point in this process, and if it does, the necessity of moving through levels

## Table 16.2:  A Curriculum for Transformation

| Level | Part One | Part Two | Part Three | Part Four |
|---|---|---|---|---|
| Program | Cognitive Course | Spiritual Practice Session | Mentor Program | Spiritual Leadership Training |
| Setting | Small group (up to 20) discussion with leader and/or guided self-study. | Weekly gathering of 10-100 people in large room with sound system. | Group of 15-20 who meet 10 weekends with Spiritual Teacher over 2 years. | Study with teacher over 2 years with practicum experiences . |
| Aims to Provide | Cognitive basis for understanding human capacity for spiritual realization and to outline the psychological process involved in transformation. | Context for committing to the practice of observing and transforming identification with the ego; for celebrating liberating shifts from ego attachments. | Intense focus on individual ego strategies for resisting and/or avoiding relationship with God, self, and others. | Preparation for persons called to spiritual service and the creation of contexts to facilitate the spiritual growth and development of others. |
| Content | Topics dealing with the psychology of transformation. | Movement, meditation, individual and group process, spiritual teaching. | Spiritual practices deepened with commitments to self-inquiry, relationship to Teacher; creative expression; dream work.<br><br>4 basic questions: Who am I? What really matters? How do I avoid relationship? How am I called to serve? | Focused attention on the questions: What motivates my spiritual leadership? Who am I being when I am being a minister?<br><br>Skills training, including legal / financial aspects<br><br>Therapy to address psychological issues. |

is obviously moot. At this stage of Being, perspective shifts and all levels disappear. A process is necessary only from the perspective of the unrealized being. For most people, however, the Curriculum for Transformation provides a step-by-step path for the spiritual seeker in the context of church.

## The Transitional Church

The Transitional Church serves as an important bridge between Old Church and New Church. By definition, a Transitional Church is one that retains many of the trappings of the Old Church—a traditional setting, a customary order of service, familiar religious observances and church activities—while offering a significant alteration in the content it delivers. The Transitional Church, like the Old Church, translates life for its members. It interprets for them what is good and meaningful. The interpretation it offers, however, is one that empowers listeners, preparing them to take on the risks inherent in transformation. The content of the Transitional Church encourages people to assume greater responsibility for their experience in life. Along with teaching the spiritual principles that govern co-creation with God, the Transitional Church also offers a cognitive understanding of the psychology of transformation, and suggests how one will be able to apply it.

The Transitional Church teaches people to meet their own needs for love, acceptance and esteem, and prepare to consider higher levels of being. Transitional Church opens the way to deeper spiritual connection by cultivating an appreciation of what a human being can be and do. It supports people in letting go of past dependencies and empowers them to take the risk to fulfill their potential. The parental dynamic still operates at the Transitional Church level. But now this shows up looking more like the mother bird who shows her baby how to take flight from the nest, and then leaves him to it.

Referring again to the analogy of the caterpillar's metamorphosis into a butterfly, the Transitional Church tells caterpillars about their destiny. It shows them how to approach the change awaiting them, provides encouragement for every step taken. Then, ideally, Transitional Church waves goodbye to the caterpillar as it spins a cocoon and begins its transformational journey to its new State of Being as a butterfly.

The difficulty with using an evolutionary framework for identifying the phases of church is that Transitional Churches don't generally want to consider themselves transitional. In a workshop I facilitate for church groups, I show congregants Maslow's Hierarchy labeled with the various needs and ask them to point out which of the need-levels they identify with. (Figure 16. 1) Usually without much hesitation they select two levels of need, Belonging and Esteem.

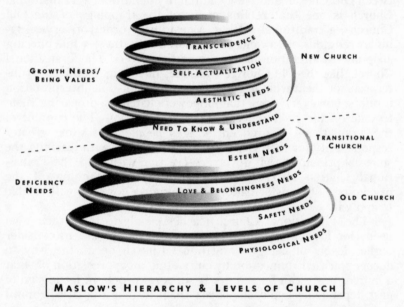

**MASLOW'S HIERARCHY & LEVELS OF CHURCH**

Figure 16.1

People drawn to the Transitional Church may have a strong need to belong to a church where they hope they will find love and esteem forever. When their church seems to offer an idealized or "healthy" version of family (to replace the one many people working at this level are conscious they never had), there is a tendency to want to make sure this replacement version doesn't fall apart the way their original family might have done. People who insist that the church meet their needs for love, acceptance and esteem (as opposed to their learning there how to meet these needs themselves), are often not interested in a possible next step beyond the Transitional Church level.

The church often becomes a preoccupation for such people. Many of them entrench themselves in lay leadership positions where they work to stabilize the church rather than encourage its possible dynamism. For them, it is definitely not a good thing when church members grow up and out of their "family." To avoid triggering issues of abandonment the church becomes, not a vehicle that enables one to travel a spiritual path leading to greater awareness experiences, but an end-in-itself that must be maintained at all costs.

From an evolutionary perspective, this is where Transitional Churches often unconsciously get caught up in their own shortcomings. Like the Old Church and, to some extent, the New Church, the Transitional Church believes in itself, identifies with its mission, and invests time and effort promoting its good ideas. In other words, Transitional Church forms an ego. The trouble the church-ego causes is similar to the trouble caused by the human ego, which is that it has unconscious as well as conscious intents, and some of these unconscious intents will tend to have a negating or limiting aspect. The Old Church and Transitional Church both share an unconscious motivation that has to do with self-preservation. That is, they are as concerned for the maintenance of their organizations as they are interested in serving their spiritual purpose, and, in practice, the former will tend to take precedence over the latter.

This is not unlike the dynamic in which the ego claims to be the entirety of who we are. The ego identifies us as a separate entity with a discrete body that can be threatened and die. Because when the body dies, so does "I," survival fears tend to justify all kinds of strategies for defending ourselves, even when the actual threat is emotional and not physical at all. We generally believe what the ego tells us; believing the ego to be "me," we don't question its assumptions.

Realized beings, though, have a different perspective, one that transcends the ego. Spiritual masters teach that *consciousness* is the primary reality. The ego arises in consciousness as a thought, not the other way around. From this realized perspective, we are separate in thought only, so no particular defense of "self" is really necessary; in fact, the ego itself is ultimately unnecessary. Of course, no self-respecting ego likes the sound of that, and it is also true the world requires a certain amount of ego for us to be able to function in it. In the best case, however, the ego eventually recognizes its fear-based limitations, and surrenders itself in service to the transcendent reality, ultimately finding peace in a state of unified being with its source, Consciousness.

Like the human ego, a church's ego has an underlying agenda that is often self-serving. Only to the extent that this agenda is dealt with in a conscious way can we really trust what the church is up to. Otherwise, we cannot assume it is only serving God, but must suspect that it is indulging in a fear-filled fantasy that rejects the true purpose of any church to facilitate spiritual realization.

When they are conscious, I believe Transitional Churches such as Unity, Religious Science, Unitarian, Creation Spirituality and other kinds of "New Thought" churches, are in the best position to support the evolution of consciousness in the world today. How can they do this? Transitional Churches need to acknowledge that they are a bridge, and not the destination.

Then, rather than grabbing and holding on to the people who come to their churches, they will do what they do best: receive those who have left the Old Church; convey an empowering message about their human potential; and provide, at the appropriate time, a graceful graduation to the next level of spiritual work. There will always be a flow of people who can use the services of a Transitional Church, so there is no real need for them to worry about having nothing to do. Transitional Churches can place what they do in the service of transformation, assured of their continuity.

There is a real need for Transitional Churches to understand the importance of the role they play in the Curriculum. I do not envision people walking in off the streets to participate in New Church services. If the New Church is to function as a Community of the Teaching, there has to be a way for people to be exposed to the Teaching and the Teacher in an introductory sort of way, and the Transitional Church setting can provide this.

To establish a way to prepare people for the New Church, I have developed a course of study that summarizes the cognitive information necessary for entry into the transformative environment of the New Church. This provides a philosophical and spiritual foundation I would want anyone who was going to do deeper work with me to have at least thought about and discussed with a trained facilitator. This course of study, then, is designed as an adjunct to regular Transitional Church services and activities, and, when completed, serves as an indication of the participant's readiness to proceed to the New Church.

Of course, no one should feel they must leave the Transitional Church setting. Because it has more of a social aspect than the New Church, some people might choose to continue to enjoy it for a long time. In general, however, most people will cycle through the Transitional Church in two to three years. This is currently the average length of participation in Unity churches, and matches my experience at Unity-Midtown. For many years we spent hours of Board meetings discussing the "problem" of people not staying longer. Now it is clear that people leave, often not because there is something wrong, but because they've outgrown what's offered. The New Church creates a place for people to go beyond Transitional Church, if and when they are ready and want to go there.

In summary, the Transitional Church appears to be like the Old Church. It has church services on Sunday mornings, celebrates holidays such as Christmas and Easter, has a church chorus, a children's program, a bookstore, and holds potluck suppers, bake sales and the like. The message, however, is uplifting and positive in tone, and the content encourages the listener to be all he or she can be. Transitional Church does not require adherence to a particular belief system, so the environment tends to be inclusive of diverse types of persons. Commitment to spiritual practices is not obligatory in the Transitional Church, yet the Transitional Church points the way to the next step where such practice forms the opening for a direct experience of God.

❧

## The New Church

The New Church is designed to facilitate the fulfillment of the human Being-needs, the need to self-actualize and transcend. It has several levels of participation beginning with Part Two of the Curriculum for Transformation. Part Two's Spiritual Practice Service provides for regular experiential events intended to open an energetic space for the direct experience of God.

The inspiration for the format I use for this grew out of a variety of experiences I encountered in my work on myself. These include conferences with Richard Moss, Core Energetics emotional release work, holotopic breathwork, mindfulness meditation, Twelve Step recovery groups, Pathwork process groups, an Experience Week at the Findhorn Foundation (a transformational community in northern Scotland), and years of individual work in therapy. The idea behind this Spiritual Practice Service is to create a two-hour experience of varying physical and emotional intensity for the purpose of inducing a heightened state of awareness. In this state participants may access an essential part of themselves and make contact with that deeper aspect in others. Additionally, an energetic dynamic builds from session to session, as the sustained commitment of the Teacher/Leader and the participants deepens the intention behind the meetings.

For ten months, I created such a service on a weekly basis at Unity-Midtown Church. It is a very simple format that can easily be adapted to a variety of venues. It was scheduled to take place at 9:30 a.m., before the 11:00 a.m. Transitional Church service, in case people wanted to participate in both services. The first service generated so much expansive energy, however, it was often difficult to get people contained enough to sit through a more traditional service afterwards. We ended up creating more of an interval between the two services to accommodate this.(One could offer the New Church service later in the day, or on another day besides Sunday altogether so as to avoid any conflicts such as this, and also to emphasize the distinct purposes of the two services.)

I used the large banquet hall in the same building as the auditorium where Unity-Midtown holds it 11:00 a.m. service. Since this a leased space, we were not able to set up a permanent sound system, so we purchased a portable one with powerful speakers, a

CD player, cassette recorder/player, and a wireless microphone. Other equipment included eight 6x8 foot carpets that were arranged in a rectangle along the perimeter of the room, and forty backjacks with pillows that were stacked in the corner of the room for use in the latter part of the service. People were asked to remove their shoes upon entering, and to leave any food or drinks outside the room.

The beginning part of the New Church Spiritual Practice Service was devoted to body awareness. Soft music was put on before the official start time, and anyone who wanted to could come early to stretch to the music or do some gentle movement. Gradually, the rhythm of the music intensified and the gentle movement transitioned into more energetic dance. People initially moved and danced alone, and then were invited to dance with others in the room, or to interact in some specific way. This part of the service continued for twenty to thirty minutes, and was followed by a period of deep relaxation with people lying, eyes closed, on the carpets. People were then invited to get backjacks or pillows and to sit in silent meditation for up to twenty minutes. At the conclusion of the meditation there was an open space for me to bring forth a spiritual teaching, or for a dialogue, or for anyone to simply share what was present in their experience. In the 9:30 service there usually would be some of each. We concluded with a resonance circle, holding hands, sensing into the space in which we had just met.

There was never an occasion when the time we allotted to our meeting felt like enough. I believe a optimum length of time for such a gathering would be at least two full hours. Because words are completely inadequate to describe what can happen in a gathering such as this, it must suffice to say that never in the forty or more of these services held in 1999 did I fail to experience the Presence described by Jesus as "there am I in the midst of them." This is why I recommend this simple form to those wishing to explore New Church practices.

This is only one of many ways to accomplish the same thing however. A helpful reference called *The Life We Are Given* by George Leonard and Michael Murphy describes another way to build a spiritual practice session. The term they use is Integral Transformative Practice, but it's just another name for this level of New Church. New Church doesn't have to take place in a church building, nor does it necessarily have to be called church in order to be what church was originally intended to be!

The important elements at this level of New Church expression are consistency of form, continuity of leadership, and committed relationship to body, mind, heart and spirit. These emphasize the relational aspect of spiritual growth and development. When there is a willingness to return to a relationship—with a form, with a teacher and others—over and over again, a deeper capacity for discovering the layers of self that resist the reality of Self develops. The practice of seeing one's many selves in this manner allows them to eventually be transcended as well.

The Teacher invites the commitment to spiritual practice, but only the participant can fulfill it. If the commitment to practice is tentative, which becomes quite clear in energized and meditative space, the Teacher may invite the participant to engage in deeper work. Facilitation of individuals' spiritual process through these issues is an integral aspect of the New Church service even within a limited time frame. And when there is committed involvement, a greater capacity for intimate sharing may arise in a relatively short time.

The New Church Spiritual Practice Service invites participation at a much deeper level than either the Old or Transitional Church. While it is possible to simply attend traditional services, the New Church service requires more than passive involvement. The New Church service is designed to bring people towards relationship—with music, people, self, the present moment—not to make relationship happen, but to bring the relationship that already is there into awareness.

The uncomfortable part of this, and what feels risky and challenging to people who aren't well-prepared for it, is that what often becomes conscious are the many ways in which we avoid relationship. We notice how our mind wanders when asked to meditate, how our eyes avoid contact when there is the opportunity to connect with another, how we giggle and socialize to distract us from a deeper kind of sharing of the heart. Awareness of these avoidance activities bring the ego's strategies into full relief, and this is very disconcerting to the ordinary sense of self. It seems strange to commit to a practice that is constantly revealing the places in ourselves that we've worked so hard to keep hidden. Yet, for those who are drawn to work at the level of the New Church, that's exactly what's called for.

The spiritual work facilitated by the New Church best suits the person who has an ego that is sufficiently developed (i.e., the person has fulfilled their Deficiency-needs, has a sense of self that does not depend on others for definition, and is open to self-actualization) to see the problems identifying exclusively with the ego poses to further development. Such a person will not particularly enjoy having their egoic identity exposed. Even if they experience emotional discomfort when this happens, however, most people working at this level are relieved to have the opportunity to get closer to their more essential self. It's like going to the dentist when you finally admit you have a cavity that needs filling. You don't enjoy the drilling, but you appreciate the effect that results from meeting the difficulty.

With spiritual work of this sort, you don't exactly have something as tangible as a filled tooth to show for your efforts. Each time the ego is discovered to be "not-who-I-am," however, the ego-thought relaxes its hold on the psyche. A sense of freedom from a false self ensues. Energy is liberated that was bound up in sustaining the fiction of "I am this" or "I am that." Aliveness surges through the body, love opens the heart, peace calms the mind.

The New Church service, for all the risk it presents to the ego-bound person, also offers a space for celebration of the spiritual reality that exists prior to and beyond the ego. This is worship at its most profound: a spontaneous outpouring of gladness of life for Life itself from the depths of the most essential Self. When worship arises from such an experience, it is obvious that it is not necessary to *believe* anything at all *about* God. You are One with It—you cannot speak accurately about it, much less make up concepts to explain it. In the experience of mystical union there is only the joy of *being* in this moment. This quality is not manufactured nor contrived by magical incantations. Joy simply arises as the experience of pure Being in any moment that identification with the ego falls away.

What threatens the ego in a New Church service opens us to our true Self. The New Church service is risky, but it is only the ego that experiences fear. And a well-defined ego actually reaches a point when it tires of being driven by its fears; when it does so, the ego becomes willing to lay itself down in what we call an act of faith. This faith is not the defensive armor against fear that Old Church cleverly disguised as the fairy tale that things will turn out fine (the way we want them to) in the end. Rather, it is a faith that is born in the presence of fear as a surrender to things as they are; it is the willingness to let go into the reality of this moment, and to see what happens.

The succeeding levels of the Curriculum for Transformation provide a structure into which individuals who find themselves called to this type of inner work may progressively deepen their commitment to Self-realization, for a call to a life of service frequently emerges as a natural outcome of increasing spiritual awareness. The basic work described above continues in these more committed contexts with an increasingly intense focus on cultivating self-inquiry, spiritual practice and committed relationship in a Community of the Teaching.

While the New Church service described above can accommodate, with a venue of adequate size, up to a hundred people, the third level of the Curriculum for Transformation is much smaller, providing experiences for only fifteen to twenty people. This allows for greater attention to the relationship between Student and Teacher, and for the development of relationship between group members. The point is not, however, to form lasting friendships or an ongoing support group. This may happen, but it is not the primary aim of these levels.

The relational aspect is introduced in a more deliberate way at this point to allow the work of observing and transforming the ego to proceed in an accelerated fashion. There's nothing like a relationship to show us how we avoid relationship, and so the context of committed relationship with Teacher and other Students continually mirrors the participant's relationship with God, or spiritual reality.

The New Church constantly aims to facilitate the awareness of what we are not conscious of. On the Part Three level, the Mentor Program, the torch that lights up this awareness burns brighter and hotter. Deep introspection at this level centers around four basic questions: Who am I? What really matters? How do I avoid relationship? How am I called to serve? At the mentoring level there are also exercises involving both spontaneous and deliberate creative expression, dream work, energy sharing, and numerous opportunities for the participant to discover the inventive ways the ego obstructs the life force so that he or she may break through that resistance.

Part Four of the New Church is Spiritual Leadership Training. It serves a small number of persons who through the inquiry "How am I called to serve?" discern they have a calling to serve the spiritual needs of others in a consecrated manner. The Spiritual Leadership Training calls them toward an even deeper relationship with God, Self and other, while providing training in specific skills for creating contexts that will support the spiritual growth and development of the groups they will attract. To gain practical experience, trainees have the opportunity to teach and speak as leaders in Transitional Church settings, and eventually to facilitate Spiritual Practice Sessions in the New Church setting.

I have no doubt there are other levels that could emerge within the framework of an evolving curriculum for transformation, but I will stop at this point. What I have described here is just one possibility for New Church expression, a kind of prototype. I offer it as an example of how the New Church acts as a crucible for the actual work of transformation in a specific, progressive program. In its essence, it's not so complicated, certainly not as clinical or formal as my description makes it seem. The New Church is really just as simple as Jesus said: "Where two or more are gathered in my name, there am I in the midst of them."

To close this description of the New Church, I'd like to share with you an excerpt from an e-mail I received in the winter of 2000. The writer was responding to a general message requesting feedback that I sent out to people who'd participated in the New Church Spiritual Practice Service in the previous year. Her response reveals the heart of much of what I've wanted to describe in these chapters:

Dear Ellie,

The reason I came to the 9:30 service was simply because it was a gathering of people doing stuff that most people don't normally do, which opened this incredible space just to be. My biggest desire in this life is just to have a space where I can simply be. You/we created this container-without-words to explore parts of ourselves that we don't usually explore.

It was a gathering of souls, an opening that just can't be explained with words. I can see now why you are experiencing difficulty writing [about the service]. So many of those 9:30 spiritual practice sessions (or whatever words you call it) were just beyond words. I want to use words like magical, mystical, spiritual, but those are not accurate either. That time of opening hearts and souls is just beyond words. I mean words just are not powerful enough. If they were we wouldn't need to gather, we could just stay home with a pile of books. It is like me trying to tell you what tofu tastes like. I can't tell you. I can only let you taste it. I guess I could tell you something that it tastes like, but what if there were nothing it tastes like. I can't tell you. So the simplicity is that... "Where two or more are gathered in my name, there am I in the midst of them."

The "I" is Jesus, who represents God, and just as the word God means so many different things to so many different people, so does what occurs when two or more are gathered. How wise of you to ask people what it was for them because the "I" is different for every person, but it is also a very important part of the one or the "we." The 9:30 service was everything and it was nothing. It was spiritual, and it was earthly (the way we moved our bodies!!!) It's like we got in touch with the divine through the physical. We honored our physical, emotional, and spiritual selves. We made space for it all. None was left out. All were allowed.

It is just that simple. A complete embrace of all that is with no judgement. Several times I found myself asking, "Why are we doing this?" Then I thought "Who cares why? Just do it!" When I am able to do that in life, I am so much more peaceful. It is a way of complete nonresistance.

Also, it is very hard for me to give my description of you in all of it. You were the first one. You were the one who had the faith first. All you did was be who you are, but yet, that was everything. I think that is our greatest challenge in life is to be ourselves no matter what. It is so much easier to be what other people want us to be. You were willing to be wrong.

...I had no idea how powerful the 9:30 service was for me, even when I was not in attendance. I have no doubt that the energy and power of that service affected everyone in our community, whether they participated or not. Okay, all that to say..."Where two or more are gathered in my name, there am I in the midst of them." It is really that simple.

All my love and commitment, Jill

As Jill so wisely observes, you have to be in the New Church experience to get the full flavor of what these words attempt to describe. I hope her letter will do what a good menu does and tantalize you enough to order up a dish of the New Church to get a taste of it for yourself.. If you like what you find, perhaps you'll even want to open a restaurant where you serve up some yummy portions yourself. Should you decide to experiment with creating a New Church setting, in the last part of this book I share some guidelines and anecdotes from my experience of founding, first, a Transitional Church, and then, a New Church.

# 17
# Guidelines for
# Creating a New Church

*I wake to sleep, and take my waking slow.*
*I learn by going where I have to go.*

**THEODORE ROETHKE**

To those who wish to create a New Church I have generated some guidelines to help you begin the creation of a
New Church. These are neither exhaustive nor specific;
they are based on my experience, and are intended to be used—
not as dogma or *the* way to do church—in the spirit of the old
"Hints from Heloise." I want to give you some down-home advice based on what I've learned in my New Church experiments.
Use this advice as a place to begin, but by all means see what
resonates with your own deep consecration and do that.

I made a lot of mistakes in my church-making efforts, and
you will too. But you will learn just as I did, what you need to
learn. Most of these guidelines were formed by my trial and
error discovery of how *not* to do things! I've come to realize it
is not a sin to make a mistake—mistakes are merely invitations
to greater consciousness—so don't get too hung up on making
yourself or others wrong because of mistakes. Remember that
the whole notion of "right" belongs to the Old Church. On the
other hand, take responsibility for what you create, be as
thoughtful and conscientious as you can—don't upset the apple
cart unnecessarily—and, definitely, make amends as they are
called for. Through your experiments and mine, we are more or
less (hopefully more) consciously evolving the New Church. We

are unfolding the possibility of what a church can be as we enter a new century, and, indeed, this new millennium.

## 1. Discover your motivation.

Why do you want to change the church you already have, or start a New Church? Have you exhausted all the possibilities within your current form, or are you simply upset with it? Unless you have truly outgrown your Old Church, the chances are you will re-create it in a disguised form if you try to do something different in reaction to it. Real change only comes about when you deeply understand yourself in relation to the desired change. So, the most important thing to do is examine your motivation for changing your current involvement.

Many people who go church-shopping, whether as congregants or clergy, have left their previous church over some unresolved issue. When I ask people why they are looking for a new church,, it is not unusual for someone to describe a difficult relationship with the minister or another church member whom they refused to deal with. Often this might have been resolved if the complaining party had been willing to take responsibility for his or her part in the situation. But many people will find it easier to complain. Beware this person's enthusiasm upon discovering you, or you may become the new target of their unhappiness. Ministers who switch churches also are likely to find a new church member with an identical personality to the one they left behind. It's more spiritually economical to simply deal with what needs to be dealt with in a present situation than to change to something new prematurely.

If upon reflection, however, you find you are relatively at peace in your current situation, or have gradually come to find less and less meaning there, it is possible your discontent is the manifestation of your personal growth and an indication of need for Something More. Now is a good time to explore what that need is. Look again at Figure 16.1. Use Maslow's Hierarchy of Needs to assess your need-level. Then see what kind of church would best support you at this stage in your life. Be honest in this, and don't assume that you will be better off in the kind of church that serves a higher level of development. It doesn't matter if you go to an Old Church, a Transitional Church or a New Church, as long as it is appropriate for meeting your needs. If you choose a church that doesn't meet your needs, you will be opening yourself up (and possibly others) to some useless and unnecessary suffering.

If as a congregant, your needs are at the upper end of the "basic" needs category, you will want to find a Transitional Church to participate with. Remember, this kind of church may only be helpful to you for a couple of years, so be alert to the signs that indicate you may be ready to move on to a New Church format. In the meanwhile, however, let the church serve you by providing opportunities to learn how to meet your needs for Love and Belongingness, Self-esteem and Esteem by Others.

If you are a clergyperson who is outgrowing the Old Church form, you might consider ministry in the Transitional Church as your next step. However, a word of caution. Please make sure you have already gotten *your* basic needs met before you start trying to minister to the needs others have at this level. It is tempting to "graduate" oneself to a leadership function to simply be in an environment supportive of your own growth. But this rarely serves those people who are coming to you for their need-fulfillment, nor will it ultimately serve you in getting your basic needs met. The best spiritual leader for a Transitional Church will probably be one whose own needs are being met in a New Church.

The New Church will serve people best who have truly out-grown and not rejected the Old Church, and who have been prepared to move beyond the Transitional Church and into the transformative environment of the New Church. The movement from Transitional to New represents a quantum shift. Deficiency needs are simply not addressed in the New Church—they are assumed to have been met in other settings. The New Church is devoted to meeting your growth- or Being-needs. It is unlikely it you will be able to step into participation as a student or teacher at this level unless you have been sufficiently prepared as explained in the Curriculum for Transformation.

The best motivation for adapting a present church, or getting involved in a new one, is appropriate need-fulfillment. Any other motivation is likely to be based in fear, albeit and unfortunately, well-disguised fear. Reveal and meet the fear, and you will have already moved closer to spiritual realization.

## 2. Start where you are.

Beginning this work is not any harder or easier than anything else. To start, you just need to do the first thing there is to be done. But don't start by trying to be something you're not. Be honest enough to acknowledge the state of ignorance in which you find yourself. Start the work there.

I founded Unity-Midtown from a space of deep disillusionment about any kind of church ministry, and only the merest glimmer of a hope that something else was possible. Evidently, belief in yourself or God or anything else is not a prerequisite to creation. So, please be outrageous in your vision of what is possible for a church. You probably have, as I did, an unconscious mental checklist of what a church should be and do. Make these "shoulds" conscious and the Old Church won't be a hidden force driving your efforts.

You also may have, as I did, a list of complaints about the Old Church and all the things you swear you'll never do like the they did. Guess what? You will! That is, unless you clean up your resentments and find a way to forgive all the ways you think you've been wronged.

But you don't have to be perfect to create a New Church or bring your Old Church into a more Transitional Church mode. Unconscious agendas and resentment lists don't disqualify you from beginning your work. It may take a while, or a lifetime, to work through these things—I've spent the better part of ten years grappling with my attachments in this arena—but one of the greatest gifts about taking on spiritual work of this sort is that it eventually puts everything you weren't conscious of (and didn't want to be) right out in front for you and everyone else to see! I don't know of a stronger motivation to be as conscious as is possible.

By the same token, if you are a spiritual leader, the people who are drawn to you also have their unconscious agendas and personal history operating. They will have the best of intentions and then, for their own reasons, do something completely contrary that hurts you and others. You will feel betrayed. Don't deny this, but don't indulge it either. You chose to work in this arena to learn how to be as you are, not to be righteous about your victimization at the hands of the people you thought you were supposed to be helping.

Don't be discouraged. In the beginning of this kind of work, everyone is discovering their capacity to come to life in faith. So there is a lot of fear, mostly fear masked with goodwill. Only by a commitment to stay and do the work of seeing what underlies the fear will you build trust in your dealings with each other. And, as you do this, you'll notice this is also how you create a new kind of church.

When I first decided to found Unity-Midtown, I made many mistakes. I didn't have a clue what to do differently in order to create a new kind of church except talk about my vision of it. Yet I wanted people's approval so badly at one point I collapsed my entire vision about the possibility of this new kind of church. But, after ten years of realizing that I—my ego, that is—would never be able to get it right according to *my* standards of rightness, I accepted the fact that, in spite of me, but definitely through me, a version of the New Church was emerging.

Just start where you are. You are a pioneer. Be humble enough to admit your ignorance of how to go about the task before you. You will learn, as Theodore Roethke wrote so wisely, to "learn by going where you need to go."

### 3. Stop! Look! Listen!

It's all too easy for both spiritual leaders and participants to get caught up in a lot of busywork when forming a church, particularly a Transitional Church. You have to find a suitable meeting place and furnish it. You have to let the world know you exist. You have to, have to, have to... the list of things that must be done seems endless.

Yet in Transitional Church and New Church it is more important that the people who form the core consciousness of their gatherings of "two or more" *be* more than *do*. Unfortunately, meditation and other practices find themselves on the bottom of most to-do lists (if they ever get there in the first place).

Consciousness work must not simply be another "have-to-do." It is a way of life! It is how anyone finds their real life. Please don't confuse the busy-ness of "doing" a church with living your real life. Busywork is an inadequate substitute. The church project can help you become more conscious, but it may also seduce you into being less conscious if you mainly stay focused on the doing part. A consistent spiritual practice will help you discern the difference and assist you in integrating your church life with your personal life.

The primary difference between a New Church and an Old Church is that the New Church insists that consciousness is the only real aim of church, while Old Church says that a bunch of other things are just as or more important. If you find yourself getting caught up in doing a lot of churchy stuff follow this guideline: Stop! Look! Listen!

*Stop* whatever you are doing that seems so important. Ask yourself, Who in me has declared this as necessary? Then, *look* at this self and see what is motivating it to act. See everything you can about this self. See that it is not the real you, but just one of your many ego-selves claiming to be you. Finally, *listen* to the silence of the infinite space from which all thoughts about what should be done arise. Let the thought of what needs to be done dissolve back into the silence. Let it all go and rest in the silence of your deep listening. When you're ready, just do or don't do, as you like. Chances are, the quality and quantity of what you think you must do will alter. You'll find yourself doing what is appropriate for you to do, not what some ego-self thinks you should.

## 4. Keep it simple.

Organizational complexity is an energy drain. Energy gets bound up, not liberated, in establishing orderly systems. Think of energy as Spirit and you can see why organized religions seem so spiritless.

A recent *New Yorker* magazine features a photo essay, by Richard Avedon, depicting holy men and women from various world religions. An Indian holy man, naked except for the large stone tied to his genitals, grins at the camera. However, neither the robed Roman cardinal nor the bejeweled Orthodox patriarch can seem to manage more than a dour grimace. The feeling I get from looking at those photos is that the actual weight carried by the naked holy man is far less of a burden than the invisible one borne by those Christian leaders.

While a certain amount of organization provides a balance of spiritedness and grounding, overly-organized systems may be a compensation for the absence of authentic spiritual experience. Unnecessary formalities bestow a false sense of identity on the essential gathering of two or more. The importance of following ritual procedures supercedes an appreciation of being in the moment. This is not say there isn't a place for discipline within a spiritual community. But make a distinction between order and the complication of your church life with a lot of rules for how things should work.

One of the strongest organizational imperatives we inherit from the Old Church is that a church should grow in numbers. Energy in a church bent on increasing numbers is generally poured into activities such as building bigger buildings, advertising campaigns, jazzier services. Church life starts looking a lot more like corporate life under these circumstances. The spiritual leader of such a church had better know something about architectural design, bank financing, media outreach— and have plenty of time to devote to committee meetings. Unfortunately, that's much of what a lot of church ministers are up to these days.

One of the main reasons I hesitated to pioneer a church was that I was clear I did not want my spiritual life to be supplanted by such organizational concerns. I wondered if it would be possible to sustain a church on a small scale, and have it support me as a fulltime spiritual leader. I learned it is possible. The hardest thing my small church community dealt with was not financial support but the belief that we should strive to have larger numbers of people involved.

My personal struggle with this had to do with pride—how could I feel I had done my best when all I had to show for it was eighty to one hundred people on a Sunday? So, periodically, I'd bang the drum for better attendance. Yet, it was precisely at the moment when I was most fully living my New Church vision that attendance dropped dramatically from eighty to twenty over the course of a month. After dealing with feelings that I was a complete failure, it finally struck me that quantity and quality do not equate. To be true to my calling, I'll walk the path with fewer people before compromising in order to have more. The depth of experience that was possible with the smaller number may not have satisfied my ego's insatiable pride, but it fulfilled a deeper longing in my heart and soul. So much so that I now feel compelled to share the good news that small is good—very, very good.

Keeping it simple means sticking to your spiritual purpose. Don't be seduced by Old Church imperatives to over-organize your church. Work with any judgements you may have of a simple operation. Understand what the most essential elements of your church are, and provide these. Leave the rest of it alone. Enjoy!

### 5.   Render to Caesar the things that are Caesar's, and to God the things that are God's.

If you want to pioneer a Transitional or New Church, you have an advantage over an already-established group. You are in a position to deliberately choose what sort of involvement you want with the world—a little or a lot. Whatever you decide, however, if you root your spiritual work in the material world you'll be a part of Spirit incarnating and evolving itself through your manifestation.

For a church in the United States this grounding generally requires relating yourself to the State through a legal structure. Although our Constitution provides for a separation of Church and State, it is through the state legal structure that churches tend to define themselves. You can be a church without going through a formal incorporation process. There is no guarantee, however, that donations to the church are considered tax-deductible unless you apply to the IRS for a recognition of your tax-exempt status. In order to do so, you need to incorporate as a non-profit organization.

You should nonetheless consider if you want your gathering of "two or more" to be so well-organized. A group may simply gather as a Community of the Teaching and not be concerned with whether their donations to the group (in support of the

Teacher) are tax-deductible. This is probably the least formal arrangement, and the simplest to maintain.

From the perspective of consciousness, however, I see an advantage in having to deal with the organizational details demanded by your state. Jesus made this point to his disciples when he answered their question about the payment of taxes to the Romans: "Render to Caesar the things that are Caesar's, and to God the things that are God's."(Mark 12:17) In other words, both the material and spiritual worlds must be honored.

Incorporation is not a difficult process. One benefit of doing so is that it invites your church group to think about and articulate its purpose. Gaining tax-exempt status requires an even deeper reflection upon, and more detailed description of, your intention and methodology. When I recently applied for this status for The New Church Ministries I was pleased to come away with more clarity about the nature of my own work.

If you want your state's recognition of your work, then you much comply with its regulations. But don't let the State limit what your church can be. Even if your church is not deemed by the IRS to be a church according to their definition, that doesn't mean you can't operate as a church. It simply means contributions can't be written off against taxes, which allows people the opportunity to give purely for the sake of giving. (In the Bahamas, where there is no tax advantage for making donations, I learned that people who want to will still give!)

You may want to experiment with other ways of supporting your church, and not want to have non-profit status at all. Imagine a church conducted on a fee-for-service basis. Unheard of for a church? At the present. But if your New Church is composed of healthy, self-responsible spiritually mature adults, there may be a time when you can be more direct about financial support than many Old and Transitional Churches currently are. Why not? Those who create New Churches may want to explore these areas once they get past the Old Church way it's always been done.

The bottom line when grounding any church in the legal and fiscal realities of whatever culture is to be certain your main priority is rendering unto God that which is God's. This means putting consciousness of Spirit first in all dealings in the world. A commitment to consciousness makes it possible to join the material with the spiritual; in the space of conscious awareness, the separation insisted upon by the State simply does not exist. A lot of room exists, then, for cooperating with, rather than getting caught up in, the complications of the material realm. So, do the necessary paperwork, pay your bills, live within your means, and Caesar will be satisfied. God already is.

## 6.   Find the Ground of your Being and stand on it.

Inevitably, where people get together for any purpose, it's easy for personalities rather than principles to rule the day. Personalities, those servants of the ego, busy themselves with strategies to secure the ego's dominant position. These tend to be political in nature. Churches, especially those modeled on the Old Church, frequently fall under the influence of ego-driven politics. In founding a church, I very much wanted to avoid this trap. And so I was caught in it. Amazing amounts of time and energy—my own and others'—went into the difficult task of extricating myself, and the New Church, from the power struggle the ego so loves to engage in.

In the case of Unity-Midtown the power struggle centered around me, in my role as minister, and the Board of Directors. In Transitional Churches like Unity there tends to be no dominant clerical hierarchy as in the Old Church. Instead, church leadership rests in the hands of more or less democratically elected Board members and the minister they hire and fire. But at Unity-Midtown the situation was a bit different in that I founded the church, and the lay leaders were, at least initially, people I invited to sit on a Steering Committee. These were men and women who expressed interest in the vision I described of a new kind of church. Two years into our church adventure, the Steering Committee and I formulated a set of bylaws as part of our incorporation process. These bylaws allowed for eight members of the Board—four to be appointed by the minister, four to be elected by the congregation.

Until this point, let me be clear, everyone who served in a lay leadership position had been a volunteer that I had either appointed or approved to fill the position. This happened in a relatively informal manner, and there was a sense of all of us working together to bring forth a common vision—the one I articulated in my teaching again and again. But out of some notion that the church should have a democratic component, I insisted those bylaws should include elected Board members, and regretted it almost as soon as we held the first election.

It seemed no one wanted to formally run for the positions. Congregants had to be cajoled into allowing themselves to be nominated. Then, for the four years we had such annual elections, the candidates who were not elected all left the church! It seemed we lost some of most involved people this way. We were left with Board members who arrived on the scene in a much different way than the ones who were appointed. They seemed to feel their mandate was to protect the congregation from my vision, although, ironically, this was the reason they and most of the people who attended the church were there in the first place!

From the day we first had Board elections, a power struggle ensued. It was not a blatant one for several years. I tried not to participate. In fact, I did my best to please my apparent opposition. But it seemed I could do nothing right in their eyes. I wasn't spiritual enough, some of them said. I was too hung up on psychology. Who did I think I was, anyway? Everything they said echoed some deep insecurity I thought I'd hidden from them. The harder I tried to please, the more they attacked.

Eventually their dissatisfaction with me emerged as such a huge issue that I was on the verge of being fired from the church I'd founded. I had terminated the employment of a secretary, a very disturbed woman who would shout obscenities over the phone to whoever was on the other end, and yell at me or speak only in sarcasms. Her insubordination was beyond the pale, and after months of trying to work things out with her, I asked the Board President to fire her.

This gave her friends on the Board all the proof they needed. I was incapable of unconditional love, they said. I should have just forgiven this woman and forgotten about it. What kind of spiritual leader are you, anyway? We don't know what you stand for!

At this point I saw the problem. My codependent attempts to please this half of the Board interfered with my ability to communicate to them what I saw as my spiritual purpose. In the absence of any real appreciation of my founding vision (they were a second generation of congregants), they inserted one of their own—and I had no place in it. I finally understood that my founding vision was a valid and beautiful one, but I had set it to one side in my attempt to get these people to like me. As a result, I compromised my vision and integrity.

When I realized this, I was able to reestablish myself in the Ground of my Being—that is, the purpose for which I started the church in the first place. Standing on this spiritual Ground, the codependent me stepped aside. I was firmly and heartfully able to reclaim the leadership of this Transitional Church. When I did so, those Board members who had taken the secretary's side resigned from the Board. Before this happened, however, they moved that the bylaws be rewritten to assure that the founding vision would always be upheld. The elected Board positions were eliminated so the spiritual leader could always count on the support of its members. Further the name was changed from Board of Directors (who feel they must direct) to a Board of Trustees, whose mandate is to support the vision held by the spiritual leader.

Doesn't this way of organizing the structure give too much power to a spiritual leader? Can one really give power to another they don't already possess? I already had access to a tremendous amount of spiritual power. It had been energizing me, as I would allow it, at least since I was first called to ministry, more likely long before. No one gave me that power, and no one took it away—this power is inside everyone equally. It's just that we aren't always conscious of it and we don't draw upon it. In this situation, I simply failed to lead the church in a powerful manner. My self-doubt, arising from a desire to please rather than be as authentically powerful as I am, got in the way.

Re-discovering the Ground of my Being was like plugging back into the original spiritual impulse to discover a new kind of church. As long as I stood upon this Ground, I had no need to engage in a power struggle, nor to force anyone to follow me who didn't want to. This power couldn't push others around, it was simply there to be used in service to my spiritual vision. Anyone was free to say no to my leadership if that's what suited them.

In this situation, the four elected Board members left the church. One came back several years later, and we were able to share how much we had both grown from that experience. The good feeling between us felt genuine.

Given how much we are conditioned by the Old Church, we may be fearful of the power surging through us from the Ground of our Being. We may hold back from being as powerful as we really are, and so deprive the world of the mutual empowerment that can belong to all beings. It may appear we are being humble in doing so, but we're merely denying the greatness of the spiritual source of our Being, and preventing it from finding expression in the world. Find the Ground of your own Being. Feel what it's like to stand on that Ground with your own two feet. Breathe deeply. Let the energy flow!

### 7.   Have the courage to change what you must.

If you long for a different sort of church, whether you want to adapt your already existing church setting, or create an opening for a New Church, you are a part of the transformation of an institution of archetypal proportions. Even small changes may seem to take a lot of effort, and you may experience, as I did, a kind of emotional fallout whenever you make a change.

A year or so into my work at Unity-Midtown I gradually became aware that, in spite of my aspiration to create a new kind of church, I was still bound by my conditioning in the Old Church. For example, I realized I had never worn anything other than a dress for Sunday Service. This was a vestige from the Catholic Church. When I was young, women couldn't wear pants to church and had to cover their heads. Others who came to Unity-Midtown were haunted by similar prohibitions. Former Southern Baptists believed they were going to hell if they smoked or danced, while the other Protestants thought church was supposed to be solemn and that good church-goers should sit down and shut up. These rules for what to do and what not to do in church were mainly unconscious, yet they tended to define the fall-back position for decisions we made about what a church was "supposed" to be. Because we were unconsciously self-conscious about whether we were doing church "right," there was a sense of holding back and the energy had a damped down feeling to it.

Once I realized that I and others were defaulting to these old beliefs about how we were supposed to be in church, I knew my job was to bring these beliefs into awareness for the whole congregation. My plan to do this involved devoting an entire Sunday Service not just to speaking about how this Old Church conditioning might limit what we believed a New Church could be—I had done this on many occasions—but to actually breaking some of the taboos we'd been living under.

On that day, I wore a brightly colored outfit with flowing pants. I recall standing on the platform as I opened the service and actually wondering if God in Heaven was going to throw lightning bolts at me. When no such divine retribution arrived, I was thrilled! Even though I truly had no conscious belief in such a silly and obviously sexist superstition, I evidently did still believe, unconsciously, that the Catholic Church had the power to define what one should or shouldn't do in church. Some part of me still looked over my shoulder for approval from Catholic authorities. (For years after leaving Catholicism, I still felt that Protestant churches weren't *real* church because they didn't include the Mass. ) It was thrilling to realize I could stand up in whatever I felt was appropriate to wear and still have "church"—to know that real church exists in the heart, not in any external trappings.

And, so, with the energy of this realization fueling me, I invited the congregation to experience some of their own taboo-breaking. I explained that instead of a group song that morning, we would put on some dance music and see what happened to our old ideas of what the Old Church had told us about how church was supposed to be. I invited everyone to put their whole body, mind and spirit into that dance, to let it be an expression of their worship of the divine. When the music—the Pointer Sisters' "Jump"—started, one person after another took to their feet, at first tentatively, with nervous looks over their shoulders, and then more wholeheartedly as they seemed to give themselves permission to "go for it." Soon the whole congregation was dancing, jumping, singing, laughing and crying. When the song was over the energy in the room felt like someone had just hit the winning homerun in the World Series. We'd blown the lid off our Old Church conditioning and everyone knew it—the result was ecstatic.

Later in the service I had a dialogue with the congregation about the experience, and people shared how challenging it had been for them to participate in this exercise. One rather soft-spoken man said he had also felt as if he might be struck down by lightning. But as he faced his fear of this, a sense of power welled up in him and he saw how much he'd let himself be held back in life by the rules he'd internalized as a young Southern Baptist. A middle-aged woman was still afraid that she'd done something wrong, but said she felt great because it had been so long since she had moved her body.

I would never be spurious in my introduction of radical experiences such as this, and I recommend that any change be grounded in a perception of deep need for a shift. There is a tendency in the contemporary Old Church to be trendy—to introduce changes that will popularize traditional religion for the sake of being more attractive to the unchurched person. The kind of changes I believe will be truly transformative ones will be ones solely designed to bring greater awareness to the participants. And this is not popular. In fact, it's often very uncomfortable for people to become conscious as whatever part of the personality is identified with the unconscious material feels threatened by the exposure.

There were always people in my congregation who would leave or feel like leaving when I offered them the opportunity to do something very different in a church service. As much as possible, then, prepare people for the changes you are going to introduce. Let them know why you think it is important. Help them anticipate their own discomfort and assure them that you will help them meet it. Then, stay present for them in their process, and don't be attached to them "getting it" in the way you think they could or should. In my experience, after a while, people begin to feel the liberating benefits of being challenged out of their conditioned ways of being.

One reason people come to the New Church is because on some level they want change, even if they balk at it initially. One way I found to work with introducing mildly transformational work on a regular basis was by incorporating it into an activity that is part of the weekly Order of Service. I used the greeting time as a way to facilitate congregants to discover their capacity for a deeper relationship to themselves, others and God, by offering them opportunities to break through their conditioned inhibitions. But I always gave individuals permission not to participate, and emphasized their responsibility to set boundaries for themselves regarding this. When the aim is to increase consciousness, even when people don't participate they may get a look at what in them doesn't want to, and achieve the aim anyway. When we surveyed the congregation periodically, most people described the greeting as the most challenging part of the service and one they'd most like to avoid. But they would frequently add a note saying they felt it was the part that caused them to grow the most.

It takes courage to make changes in the way things have always been. Initially, it feels wrong to challenge the status quo. But remember, the status quo is simply the crystallization of what was once an innovation. Our ego is always up to its tricks, and it will attempt to rigidify the changes you do find you have the courage to make. That's how rituals that may have served a transformative purpose in one setting become a drag on Spirit in another. So you also have to summon the courage to keep making changes. Don't get so attached to your creation that you're no longer sensitive when Spirit wants to move you in a new direction. Let your trust in the process of Spirit's evolution be your guide, and when you sense that trust is faltering, work with facing your own fear of letting go.

The biggest change I asked my congregation to make was to move from a traditional theatre-style seating arrangement into a circle. I had envisioned a circular meeting since my first experience of what I considered real church at a conference with Richard Moss, but could never quite visualize how to set it up in the space available to us at the Academy of Medicine. Then I visited the Jubilee! Church in Asheville, North Carolina, and saw exactly how it could be done using concentric circles of chairs. But the physical layout was only the first challenge.

Almost immediately it was apparent that the new seating arrangement would be a container for a more intimate relationship. We were not only physically closer, we also had to look at each other too! This made some people more uncomfortable than they could handle, and the attendance dropped off by about twenty percent. For those who remained, the circular arrangement evoked a different kind of service. It was less formal and tended to be more personal. In the center of the circle, an altar table was decorated each week by a different group within the congregation and often became the focal point for participation as people stepped forward to light candles, read poetry, or offer a reflection. My talks evolved more into dialogues with individuals in the congregation, and these at times became an opportunity for them to process spiritual issues they were working with in their lives. If we needed to, the non-fixed seating allowed chairs to be arranged in small groups for even more contact. Dreams were shared, stories of spiritual experiences were told. Group singing turned into meditative chants that were prolonged until they dissolved into silence.

Over the course of the fourteen months we experimented with the circular format, attrition was high. People commented that it didn't feel like church to them. It was too interactive, they missed the anonymity of passively attending church. They complained that the banquet chairs we were using weren't as comfortable as the auditorium seats, and that the room wasn't as pretty.

When people grumbled like this and stayed away, I had to decide how important it was to stay with the change that seemed to make the difference between the Transitional Church and the New Church. In fact, it was at the time of making this decision that I realized that Unity-Midtown really was operating at the level of a Transitional Church rather than a New Church. The circular form allowed me to do the best work I'd ever done facilitating a group of people, and I knew I wanted to go all the way to being a New Church. But I realized there were a good number of folks who simply didn't want to. They had a variety of reasons, but underneath it seemed they just weren't ready for what the New Church would elicit in them. At this point it seemed important not to force people into a situation they weren't prepared to handle. So I created two services: one, a full-blown Transitional Church that met back in the auditorium—more like Unity-Midtown had been in its early days; and the other, a smaller one that met in a circle with the seating on the floor using backjacks and carpets (as described in the section on the New Church).

Although some people ended up being a part of both services (since they met at different times), I have to say I did not like the idea of splitting the group. I would have preferred for people to simply deal with their discomfort and come along to experience the New Church. But many of them didn't want to and I respected that. I also honored the reality that I needed to finally live my vision as fully as possible, without compromise. One of my trainees took over the more traditional Transitional Church service while I continued to deepen the New Church format with a group of fifteen to thirty people each week.

This change, which I initially experienced as a failure to lead a large number of people toward my vision, brought me the greatest satisfaction I have ever experienced, not only in ministry but in life. It was the fulfillment of a dream to have church be what it could be—a simple yet deep gathering of two or more. Even when, from the perspective of my ego's pride, things appeared to be headed downhill, staying with the changes was just what was needed.

Some people think I am especially courageous, but I don't agree. The courage to change comes from what is deepest and most essential within you. It is simply a matter of being true to yourself and doing what you must. Real courage comes from the heart (both "courage" and "heart" share common etiology), and forms our most intimate connection with the evolutionary impulse, which you might also think of as the heart of the Universe. When you use the courage you have to change the many things you can and must to create a Transitional or New Church, the Holy Spirit has more room in which to breathe a heartful breath. You, in turn, will be inspired and energized to bring forth something new, Something More.

# 18
# Where Two Or More
# Are Gathered

*How lucky Kabir is,*
*that surrounded by all this joy*
*he sings inside his little boat.*
*His poems amount to one soul meeting another.*
*These songs are about forgetting dying and loss.*
*They rise above both coming in and going out.*

**KABIR, Translated by Robert Bly**

I began work on this book about five years into the life of the church that began as research, but which clearly now has a life of its own. I have completed this book while on a sabbatical, and, in the process of doing so, have decided I will not continue as the minister of that church. There is so much I learned at Unity-Midtown and I now want to share that with the world as best I can. One advantage of no longer working in the research laboratory is that I'm starting to understand what I set out to do ten years ago and what happened. Life now calls me to a deeper exploration of the New Church.

When writing my critique of the Old Church for the second section of this book, I became terribly depressed. Very dark, heavy, scary thoughts and feelings seemed to oppress me as I wrote those chapters. It was as if some booming voice (like that of Sister William Joseph, my eighth grade teacher) challenged me at every turn. Who do you think *you* are to say these things about *the* Church? And I couldn't answer, for I certainly had no impressive academic qualifications to do so. All I had was my own experience to go by, and this experience was deepened every time

I gathered others together with the consecration and intention to create a new kind of church. If nothing else, doing this week after week, and writing about it, has forced me to claim an inner authority. This authority is based on experience – my own and what others have shared where "two or more" have come together as the New Church—and it has led me to make these assertions:

Church, in the form we know as traditional Christianity, is rife with the distortions of the limited emotional development and spiritual understanding of those who first interpreted Jesus' intent to found a church. As a result of the widespread dissemination of the traditional Christian belief through a perceived imperative to convert the world, the Church has embedded itself so thoroughly in Western culture that one is influenced by it at every turn. Our culture's ethos follows the line of traditional Christian thought, so much so that it is hardly possible anymore to see how the capitalist and religious celebrations of Christmas differ. We live with the distortions of the traditional Church, much as a fish never questions the medium in which it swims.

And, yet, there is value in challenging the tradition we have taken for granted. One doesn't have to destroy it to do so, because understanding that religious expressions evolve in an organismic fashion liberates us from the need to form an adversarial relationship to what has gone before. The Old Church, as I have described it, can be included even as we discover the possibility (and reality) of valid new forms emerging from the same inspirational source, Jesus. In the light of a more evolved perspective—one hopes that two thousand years of trial and error have offered at least a measure of insight!—we see the necessity for *all* stages of development. The trick is not to cling too tightly to any one of those stages, but to move, when it's time, to the next, more appropriate one.

The New Church offers some simple, and perhaps obvious solutions to the problems of the Old Church. Yet because the work of advancing through the stages of Old Church, Transitional Church, and New Church involves a maturation process, these solutions are not necessarily easy ones. Growing up may be what's asked of every single human, but it is still not the easiest thing in the world to accomplish. The comfort of dependency, coupled with a seemingly natural inclination to inertia, is a real obstacle to spiritual growth for many people.

Yet, the longing for Something More than the familiar status quo exists in all of us. Our own destiny as self-actualized, Self-realized beings calls for us to become a potent force in the Universe. The New Church has emerged in response to that evolutionary urge in a variety of forms that seem far from what we've been conditioned to think of as "church." But, as I've described, these forms embody a kind of program, a generalized curriculum that will assist in the evolutionary task of increasing spiritual awareness.

Where can these new forms, specifically the ones I've described as the Transitional Church and the New Church, take us if we allow them to guide our spiritual development in this twenty-first century? I believe they can lead us to a more essential spiritual experience than most people have previously known in the Old Church, and ultimately to a God-realized state of Being in which our innate potentials are fulfilled to the benefit of all humankind.

A Gallup poll taken on Christmas Eve, 1999 reported that "Americans remain very religious, but not necessarily in conventional ways. Many feel that they do not have to follow the strict teachings of their religion and that religions have unnecessary rules and responsibilities." The Transitional Church offers a more empowered environment for those people who may be moving out of the Old Church.

Through the Transitional Church, I envision people making their peace with the wounds they've suffered as the consequence of the stricter, less-than-conscious religious traditions, and redeeming these by taking responsibility for all experiences in life. Beyond providing a setting in which to accomplish this important individual healing work, I see the Transitional Church consciously preparing these same people to move forward in their spiritual development. By allowing itself to be more than a safe place to recover from the traumas of the past, the Transitional Church can serve as a bridge between old methods and new. In so doing, the Transitional Church has the opportunity to model the kind of humility that is the hallmark of a supple but powerful spirituality. This sort of spirituality evokes service to a purpose beyond itself, rather than merely basking in the warmth of its own accomplishments.

The challenge to those churches that I believe already exist as Transitional Churches—those "New Thought" metaphysical-type churches and other liberal churches—is to cultivate a sense of what lies beyond them so as not to indulge in self-aggrandizement. People who have outgrown the Old Church will put tremendous resources, financial and otherwise, at the disposal of the Transitional Church. Consequently, it is very tempting for a Transitional Church to serve only its own immediate needs, to build bigger, better Transitional Churches, and to fully embrace big, business Churchianity. This can be avoided, however, if the Transitional Church will look beyond itself, and be open enough to see how the New Church grows out of the work done at the transitional level. With that perspective, I hope that the Transitional Church will consider its task to include supporting the level which emerges from it.

The New Church finds itself in the position of a Buddhist monk who goes out with his begging bowl each day. This simple form doesn't require much, *and* it does require something in the way of sustenance. A venue, a basic inventory of equipment, remuneration for the Teacher—these aren't a lot but they are all necessary. Because the evolutionary tenet "more depth, less span" applies, outside funding to support the work of the fewer, more intent spiritual workers helps. For the New Church to be most effective, it will appreciate such support wherever it comes from, and it seems fitting that the Transitional Church supply some of this. It is my hope that Transitional Churches will meet this sweet obligation.

What of the New Church in this twenty-first century? How will it impact our culture? Is this an idea whose time has come? First of all, if the New Church intends an evolution, not a revolution, it may be a long time before the results of the New Church can be discerned. But recall that the New Church doesn't necessarily aim for measurable results. In spite of this lack of worldly ambition, acknowledgement of simple New Church gatherings as "church" has the potential to broaden the definition of what constitutes legitimate religious and spiritual expression.

Categories such as "believers" and "non-believers" may lose meaning as we begin to conceive of a developmental continuum of religious expression, a hierarchy of spiritual experience that excludes no one (except perhaps those who would deny the validity of any other person's experience—they exclude themselves!). The adversarial contempt inherent in such categorization could be replaced by the mutual understanding *all* humans are infinite their potential. Imagine a world in which everyone believed, or didn't, according to their own lights, and found instead of discord a possible relationship with those who walk another path! The concept of religious war might, in time, become obsolete, forming the legacy of the New Church to humanity for the next millennium. If this happens, the violent past of persecutions performed in the name of the Church might also be redeemed.

In considering the implications of the New Church for people in a more individual way, I think back to what Jill wrote to me about the impact the New Church Spiritual Practice Service had on her life. I warm to the thought of others like her finding an intimate space in which to simply be themselves. As an opportunity to directly experience Christ, this simple, elegant, spiritual expression—the New Church—stands for what I believe Jesus really intended church to be. If this is all the New Church ever is, all it ever does, let us take pleasure in creating it together.

# ENDNOTES

## Chapter 8

1. Charles Fillmore, *Talks on Truth* ( Unity Village: Unity Press) Fillmore goes on to say, "Jesus Christ is still the head of His 'assembly,' and its only organization is in Spirit. Whoever attempts to organize it on earth, with creeds, tenets, or textbooks of any kind or description as authority, is in direct opposition to His work and His example....Whoever formulates a creed, or writes a book, claiming it to be an infallible guide for mankind; whoever organizes a church in which it is attempted, by rules and tenets, to save men from their evil ways; whoever attempts to offer, in any way, a substitute for the one omnipresent Spirit of God dwelling in each of us, is an obstructor of the soul's progress."

2. The Catholic Church has the most defined provisos on this subject. One's final destination depends on whether or not one is in a state of grace at the time of death. The version of Catholic dogma I grew up with said that missing Mass on Sunday was a mortal sin, in the same category with murder. If you died with a mortal sin "staining" your soul, you went directly to hell. Lesser sins, referred to as venial sins, were punishable by a period in purgatory. Hell was a permanent sentence whereas you could be paroled from purgatory. (The Protestant Reformation was sparked by Martin Luther's objection to the Church's practice of selling indulgences to obtain early release for purgatorial inmates.)

## Chapter 9

3. Ken Wilber is probably the most prolific and articulate proponent of this view of stages of psychological development. See especially *A Brief History of Everything* (Boston: Shambhala, 1996) and *One Taste* (Boston: Shambhala, 1999)

4. Recent revelations regarding Kennedy's personal shortcomings may have shaken our faith in our perceptions of him somewhat, but his public persona remains an icon nonetheless.

5. Ray Kurzweil, in *The Age of Spiritual Machines* (New York: Viking, 1999) says the technology for this will be available by 2020. One wonders when *we* will be! To answer that question, of course, requires a profound inquiry into Who am I?

6. Hubbard, *The Book of Co-Creation* (Novato, CA: Nataraj Publishing, 1993)

7. I find it ironic that the U.S. Army chose this phrase as their slogan. It is a genius marketing tool, but unfortunately its overuse tends to diminish the impact when these words are applied to human growth and development. But for some people, I suppose the Army really does provide access to fulfilling D-needs and the possibility of moving into the arena where B-values are more compelling.

8. *Man's Search for Meaning* (Boston: Beacon Press, 1959)

9. Although in practice the Roman Church's claim to the infallibility of the Pope in matters of church doctrine actually puts the Church right up there at the top with God.

10. Fox, Matthew, *Compassion* ( Minneapolis: Winston, 1979)

11. The no-hierarchy approach of New Age religions is equally distorted. As Wilber points out, anyone who says their way is better because it doesn't have a hierarchy, is already operating from one. The point is not to get rid of hierarchies but to be accurate with them and to hold those who may be more evolved to be responsible in their position. This means that those more evolved must be willing to use their increased depth of perception in a manner that honors and respects the lower levels upon which the higher level rests, even as it brings a more complex or refined perspective into being that elucidates the shortcomings of its predecessor.

## Chapter 10

12. Anthony De Mello, *The Song of the Bird* ( New York: Image Books, 1984), p. 4.

13. Marsha Sinetar, *Developing a 21st Century Mind* ( New York: Villard, 1991), p. 29

14. Henri Nouwen, *Way of the Heart* (New York: Ballantine, 1981)

15. Words attributed to Jesus in the Gospel According to Thomas: "Whoever is near to me is near to the fire."

16. De Mello, *Song*, p. 4.

## Chapter 11

17. Richard Moss, *The I That Is We* ( Berkeley: Celestial Arts, 1981), pp. 184,185

18. John A. Sanford, *The Kingdom Within* ( Philadelphia: Lippincott, 1970), p. 64

19. Stephen Mitchell, *The Gospel According to Jesus* ( New York: HarperCollins, 1991), pp. 46, 47

20. The promotional material of the Illinois megachurch, Willow Creek Community Church calls these "intentionally crafted evangelistic events."

## Chapter 12

21. *The Chalice & the Blade* (San Francisco: HarperCollins, 1987)

22. This vision, however, is still based on God as conceived of by the Old Church. A particular powerful Being separate from its creatures who might (anthropomorphically) choose this partnership. The Eastern conception of God, not as a deity, but as Being itself, allows that a relationship already exists between

the Awareness that could be called God, and the manifest and unmanifest expressions of that Awareness. The task is not to establish a relationship between "God" and "man" but to become aware of the one that already exists.

23.   There are some problems with applying Eisler's postulated gylanic model to spirituality, one of these being that it ignores that there are indeed levels of spiritual realization, and that spiritual leadership doesn't obtain when it's driven by a less-realized constituency. But gylany does hold water as a possible way to reconceive of gender relationships in the structure of religious organization, and thus impact the whole notion of dominance as a *sine qua non* of spirituality. An evolutionary approach to spiritual organization would include leaders who are willing to honor and respect those who may be less realized than they are, while not denying the greater depth of their own experience and their capacity/calling to lead.

## Chapter 13

24.   Quoted in *The Search for America's Faith* by George Gallup & David Poling, (Nashville: Abingdon, 1980).

25.   *Your Church Has Real Possibilities*, Robert Schuller.

## Chapter 16

26. This does not mean that a New Church leader is relieved of the obligation to meet ethical or legal standards. The New Church leader must be more, not less, accountable than the ordinary minister. For this reason, he or she needs a Teacher for help in discerning their own egoic interference. A leader or teacher without such supervision easily falls prey to an arrogance which undermines the ability to facilitate transformation.

⊱

# BIBLIOGRAPHY
# & SELECTED READINGS

Karen Armstrong, *A History of God* ( New York: Knopf, 1994)

Eric Berne, *Games People Play* (New York: Grove Press, 1964)

Wendell Berry, *A Place on Earth* ( New York: Farrar, Straus, & Giroux, 1983)

Jeffrey Birnbaum, "The Gospel According to Ralph" *Time*, 15 May 1995, 28-35

Robert Bly, *The Kabir Book* (Boston: The Seventies Press, 1977)

E.J. Brill, Ed. *The Gospel According to Thomas* (New York: Harper & Row, 1959)

Anthony De Mello, *The Song of the Bird* (New York: Image Books, 1984)

Riane Eisler, *The Chalice & the Blade* (San Francisco: HarperCollins, 1987)

Charles Fillmore, *Talks on Truth* (Unity Village: Unity Press)

Matthew Fox,. *Compassion* ( Minneapolis: Winston, 1979)

_____. *The Coming of the Cosmic Christ* (San Francisco: Harper & Row, 1988)

Viktor Frankl, *Man's Search for Meaning* (Boston: Beacon Press, 1959)

George Gallup & David Poling, *The Search for America's Faith* (Nashville: Abingdon, 1980)

Barbara Marx Hubbard, *The Book of Co-Creation* (Novato, CA: Nataraj Publishing, 1993)

William James, *The Varieties of Religious Experience* (New York: Penguin Books, 1982)

Tom Kavanagh, "Big-Time Religion" *Common Boundary*, September/October 1993: 20-27

Ray Kurzweil, *The Age of Spiritual Machines* (New York: Viking, 1999)

George Leonard & Michael Murphy, *The Life We Are Given* (New York: Putnam, 1995)

Douglas Lockhart, *The Dark Side of God* (Boston: Elements Books, 1999)

Martin E. Marty & R. Scott Appleby, Editors, *Fundamentalisms Observed* (Chicago: University of Chicago Press, 1991)

Abraham Maslow, *Toward a Psychology of Being* (New York: Van Nostrand Reinhold, 1968)

Stephen Mitchell, *The Gospel According to Jesus* (New York: HarperCollins, 1991)

R. Laurence Moore, *Selling God* (New York: Oxford University Press, 1994)

Richard Moss, *The I That Is We* (Berkeley: Celestial Arts, 1981)

Maurice Nicoll, *Psychological Commentaries on the Teaching of Gurdjieff & Ouspensky Vol. 1-5* (Boulder, Shambhala, 1984)

Henri Nouwen, *Way of the Heart* (New York: Ballantine, 1981)

Elaine Pagels, *The Gnostic Gospels* (New York: Random House,. 1979)

Eva Pierrakos, *The Pathwork of Self-Transformation* (New York: Bantam, 1990)

John A. Sanford, *The Kingdom Within* (Philadelphia: Lippincott, 1970)

Robert H. Schuller, *Your Church Has Real Possibilities* (Glendale, CA: Regal Books, 1974)

Marsha Sinetar, *Developing a 21st Century Mind* (New York: Villard Books, 1991)

John Shelby Spong, *Why Christianity Must Change or Die* (San Francisco: HarperCollins, 1999)

Susan Thesenga, *The Undefended Self* (Madison, VA: Pathwork Press, 1994)

Ken Wilber, *A Brief History of Everything* (Boston: Shambhala, 1996)

_____, *One Taste* (Boston: Shambhala, 1999)

All quotes from The Bible, unless otherwise noted, are from *The Oxford Annotated Bible, Revised Standard Version*, Herbert G. May & Bruce M. Metzger, Editors, (New York: Oxford University Press: 1977)

ॐ

# ACKNOWLEDGEMENTS

MY PRIMARY DEBT OF GRATITUDE for the work represented in this book is to the hundreds of people who attended Unity-Midtown Church from its inception in 1990 until Autumn of 2000. They put themselves in the New Church experiment and, whether they enjoyed the experience or not, contributed to the unfoldment of the ideas in this book. We shared life (and during the worst of the AIDS epidemic, death) in a kind of spiritual intimacy that is a rare treasure in a world, to use Ken Wilber's phrase, "gone slightly mad." For this immeasurable contribution, I am most grateful.

In particular, I want to acknowledge all of the people who served on the Board of Directors and the Board of Trustees of Unity-Midtown, and, especially, Ken Wiltsee, Deby Glidden, and Lynn Laughlin. Their commitment to serve the New Church idea at this level was a demonstration of trust and support in an idea that was often being articulated for the first time. I appreciate their willingness to bear with my clumsiness in describing and implementing this vision.

I am extremely grateful to my brother-in-law, Dr. Robert Pearson, for his consistent encouragement of this writing project. Bob took the book's ideas on their own merits and in so doing led me to understand that these ideas did not just belong to me or to my congregation. His assistance in reading and making clear editorial suggestions on two different drafts of the book were invaluable and grounded me in the reality of completing it.

Thanks to David Jones, a participant at Unity-Midtown, who stepped forward in the early days of this book to offer not only his professional editing skills but also his perspectives on the Old

Church, and to Cheryl Lezovich, who edited the most recent version. Thanks also to those who read and commented on the manuscript at various stages: Cathleen O'Connor, Dwight Harriman, Krista Vinkemulder, Megan Gilhoulie, MaryAnn Crawford, Jennifer Denning, Crystal Yarlott, and Roo Davison. Also, to Timothy Tew, who helped me find a softer approach to my concerns with the Old Church.

I especially want to acknowledge the contribution of the three people I have formally acknowledged as Teacher in my life:

Rev. Marvin Anderson showed me the light at the end of a very dark tunnel when I was in my ministerial training. He was instrumental in facilitating the healing of my cancer, and beyond ministering to me at this time, kindled my fierce desire to know Truth. He inspired me to think in original ways and affirmed my first attempts to express my ideas in writing.

Dr. Richard Moss was first introduced to me through his books, and it was while working with Richard in a conference setting that the vision for the New Church was awakened in me. Richard acknowledged my courage, and in turn, evoked in me the qualities of relationship, integrity, authority, surrender and love. I cannot recommend his work too highly—he embodies and communicates the transformational impulse in a way I've experienced with no one else. Beyond the inspiration of his presence over the past ten years, Richard has also helped me to commit and re-commit to expressing my work in practical ways.

Cynthia Schwartzberg has provided consistent, loving challenge to the images and beliefs that limited my thinking and feeling about myself and life. For years, she has held me to a standard of self-honesty I didn't think was necessary or desirable before I began therapy with her. Cynthia created the space for me to reveal myself in all my aspects, and showed me how to transform my seemingly unending negativity into constructive, loving presence. I sense her influence in this book in many ways, but particularly when I realize how much she helped me heal from my experiences in the Catholic Church and rediscover the purity and innocence of my essential self.

I am thankful for all the opportunities to develop spiritually offered to me by my own Students. These have been participants in the 9:30 Spiritual Practice Service—what I consider my first taste of an actual New Church service—as well as those who've enrolled in my Mentor Programs, and those who have been licensed or ordained through The New Church Ministries Spiritual Leadership Program.

I want to thank all my friends who were there in the bliss and the bedlam of the New Church experiment, especially: B.J. Sharp, whose collaboration with music and friendship wove the fabric of Unity-Midtown for many years; Rosemary Sharp, whose soulfulness, humor and aesthetic sense sustained me under all sorts of conditions; Robert Harold, my brother, whose clear-seeing and support helped me reclaim the New Church vision at a critical time in its development; Lucinda Patterson, my massage therapist, who had the job of helping me unwind on a weekly basis and listened with compassion, insight and support; Max Alligood, who provided grounding, grumbling and good humor from the earliest days of the church he so resisted being a part of; Revs. John Knight and Crystal Yarlott, who in sharing their challenges in ministry helped me to see some of difficulties all ministers face; Alan Goodwin, who listened to my complaints with a smile and without comment; and to the rest of my family for providing the rich context for my life—my mother, Charlotte Harold, and other siblings: Beeby Pearson, Brent Harold, and Polly Harold.

Finally, I want to thank my husband, Roo Davison, for his tremendous support of this work. Roo has relentlessly insisted that I finish this book, begun several years before I met him. He's made certain I've had the necessary time, space and resources so I've had no excuse for not working on it. He's not only been my computer consultant, but also he's washed the dishes for most of the past two years. His generosity and love, in this project and in so many other parts of my life, touch me deeply.

*Since 1983 Rev. Ellie Harold has worked with groups of spiritual seekers across the United States and in the Bahamas. Her energetic presentations sizzle with insight and sparkle with humor, arousing in listeners both a passion and a plan for realizing their full potential. For information on seminars, talks and other programs offered by Rev. Ellie Harold in the U.S. and Europe, please contact her through The New Church Ministries.*

*The New Church Ministries, founded in 1994, is a non-profit organization devoted to transforming traditional assumptions about church and promoting the spiritual growth of individuals. For clergy or groups who seek to innovate new church forms, NCM provides on-site workshops and seminars. For individuals, NCM offers a complete Curriculum for Transformation such as the one described in this book. Call or write for more information:*

The New Church Ministries
P.O. Box 803
Atlanta, GA 30091
678.421.1981

info@thenewchurch.com